A Source Book in APL

Other APL PRESS books

Algebra—An Algorithmic Treatment
APL and Insight
APL in Exposition
Calculus in a New Key
Elementary Analysis
Introducing APL to Teachers
Introduction to APL for Scientists and Engineers
Proceedings of an APL Users Conference
Resistive Circuit Theory
Starmap
1980 APL Users Meeting

A Source Book in APL

Papers by ADIN D. FALKOFF · KENNETH E. IVERSON

With an Introduction by
Eugene E. McDonnell

APL PRESS
Palo Alto
1981

Iverson, Kenneth E., "Formalism in Programming Languages," *CACM* 7 Feb 1964, Copyright 1964, Association for Computing Machinery, Inc., reprinted by permission.

"Conventions Governing Order of Evaluation," from *Elementary Functions: An Algorithmic Treatment* by Kenneth E. Iverson, ©1966, Science Research Associates, Inc. Reprinted by permission of the publisher.

"Algebra as a Language," from *Algebra—An Algorithmic Treatment* by Kenneth E. Iverson, ©1977, APL Press. Reprinted by permission.

Falkoff, A. D. and K. E. Iverson, "The Design of APL," *IBM Journal of Research and Development,* Vol. 17, No. 4, July 1973, copyright 1973 by International Business Machines Corporation; reprinted with permission.

Falkoff, Adin D. and Kenneth E. Iverson, "The Evolution of APL," *SIGPLAN Notices* 13, August 1978, Copyright 1978, Association for Computing Machinery, Inc., reprinted by permission.

Iverson, Kenneth E., "Programming Style in APL," *An APL Users Meeting, Toronto, September 18, 19, 20, 1978,* I. P. Sharp Associates Limited. Reprinted by permission.

Iverson, K. E., "Notation as a Tool of Thought," *CACM* 23, August 1980, Copyright 1980, Association for Computing Machinery, Inc., reprinted by permission.

Iverson, Kenneth E., "The Inductive Method of Introducing APL," *APL Users Meeting, Toronto, October 6, 7, 8, 1980,* I. P. Sharp Associates Limited. Reprinted by permission.

International Standard Book Number: 0-917326-10-5
APL PRESS, Palo Alto 94306

Printed in the United States of America

Contents

Introduction

Introduction

The purpose of this book is to provide background material for teachers and students of APL. In a course on APL the focus is necessarily on the details of the language and its use; it may not always be apparent what the purpose of a particular rule might be, nor how one piece of the language relates to the whole. This book is a collection of articles that deal with the more fundamental issues of the language. They appeared in widely scattered sources, over a period of many years, and are not always easy to find. They are arranged in the order of their appearance, so it is possible to get a sense of the development of the language from reading the articles in sequence.

The first article, ***Formalism in Programming Languages***, appeared before there was an implementation. The reader who knows only contemporary APL will have to master some differences in notation in order to understand it. The effort will be repaid, however, because it condenses in a very small space some information on the properties of the scalar functions which appears nowhere else. In the discussion following the paper, R.A. Brooker asks a key question, one which has followed APL through its development:

> *Why do you insist on using a notation which is a nightmare for typist and compositor and impossible to implement with punching and printing equipment currently available? What proposals have you got for overcoming this difficulty?*

The question had no good answer at the time. The best that had been proposed involved transliteration rules that would have made it very difficult to work with the language. It was not until the advent of IBM's Selectric typewriter, with its replaceable printing element, that it became possible to think of developing a special APL printing element. Jean Sammet dismissed the paper in her review of it two years later by writing, "as soon as [the author] starts to defend the work on the grounds that it is currently practical, he is on very weak grounds." By the time the review appeared, however, the very impractical notation had found its implementers, and I read the review as I was sitting at a terminal connected to a 7090 system which was the time-sharing host for something called IVSYS, the immediate precursor of what would be called APL.

The second paper is connected with the transition from a pure notation to an implemented programming language. When it was written, although implementations had begun to appear, and the APL printing element had been developed, it was still not clear what was the best way to publish the language. In the book, as you can see from the selection, use was still made of boldface and italic type styles, rather than the single font imposed by the printing element. In the answer book, however, the functions were displayed in both the old style and the new, so that the user could easily see how to translate between the two.

In the third selection, ***Algebra as a Language,*** the case is made for the superiority of APL notation over those of conventional arithmetic and algebra. It also gives a discussion of the analogies between teaching a mathematical notation and teaching a natural language, a note that will be heard again in the last selection. The paper makes clear that there is a larger purpose to APL than merely to give people something in which to program. What is intended is a thorough reform of the way mathematics is taught, given the existence of the computer.

The next two papers form a pair and can be discussed together. In the first, ***The Design of APL,*** Falkoff and Iverson give the reasons for many of the design decisions that went into APL. The occasion for the second paper, ***The Evolution of APL,*** was a conference on the history of programming languages. The criteria for a language to be represented at this conference were that it 1) was created and in use by 1967; 2) that it still be in use by 1977; and 3) that it had considerably influenced the field of computing. In the introduction to the proceedings, APL was described as follows:

> *This language has received widespread use in the past few years, increasing from a few highly specialized mathematical uses to many people using it for quite different applications, including those in business. Its unique character set, frequent emphasis on cryptic "one-liner" programs, and its effective initial implementation as an interactive system make it important. In addition, the uniqueness of its overall approach and philosophy makes it signficant.*

This quotation properly notes the success of APL in commercial areas, and also gives appropriate credit to the effectiveness of the initial implementation. One has to have lived through the trauma of early time-sharing systems to be able to appreciate how good this first APL really was. I could tell dozens of stories about how bad most early time-sharing systems were, and for each of the bad ones, I could tell a dozen stories about the good qualities of this first APL.

The last three papers have in common that they use the *direct definition* form of function definition. It is a bit early yet to say how important this concept will be, but there is beginning to be some evidence to suggest that it will have applicability in many areas of programming. At first glance, it might appear that its use would be restricted to simple mathematical functions, and might not, perhaps, be employed in large-scale programming activities. However, I have seen reasonably large report generators —involving several dozen functions—built using this form, and have seen other systems in which two or three hundred of these functions interact.

As APL enters its third decade, it promises to find a signficantly larger number of users. Those who truly wish to master it should know more than just the meanings of its primitive function symbols. This book is meant to help them!

A note on the origins of "APL"

I remember quite well the day I first heard the name APL. It was the summer of 1966 and I was working in the IBM Mohansic Laboratory, a small building in Yorktown Heights, NY. The project I was working on was IBM's first effort at developing a commercial time-sharing system, one which was called TSS. The system was showing signs of becoming incomprehensible as more and more bells and whistles were added to it. As an experiment in documentation, I had hired three summer students and given them the job of transforming the "development workbook" type of documentation we had for certain parts of the system into something more formal, namely Iverson notation, which the three students had learned while taking a course given by Ken Iverson at Fox Lane High School in Mount Kisco, NY. One of the students was Eric Iverson, Ken's son.

As I walked by the office the three students shared, I could hear sounds of an argument going on. I poked my head in the door, and

Eric asked me, "Isn't it true that everyone knows the notation we're using is called APL?" I was sorry to have to disappoint him by confessing that I had never heard it called that. Where had he got the idea it was well known? And who had decided to call it that? In fact, why did it have to be called anything? Quite a while later I heard how it was named. When the implementation effort started in June of 1966, the documentation effort started, too. I suppose when they had to write about "it," Falkoff and Iverson realized that they would have to give "it" a name. There were probably many suggestions made at that time, but I have heard of only two. A group at SRA in Chicago which was developing instructional materials using the notation was in favor of the name "Mathlab." This did not catch on. Another suggestion was to call it "Iverson's Better Math" and then let people coin the appropriate acronym. This was deemed facetious.

Then one day Adin Falkoff walked into Ken's office and wrote "A Programming Language" on the board, and underneath it the acronym "APL." Thus it was born. It was just a week or so after this that Eric Iverson asked me his question, at a time when the name hadn't yet found its way the thirteen miles up the Taconic Parkway from IBM Research to IBM Mohansic.

There was a period of time, however, when the name was in danger of having to be changed. IBM had just gotten over the experience of having to withdraw the name NPL which it had given to its "New Programming Language," because of a conflict with the use of the same initials by Britain's National Physics Laboratory. The conflict involving APL arose when a paper appeared in the 1966 AFIPS Fall Joint Computer Conference *Proceedings*. It was by George Dodd, of General Motors Research, and was entitled *APL—a language for associative data handling in PL/I.* (PL/I was the name now given to the former NPL.) In the review of this paper that appeared in *Computing Reviews 8,* for September-October 1967 (review 12,753), Saul Rosen wrote:

> *This reviewer has one suggestion that is offered quite seriously, though some readers might consider it frivolous. There already exists at least one language that is reasonably well known by its acronym APL. I refer to the language developed by Iverson for which translators and interpreters have been written on a number of computers. It would be helpful if the authors of the present article could make some minor change in the name of their processor to remove this very global ambiguity.*

George Dodd replied in a letter to the editor that appeared in *CACM 11,* for May 1968, p. 378:

> *I would like to offer a rebuttal to the last paragraph of the otherwise excellent and accurate review of* APL—a language for associative data handling in PL/I. . . . *In the review it is pointed out that there already exists one other language known by the acronym APL; that being the language developed by Kenneth Iverson of IBM. The reviewer concludes that the name of our processor should be changed to avoid a conflict of names.*
>
> *Before naming the language we conducted a thorough search of* Computing Reviews, AFIPS Reviews, *and other sources, and at that time (spring, 1966) ascertained that the APL acronym was unique. Unfortunately, Iverson's language, which is an internal IBM development project and not an announced product, has also come to be known by the same name. We feel our public reference to APL preceded Iverson's and that a more reasonable request from the reviewer would be that the name of the Iverson APL be changed.*

There was a short but fairly intense skirmish inside IBM following the George Dodd letter. I don't know all the details, but I believe the IBM branch office which handled the General

Motors account was supporting George Dodd, and the case for IBM's right to use the initials was being made by Al Rose. I don't know what became of George Dodd's processor. The issue wasn't resolved until late in 1968, and was one of the things preventing the release of APL as a product. Rose eventually won the day by making the case that Iverson had established his stake in the initials when his book ***A Programming Language*** was published in 1962, long before Dodd's use of the letters in 1966. The story goes that, at the final meeting to decide whether to release APL, the account representative said, "The Detroit branch office nonconcurs—" at which point the vice president sitting in judgment replied, "That settles it! Branch offices don't nonconcur." And so IBM retained the use of the letters.

Curiously, in view of the National Physics Laboratory's objection to the programming language named NPL, the Applied Physics Laboratory of Johns Hopkins University never made an issue, as far as I am aware, of IBM's joint use with them of the initials APL.

There is at least one other claimant to the initials. When the IBM Philadelphia Scientific Center closed in 1974, many of the APL people there moved across the continent to the San Francisco area, to work at an IBM language development location in Palo Alto. While this was going on, one of those moving picked up a copy of the *San Francisco Chronicle* which had the headline, "APL LEAVES SAN FRANCISCO." Since he had just pulled up stakes in the Philadelphia area, he was startled to see that the same thing was about to happen again in San Francisco. On closer inspection, however, it developed that the story concerned the departure of the facilities of the steamship company, American President Lines, from the docks of San Francisco to the docks across the bay in Oakland.

Eugene E. McDonnell

September 1981
Palo Alto

1 Formalism in Programming Languages

Formalism in Programming Languages*

Kenneth E. Iverson

International Business Machines Corporation, Yorktown Heights, New York

Introduction

Although the question of equivalences between algorithms expressed in the same or different languages has received some attention in the literature, the more practical question of formal identities among statements in a single language has received virtually none. The importance of such identities in theoretical work is fairly obvious. The present paper will be addressed primarily to the practical implications for a compiler.

The formal identities can be incorporated directly into a compiler, or can alternatively be used by a programmer to derive a more efficient equivalent of a program specified by an analyst. The identities cited include (1) *dualities* which permit the inclusion of only one of a dual pair as a basic operator, (2) *partitioning identities* which permit the automatic allocation of limited fast-access storage in operations on arrays, (3) *permutation identities* which permit the adoption of a processing sequence suited to the particular representation used (e.g., row list or column list of a matrix), (4) *general associativity and distributivity identities* for double operators (determined as a function of the properties of the basic operators) which permit efficient reordering of operations, (5) *transposition identities*, and (6) the automatic extension of the appropriate identities to any ad hoc operations (i.e., subroutines or procedures) defined by any user of the compiler.

The discussion will be based upon a programming language which has been presented in full elsewhere [1]. However, the relevant aspects of the language will first be summarized for reference.

* Received July, 1963. Presented at a Working Conference on Mechanical Language Structures, Princeton, N. J., August 1963, sponsored by the Association for Computing Machinery, the Institute for Defense Analyses, and the Business Equipment Manufacturers Association. This work was done at Harvard University while the author was a visiting lecturer, February through June, 1963.

The problems of transliteration and syntax which commonly dominate discussions of language will here be subordinated as follows. The symbols employed will permit the immediate determination of the *class* to which each belongs; thus literals are denoted by roman type, variables are denoted by italics (lowercase, lowercase bold, and uppercase bold for scalar, vector and matrix, respectively), and operators are denoted by distinct (usually nonalphabetic) symbols. The problems of transliteration (i.e., mapping the set of symbols employed onto the smaller set provided in a computer) and of mapping positional information (such as subscripts and superscripts) onto a linear representation therefore can, and will, be subordinated to questions of the structure of an adequate language.

The Language[1]

1. The left arrow "←" denotes "specification," and each[2] statement in the language is of the form

$$x \leftarrow \alpha$$

where x is a variable and α is some function.

2. The application of any unary operator $\bigcirc$ to a scalar argument x is denoted by $\bigcirc x$, and the application of a binary operator $\bigcirc$ to the arguments x, y is denoted by $x \bigcirc y$. The set of basic operators and symbols in shown in Table 1. The use of the same symbol for a binary and a unary operator (e.g., $x \lfloor y$ for $\min(x, y)$ and $\lfloor x$ for largest integer not exceeding x) produces no ambiguity and does conserve symbols.

As shown in Table 1, any relation is treated as an operator (denoted by the usual symbol for the relation) having the range *zero* and *one* (logical variables). Thus, for integers i and j, the operator "$=$" is equivalent to the Kronecker delta.

[1] The language described here differs from that in [1] in minor details designed to further systematize and simplify its structure.

[2] Except for branching statements, which are not relevant to the present discussion.

TABLE 1. Symbols for Basic Operators

Unary Operation	Symbol	Binary Operation	Symbols
Absolute value	$\vert$	Arithmetic operators	$+ \; - \; \times \; \div$
Minus	$-$	Arithmetic relations	$< \; \leqq \; = \; \geqq \; > \; \neq$
Floor (largest integer contained)	$\lfloor$	Max, Min	$\ulcorner \; \llcorner$
Ceiling (smallest integer containing)	$\ulcorner$	Exponentiation (y^x)	$x \sqcap y$
Logical negation	$\sim$	Residue mod m	$m \mid n$
Reciprocation ($\div x \leftrightarrow 1 \div x$)	$\div$	Logical AND, OR	$\wedge \; \vee$

TABLE 2. Unary Operations Defined on Arrays

$\nu \boldsymbol{x}$	Dimension of vector $\boldsymbol{x}$
$\nu \boldsymbol{A}$	Row dimension of matrix $\boldsymbol{A}$ (dimension of *row* vectors)
$\mu \boldsymbol{A}$	Column dimension of matrix $\boldsymbol{A}$ (dimension of *column* vectors)
⊖ ⦶ ⦸ ⊘	Transposition of matrix about axis indicated by the straight line (⦸$\boldsymbol{A}$ is ordinary transposition of $\boldsymbol{A}$)
⦶	⦶$\boldsymbol{x}$ denotes transposition of vector $\boldsymbol{x}$ (reversal of order of components)
$\perp$	Base-two value of vector

3. The ith component of a vector $\boldsymbol{x}$ is denoted by $\boldsymbol{x}_i$, the ith row vector of a matrix $\boldsymbol{M}$ by $\boldsymbol{M}^i$, the jth column vector by $\boldsymbol{M}_j$, and the (i, j)th element by $\boldsymbol{M}_j^i$. A vector may be represented by a list of its components separated by commas. Thus, the statement

$$\boldsymbol{x} \leftarrow 1, 2, 3, 4$$

specifies $\boldsymbol{x}$ as a vector of dimension 4 comprising the first four positive integers. In particular, catenation of two vectors $\boldsymbol{x}$ and $\boldsymbol{y}$ may be denoted by $\boldsymbol{x}, \boldsymbol{y}$.

4. Operators are extended component-by-component to arrays. Thus if $\bigcirc$ is any operator (unary or binary as appropriate),[3]

$$\boldsymbol{r} \leftarrow \bigcirc \boldsymbol{x} \leftrightarrow \boldsymbol{r}_i \leftarrow \bigcirc \boldsymbol{x}_i$$

$$\boldsymbol{r} \leftarrow \boldsymbol{x} \bigcirc \boldsymbol{y} \leftrightarrow \boldsymbol{r}_i \leftarrow \boldsymbol{x}_i \bigcirc \boldsymbol{y}_i$$

$$\boldsymbol{R} \leftarrow \bigcirc \boldsymbol{M} \leftrightarrow \boldsymbol{R}_j^i \leftarrow \bigcirc \boldsymbol{M}_j^i$$

$$\boldsymbol{R} \leftarrow \boldsymbol{M} \bigcirc \boldsymbol{N} \leftrightarrow \boldsymbol{R}_j^i \leftarrow \boldsymbol{M}_j^i \bigcirc \boldsymbol{N}_j^i.$$

5. The order of execution of operations is determined by parentheses in the usual way and, except for intervening parentheses, operations are executed in order from *right to left*, with no priorities accorded to multiplication or other operators.

6. Certain unary operators are defined upon vectors and matrices rather than upon scalars. These appear in Table 2 and include the *dimension* operators ν and μ as well as the *transposition* operators ⊖, ⦶, ⊘, ⦸, in which the symbols indicate the axis of transposition of a matrix.

7. It is convenient to provide symbols for certain constant vectors and matrices as shown in Table 3. The parenthetic expression indicating the dimension of each may be elided when it is otherwise determined by conformability with some known vector.

TABLE 3. Constant Vectors and Square Matrices of Dimension n

Symbol	Designated Constant	
$\boldsymbol{\epsilon}(n)$	Full vector (all 1's)	Logical Vectors
$\boldsymbol{\epsilon}^j(n)$	jth unit vector (1 in position j)	
$\boldsymbol{\alpha}^j(n)$	Prefix vector of weight j (j leading 1's)	
$\boldsymbol{\omega}^j(n)$	Suffix vector of weight j (j trailing 1's)	
$\boldsymbol{\iota}^j(n)$	Interval vector ($j, j+1, \cdots, j+n-1$)	
□(n)	Zero matrix	Logical Matrices
⧅(n)	Identity matrix (1's on diagonal)	
◳(n)	Strict upper right triangle (1's above diagonal)	
◥(n)	Upper right triangle (1's above and on diagonal)	
◲(n)	Strict lower right triangle	
⋮		
◤(n)	Upper left triangle	

8. If $\alpha(i)$ denotes one of a family of variables (e.g, scalars x^i or $\boldsymbol{x}_i$, vectors $\boldsymbol{x}^i$ or $\boldsymbol{X}^i$ or $\boldsymbol{X}_j$, or matrices ${}^i\boldsymbol{X}$) for i belonging to some index set $\boldsymbol{i}$, and if $\bigcirc$ is a binary operator, then for any set $\boldsymbol{s} \subseteq \boldsymbol{i}$,

$$\underset{i}{\overset{\boldsymbol{s}}{\bigcirc}}/\alpha(i) \leftrightarrow \alpha(\boldsymbol{s}_1) \bigcirc \alpha(\boldsymbol{s}_2) \bigcirc \cdots \bigcirc \alpha(\boldsymbol{s}_{\nu \boldsymbol{s}}).$$

If

$$\alpha(i) = \boldsymbol{x}_i \quad \text{and} \quad \boldsymbol{s} = \boldsymbol{\iota}^1(\nu \boldsymbol{x}),$$

or if

$$\alpha(i) = \boldsymbol{X}_i \quad \text{and} \quad \boldsymbol{s} = \boldsymbol{\iota}^1(\nu \boldsymbol{X}),$$

then $\boldsymbol{s}$ and i may be elided. Thus,

$$+/\boldsymbol{x} = \boldsymbol{x}_1 + \boldsymbol{x}_2 + \cdots + \boldsymbol{x}_{\nu \boldsymbol{x}},$$

$$\wedge/\boldsymbol{x} = \boldsymbol{x}_1 \wedge \boldsymbol{x}_2 \cdots \wedge \boldsymbol{x}_{\nu \boldsymbol{x}},$$

$$+/\boldsymbol{X} = \boldsymbol{X}_1 + \boldsymbol{X}_2 + \cdots + \boldsymbol{X}_{\nu \boldsymbol{X}}, \text{ etc.}$$

If $\alpha(i) = \boldsymbol{X}^i$ and $\boldsymbol{s} = \boldsymbol{\iota}^1(\mu \boldsymbol{X})$, then the $\boldsymbol{s}$ and i may be elided provided that a second slash be added to distinguish this case from the preceding one. Thus,

$$\bigcirc//\boldsymbol{X} = \boldsymbol{X}^1 \bigcirc \boldsymbol{X}^2 \bigcirc \cdots \bigcirc \boldsymbol{X}^{\mu \boldsymbol{X}}.$$

9. If α is any argument and $\bigcirc$ is any binary operator, then $\bigcirc^n/\alpha$ denotes the nth power of α with respect to $\bigcirc$.

[3] The symbol $\leftrightarrow$ will be used to denote equivalence.

Formally,

$$\bigcirc^n/\alpha \leftrightarrow \alpha \bigcirc \alpha \bigcirc \cdots \bigcirc \alpha \text{ (to } n \text{ terms).}$$

Hence $\bigcirc^1/\alpha = \alpha$, $\bigcirc^{-1}/\alpha$ is the inverse of α with respect to $\bigcirc$, and $\bigcirc^0/\alpha$ is the identity element of the operator $\bigcirc$ (if they exist).

10. If $\bigcirc_1$ and $\bigcirc_2$ are binary operators, then the *matrix product* $\boldsymbol{A} \overset{\bigcirc_1}{\bigcirc_2} \boldsymbol{B}$ is a matrix of dimension $\mu \boldsymbol{A} \times \nu \boldsymbol{B}$ defined by:

$$(\boldsymbol{A} \overset{\bigcirc_1}{\bigcirc_2} \boldsymbol{B})_j^{\,i} = \bigcirc_1/\boldsymbol{A}^i \bigcirc_2 \boldsymbol{B}_j .$$

In particular, $\boldsymbol{A} \overset{+}{\times} \boldsymbol{B}$ denotes the ordinary matrix product. Moreover, the pair $(\overset{\bigcirc_1}{\bigcirc_2})$ behaves as a binary operator on $\boldsymbol{A}$ and $\boldsymbol{B}$ and hence may be treated as a binary operator. For example, applying the notation of part 9, $(\overset{+}{\times})^{-1}/\boldsymbol{A}$ denotes the ordinary inverse of $\boldsymbol{A}$.

If the post-multiplier is a vector $\boldsymbol{x}$ (i.e., a matrix of one column), the usual conventions of matrix algebra are applied:

$$(\boldsymbol{A} \overset{+}{\times} \boldsymbol{x})_i = \boldsymbol{A}^i \overset{+}{\times} \boldsymbol{x} = +/\boldsymbol{A}^i \times \boldsymbol{x}.$$

Similarly,

$$(\boldsymbol{x} \overset{+}{\times} \boldsymbol{B})_j = \boldsymbol{x} \overset{+}{\times} \boldsymbol{B}_j \;, \quad \text{and} \quad \boldsymbol{x} \overset{+}{\times} \boldsymbol{y} = +/\boldsymbol{x} \times \boldsymbol{y}.$$

11. The *outer product* of two vectors $\boldsymbol{x}$ and $\boldsymbol{y}$ is denoted by $\boldsymbol{x} \overset{\circ}{\bigcirc} \boldsymbol{y}$ and defined as the matrix $\boldsymbol{M}$ of dimension $\nu \boldsymbol{x} \times \nu \boldsymbol{y}$ such that $\boldsymbol{M}_j^{\,i} = \boldsymbol{x}_i \bigcirc \boldsymbol{y}_j$.

12. Deletion from a vector $\boldsymbol{x}$ of those components corresponding to the zeros of a logical vector $\boldsymbol{u}$ of like dimension is called *compression* and is denoted by $\boldsymbol{u}/\boldsymbol{x}$. Compression is extended to matrices both row-by-row and column-by-column as follows:

$$\boldsymbol{Y} \leftarrow \boldsymbol{u}/\boldsymbol{X} \leftrightarrow \boldsymbol{Y}^i = \boldsymbol{u}/\boldsymbol{X}^i$$

$$\boldsymbol{Y} \leftarrow \boldsymbol{u}//\boldsymbol{X} \leftrightarrow \boldsymbol{Y}_j = \boldsymbol{u}/\boldsymbol{X}_j .$$

11. If $\boldsymbol{p}$ is any vector containing only indices of $\boldsymbol{x}$, then $\boldsymbol{x_p}$ is defined as follows:

$$\boldsymbol{y} \leftarrow \boldsymbol{x_p} \leftrightarrow \boldsymbol{y}_i = \boldsymbol{x}_{\boldsymbol{p}_i} , \quad i \in \boldsymbol{\iota}^1(\nu \boldsymbol{p}).$$

If $\boldsymbol{p}$ is a *permutation vector* (containing each of its own indices once) and if $\nu \boldsymbol{p} = \nu \boldsymbol{x}$, then $\boldsymbol{x_p}$ is a *permutation* of $\boldsymbol{x}$.

Permutation is extended to matrices by row and by column as follows:

$$\boldsymbol{Y} \leftarrow \boldsymbol{X_p} \leftrightarrow \boldsymbol{Y}^i = (\boldsymbol{X}^i)_{\boldsymbol{p}}$$

$$\boldsymbol{Y} \leftarrow \boldsymbol{X}^{\boldsymbol{p}} \leftrightarrow \boldsymbol{Y}_j = (\boldsymbol{X}_j)_{\boldsymbol{p}} .$$

12. *Left rotation* is a special case of permutation denoted by $k \uparrow \boldsymbol{x}$ and defined by

$$\boldsymbol{y} \leftarrow k \uparrow \boldsymbol{x} \leftrightarrow \boldsymbol{y}_i = \boldsymbol{x}_{(\nu \boldsymbol{x})|k+i} .$$

Right rotation is denoted by $k \downarrow \boldsymbol{x}$ and is defined analogously.

A *noncyclic* left rotation (*left shift*) denoted by $\underset{\circ}{\uparrow}$ is defined as follows:

$$k \underset{\circ}{\uparrow} \boldsymbol{x} \leftrightarrow (\sim\boldsymbol{\omega}^k) \times k \uparrow \boldsymbol{x}.$$

(The zero attached to the shaft of the arrow suggests that zeros are drawn into the "evacuated" positions). Similarly,

$$k \overset{\circ}{\downarrow} \boldsymbol{x} \leftrightarrow (\sim\boldsymbol{\alpha}^k) \times k \downarrow \boldsymbol{x}.$$

Rotations are extended to matrices in the usual way, a doubled symbol (e.g., $\Uparrow$) denoting rotation of *columns*. For example,

$$(\boldsymbol{k} \underset{\circ}{\uparrow} \boldsymbol{X})^i = \boldsymbol{k}_i \underset{\circ}{\uparrow} \boldsymbol{X}^i,$$

and $(k\boldsymbol{\varepsilon}) \underset{\circ}{\Uparrow} ⧅$ is a matrix with *ones* on the kth superdiagonal.[4]

13. Any new operator defined (e.g., by some algorithm, usually referred to as a *subroutine*) is to be denoted in accordance with Definition (2) and is extended to arrays exactly as any of the basic operators defined in the language. For example, if $x \; gcd \; y$ (or, better, $x \lfloor y$) is used to denote the greatest common divisor of integers x and y, then $\boldsymbol{x} \lfloor \boldsymbol{y}$, $\lfloor / \boldsymbol{x}$, and $\boldsymbol{X} \overset{\lfloor}{\times} \boldsymbol{y}$ are automatically defined. Moreover, if $\boldsymbol{n}$ is a vector of integers and $\boldsymbol{F}^i$ represents the prime factorization of $\boldsymbol{n}_i$ with respect to the vector of primes $\boldsymbol{p}$ (that is, $\boldsymbol{n} = \boldsymbol{F} \overset{\times}{\cap} \boldsymbol{p}$), then clearly $\lfloor / \boldsymbol{n} = (\, \llcorner//\boldsymbol{F}) \overset{\times}{\cap} \boldsymbol{p}$. Similarly, if $x \lceil y$ denotes the l.c.m. of x and y, then $\lceil / \boldsymbol{n} = (\, \ulcorner//\boldsymbol{F}) \overset{\times}{\cap} \boldsymbol{p}$.

Array Operations in a Compiler

The systematic extension of the familiar vector and matrix operations to all operators, and the introduction of the generalized matrix product, greatly increase the utility and frequency of use of array operations in programs, and therefore encourages their inclusion in the source language of any compiler. Array operations can, of course, be added to the repertoire of any source language by providing library or ad hoc subroutines for their execution However, the general array operations spawn a host of useful identities, and these identities cannot be mechanically employed by the compiler unless the array operations are denoted in such a way that they are easily recognizable.

The following example illustrates this point. Consider the vector operation

$$\boldsymbol{x} \leftarrow \boldsymbol{x} + \boldsymbol{y}$$

and the equivalent subroutine (expressed in ALGOL and using $\nu \boldsymbol{x}$ as a known integer):

for $i = 1$ **step** 1 **until** $\nu \boldsymbol{x}$ **do**

$x(i) := x(i) + y(i)$

[4] The $\boldsymbol{\varepsilon}$ may be elided.

It would be difficult to make a compiler recognize all legitimate variants of this program (including, for example, an arbitrary order of scanning the components), and to make it distinguish the quite different and essentially sequential program:

for $i = 1$ **step** 1 **until** $\nu \boldsymbol{x} - 1$ **do**

$x(i+1) := x(i) + y(i)$

The foregoing programs could perhaps be analyzed by a compiler, but they are merely simple examples of much more complex scan procedures which would occur in, say, a matrix product subroutine. A somewhat more complex case is illustrated by the vector operation $\boldsymbol{z} \leftarrow k \uparrow \boldsymbol{x}$, and the equivalent ALGOL program:

for $i = 1$ **step** 1 **until** $\nu \boldsymbol{x}$ **do begin**

if $i + k \leqq \nu \boldsymbol{x}$ **then** $j := i + k$;

else $j := i + k - \nu \boldsymbol{x}$;

$z(j) := x(i)$; **end**

Finally, there is a distinct advantage in incorporating array operations by providing a single general scan for each *type* (e.g., vector, matrix, and matrix product) and treating the operator (or operators) as a parameter. It then matters not whether each operator is effected by a one-line subroutine (i.e., a machine instruction) or a multi-line subroutine, or whether it is incorporated in the array operation as an open or a closed subroutine. If several types of representations are permitted for variables (e.g., double precision, floating point, chained vectors), then a scan routine may have to be provided for each type of representation.

Identities

The identities fall naturally into five main classes: duality, partitioning (selection), permutation, associativity and distributivity, and transposition. A few examples of each class will be presented together with a brief discussion of their uses.

In discussing identities it will be convenient to employ the symbols $\bigcirc$, $\bigcirc_1$, $\bigcirc_2$, ρ, σ, and τ to denote operators, and to define certain functions and relations on operations as follows. The (unary) logical functions $\alpha\bigcirc$ and $\gamma\bigcirc$ are equal to unity iff $\bigcirc$ is associative and $\bigcirc$ is commutative, respectively. The relation $\bigcirc_1\delta\bigcirc_2$ holds iff $\bigcirc_1$ distributes over $\bigcirc_2$, and $\bigcirc_1\alpha\bigcirc_2$ holds iff $\bigcirc_1$ *associates with* $\bigcirc_2$, that is,

$$(x\bigcirc_1 y)\bigcirc_2 z \leftrightarrow x\bigcirc_1(y\bigcirc_2 z).$$

This latter is clearly a generalization of associativity, that is, $\bigcirc_1\alpha\bigcirc_1 \leftrightarrow \alpha\bigcirc_1$. Finally, the unary operator δ applied to the operator $\bigcirc_1$ (denoted by $\delta\bigcirc_1$) produces the operator $\bigcirc_2$ which is *dual to* $\bigcirc_1$ in the sense defined in Table 4 (which summarizes these functions) and in Subsection (a) below.

TABLE 4. OPERATIONS AND RELATIONS DEFINED ON OPERATORS

Self-associativity	$\alpha\bigcirc = 1$ iff $x\bigcirc(y\bigcirc z) \leftrightarrow (x\bigcirc y)\bigcirc z$
Commutativity	$\gamma\bigcirc = 1$ iff $x\bigcirc y \leftrightarrow y\bigcirc x$
Distributivity	$\bigcirc_1\delta\bigcirc_2 = 1$ iff $x\bigcirc_1(y\bigcirc_2 z) \leftrightarrow (x\bigcirc_1 y)\bigcirc_2(x\bigcirc_1 z)$
Associativity	$\bigcirc_1\alpha\bigcirc_2 = 1$ iff $x\bigcirc_1(y\bigcirc_2 z) \leftrightarrow (x\bigcirc_1 y)\bigcirc_2 z$
Dual wrt τ	$\delta\bigcirc$ is an operator such that $(\delta\bigcirc)x \leftrightarrow \tau\bigcirc\tau x$ if $\bigcirc$ is unary; $x(\delta\bigcirc)y \leftrightarrow \tau((\tau x)\bigcirc(\tau y))$ if $\bigcirc$ is binary.

All of the identities are based upon the fundamental properties of the elementary operators summarized in Tables 5–8. Table 5 shows the vector $\boldsymbol{a}$ of binary arithmetic operators and below it two logical matrices describing its properties of distributivity and associativity. These matrices show, for example, that $\boldsymbol{a}_3$ (that is, $\times$) distributes over $+$ and $-$, that $\lceil$ and $\lfloor$ distribute over themselves and each other, and that $\times$ associates with itself and $\div$. The first four rows of the table show the self-associativity of $\boldsymbol{a}$ (equal to the diagonal of the outer product matrix $\boldsymbol{a} \overset{\circ}{\alpha} \boldsymbol{a}$), the commutativity, and the dual operators, wrt $\div$ and $-$, respectively.

Table 6 shows three alternative ways of denoting the 16 binary logical functions: as the vector of operators $\boldsymbol{l}$, as the matrix $\boldsymbol{T}$ of characteristic vectors ($\boldsymbol{T}_i$ is the characteristic vector of operator $\boldsymbol{l}_i$), and as the vector $\perp\!\!\!\perp \boldsymbol{T}$ obtained as the base-two values (expressed in decimal) of the columns of $\boldsymbol{T}$. The symbols employed in $\boldsymbol{l}$ include the familiar symbols $\vee$ and $\wedge$ for *or* and *and*, ∇ and Δ for their complements (i.e., the Pierce function and the Sheffer stroke), **0** and **1** for the zero and identity functions, the six numerical relations $\leqq$, $<$, $=$, $\geqq$, $>$,

TABLE 5. PROPERTIES OF THE BINARY ARITHMETIC OPERATORS

	1	0	1	0	1	1	0	0	$\alpha\boldsymbol{a}$
	1	0	1	0	1	1	0	0	$\gamma\boldsymbol{a}$
			$\times$	$\div$	$\lfloor$	$\lceil$			$\delta\boldsymbol{a}$ (wrt $\div$)
	$+$	$-$			$\lfloor$	$\lceil$			$\delta\boldsymbol{a}$ (wrt $-$)
	$+$	$-$	$\times$	$\div$	$\lceil$	$\lfloor$	$\vert$	$\sqcap$	$\boldsymbol{a}$
Distributivity $+$	0	0	0	0	1	1	0	0	$\boldsymbol{a}\overset{\circ}{\delta}\boldsymbol{a}$†
$-$	0	0	0	0	r	r	0	0	
$\times$	1	1	0	0	0	0	1	0	
$\div$	r	r	0	0	0	0	r	0	
$\lceil$	0	0	0	0	1	1	0	0	
$\lfloor$	0	0	0	0	1	1	0	0	
$\vert$	0	0	0	0	0	0	0	0	
$\sqcap$	0	0	l	l	l	l	0	0	
Associativity $+$	1	1	0	0	0	0	0	0	$\boldsymbol{a}\overset{\circ}{\alpha}\boldsymbol{a}$
$-$	0	0	0	0	0	0	0	0	
$\times$	0	0	1	1	0	0	0	0	
$\div$	0	0	0	0	0	0	0	0	
$\lceil$	0	0	0	0	1	0	0	0	
$\lfloor$	0	0	0	0	0	1	0	0	
$\vert$	0	0	0	0	0	0	0	0	
$\sqcap$	0	0	0	0	0	0	0	0	

† l and r denote left and right distributivity.

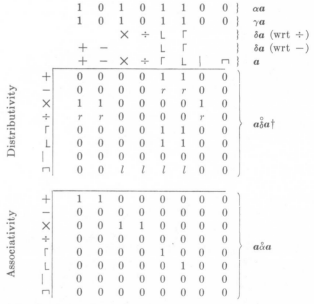

TABLE 6. PROPERTIES OF THE BINARY LOGICAL OPERATORS

1	1	0	1	0	1	1	1	0	1	0	0	0	0	0	1	} $\boldsymbol{\alpha l}$
1	1	0	0	0	0	1	1	1	1	0	0	0	0	1	1	} $\boldsymbol{\gamma l}$
1	$\vee$	$\geqq$	$\boldsymbol{\alpha}$	$\leqq$	$\boldsymbol{\omega}$	$=$	$\wedge$	Δ	$\neq$	$\bar{\boldsymbol{\omega}}$	$>$	$\bar{\boldsymbol{\alpha}}$	$<$	∇	**0**	} $\delta\boldsymbol{l}$*
0	0	0	0	0	0	0	0	1	1	1	1	1	1	1	1	$\boldsymbol{T}$
0	0	0	0	1	1	1	1	0	0	0	0	1	1	1	1	
0	0	1	1	0	0	1	1	0	0	1	1	0	0	1	1	
0	1	0	1	0	1	0	1	0	1	0	1	0	1	0	1	

Distributivity		**0**	$\wedge$	$>$	$\boldsymbol{\alpha}$	$<$	$\boldsymbol{\omega}$	$\neq$	$\vee$	∇	$=$	$\bar{\boldsymbol{\omega}}$	$\geqq$	$\bar{\boldsymbol{\alpha}}$	$\leqq$	Δ	**1**	} $\boldsymbol{l}$
		0	1	2	3	4	5	6	7	8	9	10	11	12	13	14	15	} $\perp\!\!\perp\boldsymbol{T}$
0	0	1	1	1	1	1	1	1	1	0	0	0	0	0	0	0	0	$\boldsymbol{l}\overset{\circ}{\delta}\boldsymbol{l}$
$\wedge$	1	1	1	1	1	1	1	1	1	0	0	0	0	0	0	0	0	
$>$	2	0	0	0	1	0	1	0	0	0	0	0	0	0	0	0	0	
$\boldsymbol{\alpha}$	3	0	1	0	1	0	1	0	1	0	0	0	0	0	0	0	0	
$<$	4	1	1	1	1	1	1	1	1	0	0	0	0	0	0	0	0	
$\boldsymbol{\omega}$	5	1	1	1	1	1	1	1	1	1	1	1	1	1	1	1	1	
$\neq$	6	0	0	0	1	0	1	0	0	0	0	1	0	1	0	0	0	
$\vee$	7	0	1	0	1	0	1	0	1	0	1	0	1	0	1	0	1	
∇	8	0	0	0	1	0	1	0	0	0	0	0	0	0	0	0	0	
$=$	9	0	0	0	1	0	1	0	0	0	0	1	0	1	0	0	0	
$\bar{\boldsymbol{\omega}}$	10	0	0	0	1	0	1	0	0	0	0	1	0	1	0	0	0	
$\geqq$	11	0	0	0	1	0	1	0	0	0	0	0	0	0	0	0	0	
$\bar{\boldsymbol{\alpha}}$	12	0	1	0	1	0	1	0	1	0	0	0	0	0	0	0	0	
$\leqq$	13	0	1	0	1	0	1	0	1	0	1	0	1	0	1	0	1	
Δ	14	0	0	0	1	0	1	0	0	0	0	0	0	0	0	0	0	
1	15	0	1	0	1	0	1	0	1	0	1	0	1	0	1	0	1	

Associativity		**0**	$\wedge$	$>$	$\boldsymbol{\alpha}$	$<$	$\boldsymbol{\omega}$	$\neq$	$\vee$	∇	$=$	$\bar{\boldsymbol{\omega}}$	$\geqq$	$\bar{\boldsymbol{\alpha}}$	$\leqq$	Δ	**1**	} $\boldsymbol{l}$
		0	1	2	3	4	5	6	7	8	9	10	11	12	13	14	15	} $\perp\!\!\perp\boldsymbol{T}$
0	0	1	1	1	1	0	0	0	0	0	0	0	0	0	0	0	0	$\boldsymbol{l}\overset{\circ}{\alpha}\boldsymbol{l}$
$\wedge$	1	1	1	1	1	0	0	0	0	0	0	0	0	0	0	0	0	
$>$	2	0	0	0	1	0	0	0	0	0	0	0	0	0	0	0	0	
$\boldsymbol{\alpha}$	3	0	0	0	1	0	0	0	0	0	0	0	0	0	0	0	0	
$<$	4	1	1	1	1	0	0	0	0	0	0	0	0	0	0	0	0	
$\boldsymbol{\omega}$	5	1	1	1	1	1	1	1	1	1	1	1	1	1	1	1	1	
$\neq$	6	0	0	0	1	0	0	1	0	0	1	0	0	1	0	0	0	
$\vee$	7	0	0	0	1	0	0	0	1	0	0	0	1	0	0	0	1	
∇	8	0	0	0	1	0	0	0	0	0	0	0	0	0	0	0	0	
$=$	9	0	0	0	1	0	0	1	0	0	1	0	0	1	0	0	0	
$\bar{\boldsymbol{\omega}}$	10	0	0	0	1	0	0	1	0	0	1	0	0	1	0	0	0	
$\geqq$	11	0	0	0	1	0	0	0	0	0	0	0	0	0	0	0	0	
$\bar{\boldsymbol{\alpha}}$	12	0	0	0	1	0	0	0	0	0	0	0	0	0	0	0	0	
$\leqq$	13	0	0	0	1	0	0	0	1	0	0	0	1	0	0	0	1	
Δ	14	0	0	0	1	0	0	0	0	0	0	0	0	0	0	0	0	
1	15	0	0	0	1	0	0	0	1	0	0	0	1	0	0	0	1	

* Duality with respect to $\sim$.

$\neq$, and the symbols $\boldsymbol{\alpha}$, $\boldsymbol{\omega}$, $\bar{\boldsymbol{\alpha}}$, and $\bar{\boldsymbol{\omega}}$ for the four "unary" functions, that is, $x\boldsymbol{\alpha}y = x$, $x\boldsymbol{\omega}y = y$, $x\bar{\boldsymbol{\alpha}}y = \bar{x}$ and $x\bar{\boldsymbol{\omega}}y = \bar{y}$.

The remaining portion of Table 6 is arranged like Table 5. Since $((\boldsymbol{\alpha l}) \wedge \boldsymbol{\gamma l})/\boldsymbol{l} = (\boldsymbol{0}, \wedge, \neq, \vee, =, \boldsymbol{1})$, it follows that the only nontrivial associative commutative logical operators are $\boldsymbol{g} = (\wedge, \vee, \neq, =)$. The properties of this particularly useful subset (abstracted from Table 6) are summarized in Table 7.

Certain functions of the matrices $\boldsymbol{l}\overset{\circ}{\alpha}\boldsymbol{l}$ and $\boldsymbol{l}\overset{\circ}{\delta}\boldsymbol{l}$ are also of interest—for example, the matrix $(\boldsymbol{l}\overset{\circ}{\alpha}\boldsymbol{l}) > (\boldsymbol{l}\overset{\circ}{\delta}\boldsymbol{l})$ shows that there are only six operator pairs which are associative and not distributive, namely, $(\neq, \neq)$ $(\neq, =)$, $(=, \neq)$, $(=, =)$, $(\bar{\boldsymbol{\omega}}, \neq)$ and $(\bar{\boldsymbol{\omega}}, =)$.

(a) DUALITIES

A unary operator τ is said to be *self-inverse* if $\tau\tau x \leftrightarrow x$. If ρ, σ and τ are unary operators, if τ is self-inverse, and if $\rho x \leftrightarrow \tau\sigma\tau x$, then $\sigma x \leftrightarrow \tau\rho\tau x$, and ρ and σ are said to be *dual*[5] *with respect to* τ. The floor and ceiling operators $\lfloor$ and $\lceil$ are obviously dual with respect to the minus operator. Duality clearly extends to arrays, e.g.,

$$\lceil \boldsymbol{x} \leftrightarrow - \lfloor - \boldsymbol{x}.$$

The duals of unary operators are shown in Table 8 as the vector $\delta\boldsymbol{c}$.

If ρ and σ are binary operators, if τ is a self-inverse unary operator, and if

$$\rho x \leftrightarrow \tau(\tau x)\sigma(\tau y),$$

then ρ and σ are said to be *dual with respect to* τ. The max and min operators ($\lceil$ and $\lfloor$) are dual with respect to minus, and *or* and *and* ($\vee$ and $\wedge$) are dual with respect to negation ($\sim$), as are the relations $\neq$ and $=$.

Dual operators are displayed in the vectors $\delta\boldsymbol{a}$ and $\delta\boldsymbol{l}$ of Tables 5 and 6. Each of the 16 logical operators has a dual:

$$\delta\boldsymbol{l}_i = \boldsymbol{l}_{\perp \oplus \sim \boldsymbol{T}_i}\,.$$

The duality of binary operators ρ and σ also extends to vectors and matrices. Moreover, when they are used in reduction, the following identities hold:

$$\rho/\boldsymbol{x} \leftrightarrow \tau\sigma/\tau\boldsymbol{x},$$

$$\rho/\boldsymbol{X} \leftrightarrow \tau\sigma/\tau\boldsymbol{X},$$

$$\rho//\boldsymbol{X} \leftrightarrow \tau\sigma//\tau\boldsymbol{X}.$$

TABLE 7. PROPERTIES OF THE NONTRIVIAL ASSOCIATIVE COMMUTATIVE LOGICAL OPERATORS

	$\wedge$	$\vee$	$\neq$	$=$ } $\boldsymbol{g}$	
$\wedge$	1	1	1	0	$\boldsymbol{g}\overset{\circ}{\delta}\boldsymbol{g}$
$\vee$	1	1	0	1	
$\neq$	0	0	0	0	
$=$	0	0	0	0	
$\wedge$	1	0	0	0	$\boldsymbol{g}\overset{\circ}{\alpha}\boldsymbol{g}$
$\vee$	0	1	0	0	
$\neq$	0	0	1	1	
$=$	0	0	1	1	

TABLE 8. PROPERTIES OF THE UNARY OPERATORS

$\vert$	$\lfloor$	$\lceil$	$-$	$\div$	$\sim$	} $\boldsymbol{c}$
	$\lceil$	$\lfloor$	$-$	$\div$		} $\delta\boldsymbol{c}$ (wrt $-$)
			$-$	$\div$		} $\delta\boldsymbol{c}$ (wrt $\div$)
					$\sim$	} $\delta\boldsymbol{c}$ (wrt $\sim$)

[5] Abbreviated as "dual wrt".

For example ,

$$\lfloor/\boldsymbol{x} = -\lceil/-\boldsymbol{x},$$

and

$$\wedge/\boldsymbol{x} = \sim\vee/\sim\boldsymbol{x} \text{ (DeMorgan's Law).}$$

The basic reduction identity (namely, $\rho/\boldsymbol{x} \leftrightarrow \tau\sigma/\tau\boldsymbol{x}$) leads immediately to the following family of identities for the matrix product:

$$\boldsymbol{A}\,{}^{\circ_1}_{\circ_2}\,\boldsymbol{B} \leftrightarrow \tau(\tau\boldsymbol{A})\,{}^{\delta_{\circ_1}}_{\delta_{\circ_2}}(\tau\boldsymbol{B}).$$

For the logical operators, the family comprises 256 identities, of which 144 are nontrival.

Duality relations can be specified for a compiler by a table incorporating $\boldsymbol{l}$ and $\delta\boldsymbol{l}$, and can be employed to obviate the inclusion of a subroutine for one of the dual pair or to transform a source statement to an equivalent form more efficient in execution. For example, in a computer such as the IBM 7090 (which executes an *or* between registers (i.e., logical vectors) much faster than a corresponding *and*, and which quickly performs an *or* over a register (i.e., a test for non-zero)), the operation $\sim(\sim\boldsymbol{x}) \overset{\wedge}{\wedge} \boldsymbol{y}$ is more efficiently executed as the equivalent operation $\boldsymbol{x} \overset{\vee}{\vee} \sim\boldsymbol{y}$, obtained by duality.

(b) Partitioning

Partitioning identities, which permit a segment of a vector result to be expressed in terms of segments of the argument vectors, are of obvious utility in the efficient allocation of limited capacity high-speed storage.

If $\boldsymbol{z} \leftarrow \boldsymbol{x} \bigcirc \boldsymbol{y}$, then $\boldsymbol{u}/\boldsymbol{z} \leftarrow (\boldsymbol{u}/\boldsymbol{x}) \bigcirc (\boldsymbol{u}/\boldsymbol{y})$, where $\boldsymbol{u}$ is an arbitrary (but conformable) logical vector. This simple identity applies for any binary operator $\bigcirc$ and permits any vector operation to be partitioned or segmented at will. A similar identity holds for unary operators.

From the definition of the matrix product it is clear that for any binary operators ρ and σ,

$$\boldsymbol{u}/\boldsymbol{A}\,{}^{\rho}_{\sigma}\,\boldsymbol{B} \leftrightarrow \boldsymbol{A}\,{}^{\rho}_{\sigma}\,\boldsymbol{u}/\boldsymbol{B},$$

and

$$\boldsymbol{u}//\boldsymbol{A}\,{}^{\rho}_{\sigma}\,\boldsymbol{B} \leftrightarrow (\boldsymbol{u}//\boldsymbol{A})\,{}^{\rho}_{\sigma}\,\boldsymbol{B}.$$

If ρ is any associative commutative operator (i.e., $\alpha\rho = \gamma\rho = 1$), then

$$\rho/\boldsymbol{x} \leftrightarrow (\rho/\overline{\boldsymbol{u}}/\boldsymbol{x})\rho(\rho/\boldsymbol{u}/\boldsymbol{x}),$$

where $\overline{\boldsymbol{u}}$ is used as an alternative notation for $(\sim\boldsymbol{u})$. Consequently,

$$\boldsymbol{A}\,{}^{\mu}_{\sigma}\,\boldsymbol{B} \leftrightarrow ((\overline{\boldsymbol{u}}/\boldsymbol{A})\,{}^{\rho}_{\sigma}\,(\overline{\boldsymbol{u}}//\boldsymbol{B}))\rho((\boldsymbol{u}/\boldsymbol{A})\,{}^{\rho}_{\sigma}\,(\boldsymbol{u}//\boldsymbol{B})).$$

Since the distributivity of σ and ρ is not involved, the foregoing identity (which is a simple generalization of the familiar identity for the product of partitioned matrices) applies to most of the common arithmetic and logical operators.

The identity for the two-way partitioning effected by $\boldsymbol{u}$ and $\overline{\boldsymbol{u}}$ can obviously be extended to a $(\mu\boldsymbol{P})$-way partitioning effected by a logical *partition* matrix $\boldsymbol{P}$ (defined by $\boldsymbol{\varepsilon} = +//\boldsymbol{P}$) as follows:

$$\boldsymbol{A}\,{}^{\rho}_{\sigma}\,\boldsymbol{B} \leftrightarrow \rho_i^{\iota^1(\mu\boldsymbol{P})}/(\boldsymbol{P}^i/\boldsymbol{A})\,{}^{\rho}_{\sigma}\,(\boldsymbol{P}^i//\boldsymbol{B}).$$

This is the form most useful in allocating storage; if fast-access storage for $2n$ components of $\boldsymbol{A}$ and $\boldsymbol{B}$ were available, $\boldsymbol{P}$ would normally be chosen such that $\boldsymbol{P}^i = (n \times i) \downarrow \boldsymbol{\omega}^n$.

(c) Permutation

In this section, $\boldsymbol{p}$, $\boldsymbol{q}$ and $\boldsymbol{r}$ will denote permutation vectors of appropriate dimensions.

If $\bigcirc$ is any binary operator, then

$$(\boldsymbol{x} \bigcirc \boldsymbol{y})_{\boldsymbol{p}} \leftrightarrow \boldsymbol{x}_{\boldsymbol{p}} \bigcirc \boldsymbol{y}_{\boldsymbol{p}},$$

i.e., permutation distributes over any binary operator. For any unary operator $\bigcirc$,

$$(\bigcirc\boldsymbol{x})_{\boldsymbol{p}} \leftrightarrow \bigcirc(\boldsymbol{x}_{\boldsymbol{p}}),$$

and permutation therefore commutes with any unary operator. Consider, for example, a vector $\boldsymbol{x}$ whose components are arranged in increasing order on some function $g(\boldsymbol{x}_i)$ [e.g., lexical order so as to permit binary search] but is represented by (i.e., stored as) the vector $\boldsymbol{y}$ in arbitrary order and the permutation vector $\boldsymbol{p}$ such that $\boldsymbol{x} = \boldsymbol{y}_{\boldsymbol{p}}$. Then the operation $\boldsymbol{z} \leftarrow \bigcirc\boldsymbol{x}$ may be executed as $\boldsymbol{w} \leftarrow \bigcirc\boldsymbol{y}$, where $\boldsymbol{z} = \boldsymbol{w}_{\boldsymbol{p}}$.

For any binary operators ρ and σ,

$$(\boldsymbol{A}\,{}^{\rho}_{\sigma}\,\boldsymbol{B})_{\boldsymbol{q}}{}^{\boldsymbol{p}} \leftrightarrow \boldsymbol{A}^{\boldsymbol{p}}\,{}^{\rho}_{\sigma}\,\boldsymbol{B}_{\boldsymbol{q}}. \qquad (1)$$

Moreover, if $\alpha\rho = \gamma\rho = 1$, then $\rho/\boldsymbol{x} \leftrightarrow \rho/\boldsymbol{x}_{\boldsymbol{p}}$, and consequently

$$\boldsymbol{A}_{\boldsymbol{r}}\,{}^{\rho}_{\sigma}\,\boldsymbol{B}^{\boldsymbol{r}} \leftrightarrow \boldsymbol{A}\,{}^{\rho}_{\sigma}\,\boldsymbol{B}. \qquad (2)$$

Finally, then

$$(\boldsymbol{A}\,{}^{\rho}_{\sigma}\,\boldsymbol{B})_{\boldsymbol{q}}{}^{\boldsymbol{p}} \leftrightarrow \boldsymbol{A}^{\boldsymbol{p}}_{\boldsymbol{r}}\,{}^{\rho}_{\sigma}\,\boldsymbol{B}_{\boldsymbol{q}}{}^{\boldsymbol{r}}.$$

This single identity permits considerable freedom in transforming a matrix product operation to a form best suited to the access limitations imposed by the representation (i.e., storage allocation) used for $\boldsymbol{A}$ and $\boldsymbol{B}$ (e.g., row-by-row and column-by-column lists).

For the special case $\boldsymbol{q} = \boldsymbol{\iota}^1$, $\boldsymbol{A} = \boxbslash$, $\rho = +$, and $\sigma = \times$, equation (1) reduces to the well-known method of permuting the columns of a matrix by ordinary premultiplication by a permutation matrix $\boxbslash^{\boldsymbol{p}}$, that is,

$$\boldsymbol{B}^{\boldsymbol{p}} \leftrightarrow \boxbslash^{\boldsymbol{p}}\,{}^{+}_{\times}\,\boldsymbol{B}.$$

The fact that $\boxbslash^{\boldsymbol{p}}$ and $\oslash\boxbslash^{\boldsymbol{p}}$ are inverse permutations (i.e., $(\oslash\boxbslash^{\boldsymbol{p}})\,{}^{+}_{\times}\,\boxbslash^{\boldsymbol{p}} = \boxbslash$) is obtainable directly from equation (2) and the fact that $\oslash\boxbslash^{\boldsymbol{p}} = (\oslash\boxbslash)_{\boldsymbol{p}} = \boxbslash_{\boldsymbol{p}}$.

The rotation operators $\uparrow$, $\downarrow$, $\Uparrow$, $\Downarrow$ are special cases of permutations; consequently,

$$j \Uparrow k \uparrow \boldsymbol{A}\,{}^{\rho}_{\sigma}\,\boldsymbol{B} \leftrightarrow (j \Uparrow \boldsymbol{A})\,{}^{\rho}_{\sigma}\,(k \uparrow \boldsymbol{B}).$$

Moreover, this identity still holds when the cyclic rotation operators are replaced by the corresponding noncyclic operators $\underset{\circ}{\uparrow}$, $\overset{\circ}{\downarrow}$, $\underset{\circ}{\Uparrow}$, and $\overset{\circ}{\Downarrow}$. In particular,

$$j \underset{\circ}{\Uparrow} \boldsymbol{B} = j \underset{\circ}{\Uparrow} (\boxbslash \overset{+}{\times} \boldsymbol{B}) = (j \underset{\circ}{\Uparrow} \boxbslash) \overset{+}{\times} \boldsymbol{B},$$

and if

$$\boldsymbol{B} = h \underset{\circ}{\Uparrow} \boxbslash,$$

then

$$(h + j) \underset{\circ}{\Uparrow} \boxbslash = j \underset{\circ}{\Uparrow} h \underset{\circ}{\Uparrow} \dot{\boxbslash} = (j \underset{\circ}{\Uparrow} \boxbslash) \overset{+}{\times} (h \underset{\circ}{\Uparrow} \boxbslash),$$

a well-known identity for the superdiagonal matrices $h \underset{\circ}{\Uparrow} \boxbslash$ and $k \underset{\circ}{\Uparrow} \boxbslash$.

(d) Associativity and Distributivity of Double Operators

If $\alpha\rho = \gamma\rho = \sigma\delta\rho = 1$, then $\alpha(^{\rho}_{\sigma}) = 1$; that is,

$$\boldsymbol{A}_{\sigma}(\boldsymbol{B}^{\rho}_{\sigma}\boldsymbol{C}) \leftrightarrow (\boldsymbol{A}^{\rho}_{\sigma}\boldsymbol{B})^{\rho}_{\sigma}\boldsymbol{C}.$$

Moreover, $(^{\rho}_{\sigma})\delta\rho = 1$; that is

$$\boldsymbol{A}^{\rho}_{\sigma}(\boldsymbol{B}\rho\boldsymbol{C}) \leftrightarrow (\boldsymbol{A}^{\rho}_{\sigma}\boldsymbol{B})\rho(\boldsymbol{A}^{\rho}_{\sigma}\boldsymbol{C}).$$

For example, if $\boldsymbol{C}$ is the connection matrix of a directed graph, then $\boldsymbol{B} = \boldsymbol{C} \overset{\vee}{\wedge} \boldsymbol{C}$ is the matrix of connections of length *two*; the operator $(\overset{\vee}{\wedge})$ is associative and distributes over $\vee$. Similarly, if $\boldsymbol{D}$ is a distance matrix ($\boldsymbol{D}^{i}_{j}$ is the distance from point i to point j), then $\boldsymbol{E} = \boldsymbol{D} \overset{\llcorner}{+} \boldsymbol{D}$ is the matrix of minimum distance for trips of two legs; $\left(\overset{\llcorner}{+}\right)$ is associative and distributes over $\llcorner$.

The associativity of matrix product operators can be very helpful in arranging an efficient sequence of calculations on matrices stored row-by-row or column-by-column. For the logical operators, the number of associative double operators is given by the expression

$$+/+/(\alpha\boldsymbol{l})/\boldsymbol{l}\overset{\circ}{\circ}\boldsymbol{l}$$

which (according to Table 6) has the value 66.

(e) Transpositions

Of the unary transposition operators, ⊖ and ⌽ are special cases of permutation, but ⍉ and ⊘ are not. Table 9 shows the multiplication table for the group generated by these four transpositions. The notation chosen for the four added operators is clear: ○ denotes the identity, ⊕ ↔ ⌽⊖ ↔ ⊖⌽, ⧀ ↔ ⊘⊖ (90° axial left rotation), and ⧁ ↔ ⍉⊖ (axial right rotation). Since ⊕ ↔ ⊘⍉, it could as well have been denoted by ⊗.

The following illustrate the many transposition identities:

$$⌽\boldsymbol{A}^{\rho}_{\sigma}\boldsymbol{B} \leftrightarrow \boldsymbol{A}^{\rho}_{\sigma}⌽\boldsymbol{B} \qquad (3)$$

$$⊖\boldsymbol{A}^{\rho}_{\sigma}\boldsymbol{B} \leftrightarrow (⊖\boldsymbol{A})^{\rho}_{\sigma}\boldsymbol{B} \qquad (4)$$

TABLE 9. Group of Transpositions (rotations of the square)

t∘.t \ t	○	⌽	⊖	⍉	⊘	⊕	⧀	⧁
○	○	⌽	⊖	⍉	⊘	⊕	⧀	⧁
⌽	⌽	○	⊕	⧁	⧀	⊖	⊘	⍉
⊖	⊖	⊕	○	⧀	⧁	⌽	⍉	⊘
⍉	⍉	⧀	⧁	○	⊕	⊘	⌽	⊖
⊘	⊘	⧁	⧀	⊕	○	⍉	⊖	⌽
⊕	⊕	⊖	⌽	⊘	⍉	○	⧁	⧀
⧀	⧀	⍉	⊘	⊖	⌽	⧁	⊕	○
⧁	⧁	⊘	⍉	⌽	⊖	⧀	○	⊕

$$\boldsymbol{A}^{\rho}_{\sigma}\boldsymbol{B} \leftrightarrow (⌽\boldsymbol{A})^{\rho}_{\sigma}(⊖\boldsymbol{B}) \quad \text{if} \quad \alpha\rho = \gamma\rho = 1 \qquad (5)$$

$$⍉(\boldsymbol{A}^{\rho}_{\sigma}\boldsymbol{B}) \leftrightarrow (⍉\boldsymbol{B})^{\rho}_{\sigma}(⍉\boldsymbol{A}) \quad \text{if} \quad \gamma\sigma = 1 \qquad (6)$$

$$⊕(\boldsymbol{A}^{\rho}_{\sigma}\boldsymbol{B}) \leftrightarrow (⊘\boldsymbol{B})^{\rho}_{\sigma}(⊘\boldsymbol{A}) \quad \text{if} \quad \alpha\rho = \gamma\rho = \gamma\sigma = 1. \qquad (7)$$

Identities (3)–(5) are special cases of the permutation identities and permit freedom in the order of scan, which may be important if a backward-chained representation is employed for the vectors involved. Identity (6) is the generalization of the well-known transposition identity of matrix algebra. Identity (7) is obtained directly from (6) by the application of (3), (4) and (5).

Conclusion

The use of a programming language in which elementary operations are extended systematically to arrays provides a wealth of useful identities. If the array operations are incorporated directly in a compiler for the language, these identities can be automatically applied in compilation, using a small number of small tables describing the fundamental properties of the elementary operators. Moreover, the identities can be extended to any ad hoc operators specified by the source program, provided only that the fundamental characteristics (associativity, etc.) of the ad hoc operators are supplied.

Exploitation of the identities within the compiler will, of course, increase the complexity of the compiler, and one would perhaps incorporate only a selected subset of them. However, the possibility of later extensions to exploit further identities is of some value. Finally, the identities are extremely useful to the *programmer* (as opposed to the *analyst* who specifies the overall procedure and who may use the identities in theoretical work), since the tricks used by the programmer, as in allocating storage (partitioning) or modifying the sequence of a scan (permutation), are almost invariably special cases of the more general identities outlined here.

REFERENCE

1. Iverson, Kenneth E. *A Programming Language*. Wiley, 1962.

DISCUSSION

Gorn: Some almost ancient sources of generalized operators are: Whitehead, *Universal Algebra*, and Grassman, *Die Ausdehnungslehre*. Some more modern sources are: Bourbaki *Algebra*, Forder, *Calculus of Extension*, and Bodewig, *Matrix Calculus*.

Backus: Why this comment?

Gorn: The paper presents generalized relationships among operators. The cited references are directly concerned with such questions.

Brooker: Why do you insist on using a notation which is a nightmare for typist and compositor and impossible to implement with punching and printing equipment currently available? What proposals have you got for overcoming this difficulty?

Iverson: Transliteration is, of course, essential, but I have avoided its treatment first, because a suitable scheme is highly dependent on the particular equipment available, and second, because it is extremely simple. If, for example, you have the stamina of Algol and Mad users (who tirelessly write PROCEDURE and WHENEVER), then you can use the distinct names that I have given (for conversational purposes) to each of the operators. Anyone who prefers briefer symbols can (as I have) easily design schemes which are brief, simple and mnemonic.

Gorn: This question of transliteration: I'm not talking about this paper in particular. In general it is a problem that is always with us. There is a danger that as the transliteration rules become more complicated replacement productions; we rapidly fall into a recognition problem, a translation problem and possibly an unsolvable word problem.

Iverson: Yes, one should distinguish the recognition of identifiers from the syntax, which is of more concern to the ultimate user.

Brooker: It is not obvious to me that these two symbols for FLOOR and CEILING have a great deal of mnemonic value.

Iverson: Yes, but once you have read it, you can remember it.

Gorn: But the more redundance you put in the symbolism of a language, the more equivalence problems you have.

Iverson: Not problems, I suggest that these are assets. In the extreme we could go back to the Assign and the Sheffer stroke, let's say, and then we have no problems.

Ross: I don't remember who asked the original question about notation, but I submit that they find themselves a sugar-daddy or someone with a few thousand bucks and get themselves a display console such as we're getting with programmable characters. You can even publish from it by taking pictures. I don't see why we should let mechanics influence our progress at all.

Iverson: Someone who is interested in standardization would not like that comment—a 48-character set is the thing you know. The limitation on the available character set, I think, is more of a transient phenomenon than the algorithms we want to describe.

Ross: With our console the 48 characters are available, and there is another mode where you can program any bit patterns you want in a matrix; we are doing this specifically for this purpose because we feel that the notation that goes along with the set of ideas should be usable.

Bauer: I would say that compared with some other existing proposals for matrix extensions such as that of Ershov this is a much more closed consistent system. No one can say today how far we will go in using such a language in the near future.

Iverson: Let me comment that it is useful to distinguish two reasons for learning a language; one is for description and analysis and the other is for automatic execution. I submit that this kind of formalism is extremely helpful in analyzing difficult problems without worrying about whether one wants to execute the resulting program. As a matter of fact, I would use this as a preliminary before going into some language that is executable.

Gorn: As I have it, the descriptive language you have *does* have direct translation properties into command language.

Holt: I would like to translate that comment of Ken's about description, analysis, and execution in the following way: Programming languages are machine-dependent—one is appropriate for the human processor and another for the computer.

Iverson: Well, I would disagree with that because I would use exactly the same notation for describing the computer. In fact, I've done it for the 7090 or most of the 7090, and other machines as well. In fact, you can say the instruction set of the machine is another form of language with a slave to execute it.

Holt: Then, what was the meaning of your comment?

Iverson: At this point, for example, this is not a source language in the sense that there is a mechanism available for translating it into some other language. There is no convenient way for automatic execution by translation or direct execution. Now I suggest that the notation is worthwhile just for analysis even though later we have to do a hand translation into some executable language.

Green: If I may interrupt for a moment, I think we should limit the discussion on notation to the next five minutes. And we should get to other questions.

Tompkins: There exist problems around here which were coded first in essentially this language and then were translated with great care into Fortran, for example.

Perlis: How should this language be used *on* computers? For what class of problems—*on* or *off* computers? Thus, it's not quite clear to me that a mathematical proof of an algorithm written in Fortran (the same algorithm if you will) is any more difficult than a mathematical proof of one of your algorithms. Algorithms are written for two reasons: 1) execution by computer: which means that it is pointless to write it if you cannot execute it on a computer, and 2) for description and analysis. Now if the description is difficult to read, then it fails somewhat. If, in addition, analysis is as difficult, say, as in Algol, then the virtue of the language is questionable.

A last question: You haven't discussed at all the way you describe data. It is not clear that you have a notation for describing data, though you have a great wealth of notation for manipulating data once it is described. Now Algol will obviously be extended to include matrix and vector operations in expressions. So my question is: for what classes of problems, remembering you have no data description, is your description better than "Algolic" descriptions?

Iverson: I'm not sure if I can really separate all these points. The question of representation (data description) is too lengthy to treat here. To save time, let me say that I discuss it in Chapter 3 of my book. This discussion is fairly limited, but adequate.

Concerning the virtues of the language for description and analysis, I can only say that I have found it very useful in many diverse areas, including machine description, search procedures, symbolic logic, sorting and linear programming. Now it is a separate problem as to whether you want to incorporate the complete generality of the language in any particular compiler—but I suggest that it is desirable to have a more general system that you retract from for any particular compiler rather than adding ad hoc provisions to more limited languages.

As to the question of proofs, you can, of course, translate a proof in any language to any other language, but I suggest that the proofs I give are the kind that are immediately obvious to any mathematician. There is, of course, the question of to whom you want your proofs to be obvious. Likewise, for difficulty of reading, the question is, "for whom?" And I suggest that anybody who has ever dealt with matrix operations finds this notation very easy to read.

Perlis: But is it fair to say then that if one is going to create or extend a language that the direction of extension really isn't critical—that the accent should not be put on operations so much, but on data representation or sequence rules?

Iverson: No, I disagree.

Gorn: Since you are supporting an infix notation for binary operators, would it not be useful to have some control operators in the language which would correspond to the combinatory logician's "Application" operation? Also operators for insertion and deletion of parentheses, and operators to adjust priorities in the scopes of other operators, e.g. to construct precedence matrices of the type discussed by Floyd?

Iverson: Let me give a sort of general answer to this sort of thing. You're probably talking about some specialized application for which you want special operators. I submit that no one can design a language that is equally useful for everybody. Instead, what you would like to have is a single core which you can extend in a straightforward manner.

In so far as precedence and hierarchy are concerned, I have not found any great need for them in my work, but I can understand why you might want to use them in compilers. In fact, I think such hierarchy should be included in a tabular form so that it is easily changeable.

Holt: The presentation is a marvelous demonstration of the power of notation in the hands of a very clever man. Conclusions: (1) Let us teach this skill to clever people. (2) Let us create machine mechanisms to respond to notational inventions.

Iverson: On the contrary, the basic notions are very simple and should be introduced at high school level to provide a means for describing algorithms explicitly. For example, the vector can be introduced as a convenient means for naming a *family* of variables and can be used by the student (together with a few very simple operators) to work out explicit algorithms for well-known operations such as decimal addition, polynomial evaluation, etc. A little notation and much care in requiring explicit algorithms would, in fact, clarify and simplify the presentation of elementary mathematics and obviate the teaching of programming as such.

Gosden: Many of the equivalences only become useful and powerful when time dependency is included. For example, each operation on any array implies serial or parallel execution component by component. How can you cover this for serial or parallel statements? Obviously, there are many tricks that are time (or series) dependent in array operations. How do they relate to dualities and equivalences, etc.

Iverson: Parallel operation is implied by any vector operation; serial operation can be made explicit by a program showing the specified sequence of operations on components. Distinctions of this type (employing the present notation) are made clear in Falkoff's "Algorithms for Parallel Search Memories" [*J. ACM*, Oct. 1962].

More complex simultaneity can be expressed by a collection of programs operating concurrently, all mutually independent but for interaction through certain (interlock) variables common to some two or more programs. Explicit dependence on real time can be introduced by incorporating, as one of this collection of programs, a program describing a clock (i.e., oscillator)-driven counter.

Gorn: Does your generalized operator notation for matrices lead to a simpler proof of the generalized Laplace expansion of determinants?

Iverson: For a given logical vector **u**, the Laplace expansion of the determinant $\delta\mathbf{A}$ can be expressed as

$$\delta\mathbf{A} = (+_i/((\delta\mathbf{u}/\mathbf{S}^i//\mathbf{A}) \times (\delta\overline{\mathbf{u}}/\overline{\mathbf{S}}^i//\mathbf{A}) \times \rho'\mathbf{S}^i)) \times \rho'\mathbf{u},$$

where **S** is a logical matrix whose rows represent all partitions of weight $+/\mathbf{u}$, where $\rho'\mathbf{v} = \rho(\mathbf{v}/\boldsymbol{\iota}^1, \overline{\mathbf{v}}/\boldsymbol{\iota}^1)$ is the "parity" of the logical vector **v**, and $\rho\mathbf{p}$ is the *parity* of the permutation vector **p**, defined as $+1$ or -1 according as the parity of **p** is even or odd. Since

$$\delta\mathbf{A} = +_i/((\times/\boxbslash^{\mathbf{P}^i}/\mathbf{A}) \times \rho\mathbf{P}^i)$$

(where **P** is the matrix whose $(\nu\mathbf{A})!$ rows exhaust all permutations of dimension $\nu\mathbf{A}$, and where compression by a logical matrix **U** is defined in the obvious way as the catenation of the vectors $\mathbf{U}^i/\mathbf{A}^i$), then the usual proof of the Laplace expansion (i.e. showing that a typical term of either expansion occurs in the other) can be carried through directly with the aid of the following fact: if **u** is any logical vector and **p** is a permutation of like dimension, then there exists a unique triple **v**, **q**, **r**, such that

$$\boxbslash^{\mathbf{q}} = \mathbf{u}/\mathbf{v}//\boxbslash^{\mathbf{p}}, \quad \text{and} \quad \boxbslash^{\mathbf{r}} = \overline{\mathbf{u}}/\overline{\mathbf{v}}//\boxbslash^{\mathbf{p}}.$$

[The vectors **v** and **u** are clearly related by the expressions $\mathbf{v} = \boxbslash^{\mathbf{p}} \overset{\vee}{\underset{\wedge}{}} \mathbf{u}$, and $\mathbf{u} = \mathbf{v} \overset{\vee}{\underset{\wedge}{}} \boxbslash^{\mathbf{p}}$, and moreover, $\rho\mathbf{p} = (\rho'\mathbf{u}) \times (\rho'\mathbf{v}) \times (\rho\mathbf{q}) \times (\rho\mathbf{r})$].

The special matrices occurring in the foregoing can all be specified formally in terms of the matrix $\mathbf{T}(\mathrm{b}, \mathrm{n})$ defined as follows: $\mathbf{T}_j{}^i \in \boldsymbol{\iota}^0(\mathrm{b})$, $\mu\mathbf{T} = b^n$, $\nu\mathbf{T} = n$, and $b\perp\mathbf{T} = \boldsymbol{\iota}^0$, where $b\perp\mathbf{x}$ denotes the base-b value of the vector **x**. Thus $\mathbf{S} = (+/\mathbf{u} = +/\mathbf{M})//\mathbf{M}$, where $\mathbf{M} = \mathbf{T}(2, \nu\mathbf{A})$ and $\mathbf{P} = (\wedge/\sigma/\mathbf{M})//\mathbf{M}$, where $\mathbf{M} = \mathbf{T}(\nu\mathbf{A}, \nu\mathbf{A})$, and $\sigma/\mathbf{x}$ is the *set selection* operation [1, p. 23].

Moreover, the parity function $\rho\mathbf{p}$ may be defined formally as $\rho\mathbf{p} = \bar{u} - u$, where $u = 2 \mid +/\square/(\mathbf{p} \overset{\circ}{>} \mathbf{p})$.

Dijkstra: How would you represent a more complex operation, for example, the sum of all elements of a matrix **M** which are equal to the sum of the corresponding row and column indices?

Iverson: $++/(\mathbf{M} = \boldsymbol{\iota}^1 \overset{\circ}{+} \boldsymbol{\iota}^1)//\mathbf{M}$

List of Conferees, Working Conference on Language Structures, August 14–16, 1963

P. Abrahams, International Electric Corp.; R. W. Allard, Control Data Corp.; John W. Backus, IBM; F. Bauer, Math. Inst. der TH Munchen; R. Bosak, Inst. for Defense Analyses; R. A. Brooker, IBM; L. L. Bumgarner, Oak Ridge Nat. Lab.; W. H. Burge, Univac Div., Sperry Rand; T. E. Cheatham, Jr., Computer Associates, Inc.; H. B. Curry, Pennsylvania State U.; E. W. Dijkstra, Technological U., Eindhoven; Arthur Evans, Carnegie Inst. of Technology; R. J. Evey, IBM; J. Fennell, Logistics Research Project; Robert W. Floyd, Computer Associates, Inc.; Donald B. Gillies, U. of Illinois; Ruth Goodman, Westinghouse Corp.; S. Gorn, U. of Pennsylvania; John Gosden, Auerbach Electronics Corp.; Robert M. Graham, U. of Michigan; Julien Green, IBM; Sheila Greibach, Harvard U.; John W. Guy, Nat. Security Agency; Leonard H. Haines, MIT; A. W. Holt, U. of Pennsylvania; P. Z. Ingerman, Westinghouse Electric Corp.; R. Itturiaga, Carnegie Inst. of Technology; E. T. Irons, Inst. for Defense Analyses; K. E. Iverson, IBM; Walter W. Jacobs, Inst. for Defense Analyses; Charles Katz, General Electric; R. A. Kirsch, Nat. Bur. Standards; Rainer Kogon, IBM; B. M. Leavenworth, IBM; M. Henri Leroy, Cie Bull; L. Lombardi, MIT; William H. Marlow, Logistics Research Project; E. J. McCluskey, Princeton U.; M. A. Melkanoff, U. of California; J. N. Merner, Burroughs Corp.; G. J. Mitchell, Inst. for Defense Analyses; A. Newell, Carnegie Inst. of Technology; M. Paul, Math. Inst. der TH Munchen; A. J. Perlis, Carnegie Inst. of Technology; George Radin, IBM; Gene F. Rose, System Development Corp.; D. T. Ross, MIT; Bernard D. Rudin, Lockheed Aircraft Corp.; R. A. Sibley, Jr., IBM; K. H. Speierman, Burroughs Corp.; T. B. Steel, System Development Corp.; C. B. Tompkins, U. of California; Hale F. Trotter, Princeton U.; R. E. Utman, Business Equipment Mfrs. Assoc.; S. Warshall, Computer Associates, Inc.; J. H. Wegstein, Nat. Bur. Standards; J. Weizenbaum, General Electric; M. V. Wilkes, Univ. Math. Laboratory, Cambridge; Kenneth A. Wolf, Control Data Corp.

2 Conventions Governing Order of Evaluation

Conventions Governing Order of Evaluation

KENNETH E. IVERSON

The common conventions for the evaluation of unparenthesized expressions include the rules that (1) in a multilevel expression such as $\frac{a+b}{c \div d}$, each line is evaluated before the function connecting the lines is evaluated; (2) subject to the first rule, multiplication and division are performed before addition and subtraction; (3) subject to the first two rules, evaluation proceeds from left to right; (4) division can be represented by three distinct but synonymous symbols $\left(a \div b,\ a / b,\ \text{and } \frac{a}{b}\right)$; and (5) multiplication can be represented by two distinct but synonymous symbols ($a \times b$ and $a \cdot b$), or the symbol can be elided. The one convention used in this book is that (subject to parentheses) evaluation proceeds from right to left. This appendix treats the major reasons for this choice.

The common conventions are usually defended on the grounds that they are simple and well known and that their use significantly simplifies the reading and writing of expressions. Because of the familiarity of certain common constructions, these conventions appear simple, but this simplicity is illusory and vanishes on closer examination. Inquiries among students and colleagues have shown such disagreement on the interpretation of the conventions as to dispel the notion that they are well known. Finally, the much simpler convention adopted in this text proves at least as effective in simplifying the reading and writing of expressions.

Consider, for example, the expressions $x \div y \times z$ and $x \div yz$. According to the rules, both are equivalent to the expression $(x \div y) \times z$. However, yz is frequently used as an expression for multiplication which is performed first regardless of other rules. Furthermore, the dot notation for multiplication yields the expression $x \div y \cdot z$, which (according to the interpretations encountered) seems to fall midway between the other cases. Proponents of the common convention protest that such expressions would be parenthesized anyway for clarity; but then the convention seems to lose most of its value.

Matters are further complicated by the alternative notations for division. For example, $x \div y \div z$ and $x \div y / z$ should have the same interpretation, but frequently they do not. Similarly, the formally equivalent expressions $x + a \div y + b$ and $x + a / y + b$ frequently receive different interpretations. It is interesting to consider the different possible evaluations of the following expressions which, according to rule 3, are equivalent:

$x \div y \times z$	$x \div y \cdot z$	$x \div yz$
$x / y \times z$	$x / y \cdot z$	x / yz

The common convention also appears to include a number of tacit rules that writers obey automatically. For example, xy may be written for $x \times y$, and any variable should be replaceable by a numerical value. However, while the expression $3y$ is commonplace, most readers would find the expressions $x3$ and $3\ 4$ jarring and perhaps inadmissible as expressions for $x \times 3$ and 3×4.

In spite of these defects, the common conventions are reasonably convenient when applied to simple expressions involving only the four basic arithmetic functions, but more serious difficulties arise in their haphazard extension to other functions. For example, the expression $\sin n \times \cos m$ would be interpreted as $(\sin n) \times (\cos m)$, whereas $\sin n \times \pi$ would be interpreted as $\sin (n \times \pi)$. Moreover, the expression $a^{b^{c^d}}$ is usually interpreted as $a^{(b^{(c^d)})}$ rather than as $((a^b)^c)^d$ (that is, from right to left rather than from left to right according to rule 3), apparently because the latter case can be expressed by the equivalent expression $a^{b \times c \times d}$. In the notation used in this book the first case would be expressed as either $a * b * c * d$ or $*/ a , b , c , d$ and the second as either $a * b \times c \times d$ or $a * \times/ b , c , d$.

As further functions are introduced (for example, absolute value, maximum, minimum, residue, the relations, logical functions, and the circular functions), the complexity grows and the utility of any relative priority of execution among the functions decreases. Mathematical texts handle this problem either by liberal use of parentheses or by *ad hoc* (and frequently unstated) conventions. Programming languages, which must face the issue more formally, have usually treated the problem by establishing a hierarchy of priorities among the functions such that any function is evaluated before all others having lower priorities. Such a system is usually very complex (Algol, one of the best known, has nine priority levels) and can therefore be used efficiently only by a programmer who employs it frequently. The occasional (and the prudent) programmer avoids the whole issue by including all the parentheses that would have been required with no convention.

Further examples of the complexity and ambiguity of the common conventions could be easily adduced. However, the skeptical reader will find it more instructive to scan various textbooks trying to formulate precisely the rules used (stated or implied) and applying them rigorously.

The question of the efficacy of the common convention in reducing the need for parentheses will now be addressed. Any convention will reduce the need for parentheses, but the important question is how the common convention compares in this respect with other conventions, and in particular with the notation used in this text.

The utility of the common convention stands forth well in the expression for a polynomial. For example, in the expression

$$ax^p + bx^q + cx^r$$

it would be awkward to have to enclose each term in parentheses. However, in the present notation this would be written as

$$+/\ (a\ ,b\ ,c)\times x * p\ ,q\ ,r$$

or, if the vectors of coefficients and exponents were denoted by $\boldsymbol{c}$ and $\boldsymbol{e}$ respectively, then it would be written as

$$+/\ \boldsymbol{c}\times x * \boldsymbol{e}$$

These forms make clear the structure of the polynomial while permitting suppression of detail by using vectors; the corresponding expression in conventional notation is

$$\boldsymbol{c}_1\times x^{e_1} + \boldsymbol{c}_2\times x^{e_2} + \ldots + \boldsymbol{c}_n\times x^{e_n},$$

where n is the magic variable that denotes the dimensions of all vectors.

The expression (derived in Chapter 4) for the efficient evaluation of a polynomial such as $(a\ ,b\ ,c\ ,d\ ,e\ ,f)\ \Pi\ x$ provides a further example. In the notation used in this text it appears (without parentheses) as

$$(a\ ,b\ ,c\ ,d\ ,e\ ,f)\ \Pi\ x\equiv a+x\times b+x\times c+x\times d+x\times e+x\times f$$

whereas in the common convention it would appear as

$$(a\ ,b\ ,c\ ,d\ ,e\ ,f)\ \Pi\ x$$
$$\equiv a+x\times\ (b+x\times\ (c+x\times\ (d+x\times\ (e+x\times f))))$$

Further examples could be adduced, but again the skeptical reader will find it more instructive to formulate a set of *precise* rules based on the common convention and to translate into the resulting notation the expressions appearing in the present text.

There is one further argument against imposing a priority among functions in the present notation. If F and G are dyadic functions, then the expression $F/\ \boldsymbol{x}\ G\ \boldsymbol{y}$ would have either of two interpretations (that is, $(F/\ \boldsymbol{x})\ G\ \boldsymbol{y}$ or $F/\ (\boldsymbol{x}\ G\ \boldsymbol{y})$), depending upon the relative priorities of F and G. These two interpretations differ markedly in form and would therefore lead to confusion. For example, $+/\ \boldsymbol{x}\times\boldsymbol{y}$ would be interpreted as $+/\ (\boldsymbol{x}\times\boldsymbol{y})$ whereas the similar expression $\times/\ \boldsymbol{x}+\boldsymbol{y}$ would be interpreted as $(\times/\ \boldsymbol{x})+\boldsymbol{y}$. Similar remarks apply to the matrix product $\boldsymbol{M}\ F\ .\ G\ \boldsymbol{N}$ (defined in Chapter 9).

The reasons for choosing a right-to-left instead of a left-to-right convention are:

1. The usual mathematical convention of placing a monadic function to the left of its argument leads to a right-to-left execution for monadic functions; for example, $F\ G\ x \equiv F\ (G\ x)$.
2. The notation $F/\ \boldsymbol{z}$ for reduction (by any dyadic function F) tends to require fewer parentheses with a right-to-left convention. For example, expressions such as $+/\ (\boldsymbol{x}\times\boldsymbol{y})$ or $+/\ (\boldsymbol{u}/\boldsymbol{x})$ tend to occur more frequently than $(+/\ \boldsymbol{x})\times\boldsymbol{y}$ and $(+/\ \boldsymbol{u})\ /\ \boldsymbol{x}$.
3. An expression *evaluated* from right to left is the easiest to *read* from left to right. For example, the expression

$$a + x \times b + x \times c + x \times d + x \times e + x \times f$$

(for the efficient evaluation of a polynomial) is read as a plus the entire expression following, or as a plus x times the following expression, or as a plus x times b plus the following expression, and so on.

4. In the definition

$$F/\boldsymbol{x} \equiv \boldsymbol{x}_1 \, F \, \boldsymbol{x}_2 \, F \, \boldsymbol{x}_3 \, F \ldots F \, \boldsymbol{x}_{\rho \boldsymbol{x}}$$

the right-to-left convention leads to a more useful definition for nonassociative functions F than does the left-to-right convention. For example, $-/\boldsymbol{x}$ denotes the alternating sum of the components of $\boldsymbol{x}$, whereas in a left-to-right convention it would denote the first component minus the sum of the remaining components. Thus if $\boldsymbol{d}$ is the vector of decimal digits representing the number n, then the value of the expression $0 = 9|+/\boldsymbol{d}$ determines the divisibility of n by 9; in the right-to-left convention, the similar expression $0 = 11|-/\boldsymbol{d}$ determines divisibility by 11.

3 *Algebra as a Language*

Algebra as a Language

KENNETH E. IVERSON

A.1 INTRODUCTION

Although few mathematicians would quarrel with the proposition that the algebraic notation taught in high school is a language (and indeed the primary language of mathematics), yet little attention has been paid to the possible implications of such a view of algebra. This paper adopts this point of view to illuminate the inconsistencies and deficiencies of conventional notation and to explore the implications of analogies between the teaching of natural languages and the teaching of algebra. Based on this analysis it presents a simple and consistent algebraic notation, illustrates its power in the exposition of some familiar topics in algebra, and proposes a basis for an introductory course in algebra. Moreover, it shows how a computer can, if desired, be used in the teaching process, since the language proposed is directly usable on a computer terminal.

A.2 ARITHMETIC NOTATION

We will first discuss the notation of arithmetic, i.e., that part of algebraic notation which does not involve the use of variables. For example, the expressions `3-4` and `(3+4)-(5+6)` are arithmetic expressions, but the expressions `3-X` and `(X+4)-(Y+6)` are not. We will now explore the anomalies of arithmetic notation and the modifications needed to remove them.

Functions and symbols for functions. The importance of introducing the concept of "function" rather early in the mathematical curriculum is now widely recognized. Nevertheless, those functions which the student encounters first are usually referred to not as "functions" but as "operators". For example, absolute value (`|-3|`) and arithmetic negation (`-3`) are usually referred to as operators. In fact, most of the functions which are so fundamental and so widely used that they have been assigned some graphic symbol are commonly called operators (particularly those functions such as plus and times which apply to two arguments), whereas the less common functions which are usually referred to by writing out their names (e.g., Sin, Cos, Factorial) are called functions.

This practice of referring to the most common and most elementary functions as operators is surely an unnecessary obstacle to the understanding of functions when that term is first applied to the more complex functions encountered. For this reason the term "function" will be used here for all functions regardless of the choice of symbols used to represent them.

The functions of elementary algebra are of two types, taking either one argument or two. Thus addition is a function of two arguments (denoted by *X*+*Y*) and negation is a function of one argument (denoted by -*Y*). It would seem both easy and reasonable to adopt one form for each type of function as suggested by the foregoing examples, that is, the symbol for a function of two arguments occurs between its arguments, and the symbol for a function of one argument occurs before its argument. Conventional notation displays considerable anarchy on this point:

1. Certain functions are denoted by any one of several symbols which are supposed to be synonomous but which are, however, used in subtly different ways. For example, in conventional algebra *X*×*Y* and *XY* both denote the product of *X* and *Y*. However, one would write either 3×*Y* or 3*X* or *X*×3, or 3×4, but would not likely accept *X*3 as an expression for *X*×3, nor 3 4 as an expression for 3×4. Similarly, *X*÷*Y* and *X*/*Y* are supposed to be synonomous, but in the sentence "Reduce 8/6 to lowest terms", the symbol / does not stand for division.

2. The power function has no symbol, and is denoted by position only, as in X^N. The same notation is often used to denote the *N*th element of a family or array *X*.

3. The remainder function (that is, the integer remainder on dividing *X* into *Y*) is used very early in arithmetic (e.g., in factoring) but is commonly not recognized as a function on a par with addition, division, etc., nor assigned a symbol. Because the remainder function has no symbol and is commonly evaluated by the method of long division, there is a tendency to confuse it with division. This confusion is compounded by the fact that the term "quotient" itself is ambiguous, sometimes meaning the quotient and sometimes the integer part of the quotient.

4. The symbol for a function of one argument sometimes occurs before the argument (as in -4) but may also occur after it (as in 4! for factorial 4) or on both sides (as in |*X*| for absolute value of *X*).

Table A.1 shows a set of symbols which can be used in a simple consistent manner to denote the functions mentioned thus far, as well as a few other very useful basic functions such as maximum, minimum, integer part, reciprocal, and exponential. The table shows two uses for each symbol, one to denote a monadic function (i.e., a function of one argument), and one to denote a dyadic function (i.e., a function of two arguments). This is simply a systematic exploitation of the example set by the familiar use of the minus sign, either as a dyadic function (i.e., subtraction as in 4-3) or as a monadic function (i.e., negation as in -3). No function symbol is permitted to be elided; for example, *X*×*Y* may not be written as *XY*.

A little experimentation with the notation of Table A.1 will show that it can be used to express clearly a

<table>
<tr><th colspan="2">Monadic form fB</th><th>f</th><th colspan="2">Dyadic form AfB</th></tr>
<tr><th>Definition or example</th><th>Name</th><th></th><th>Name</th><th>Definition or example</th></tr>
<tr><td>+3 ←→ 0+3</td><td>Plus</td><td>+</td><td>Plus</td><td>2+3.2 ←→ 5.2</td></tr>
<tr><td>-3 ←→ 0-3</td><td>Negative</td><td>-</td><td>Minus</td><td>2-3.2 ←→ ¯1.2</td></tr>
<tr><td>×3 ←→ (3>0)-(3<0)</td><td>Signum</td><td>×</td><td>Times</td><td>2×3.2 ←→ 6.4</td></tr>
<tr><td>÷3 ←→ 1÷3</td><td>Reciprocal</td><td>÷</td><td>Divide</td><td>2÷3.2 ←→0.625</td></tr>
<tr><td>B | ⌈B | ⌊B
3.14 | 4 | 3</td><td>Ceiling</td><td>⌈</td><td>Maximum</td><td>3⌈7 ←→ 7</td></tr>
<tr><td>¯3.14 | ¯3 | ¯4</td><td>Floor</td><td>⌊</td><td>Minimum</td><td>3⌊7 ←→ 3</td></tr>
<tr><td>*3 ←→ (2.71828∘∘)*3</td><td>Expon-
ential</td><td>*</td><td>Power</td><td>2*3 ←→ 8</td></tr>
<tr><td>⍟*5 ←→ 5 ←→ *⍟5</td><td>Natural
logarithm</td><td>⍟</td><td>Loga-
rithm</td><td>10⍟3←→Log 3 base 10
10⍟3←→(⍟3)÷⍟10</td></tr>
<tr><td>|¯3.14 ←→ 3.14</td><td>Magnitude</td><td>|</td><td>Remain-
der</td><td>3|8 ←→ 2</td></tr>
</table>

Table A.1

number of matters which are awkward or impossible to express in conventional notation. For example, *X*÷*Y* is the quotient of *X* divided by *Y*; either ⌊(*X*÷*Y*) or ((*X*-(*Y*|*X*))÷*Y* yield the integer part of the quotient of *X* divided by *Y*; and *X*⌈(-*X*) is equivalent to |*X*.

In conventional notation the symbols <, ≤, =, ≥, >, and ≠ are used to state relations among quantities; for example, the expression 3<4 asserts that 3 <u>is</u> less than 4. It is more useful to employ them as symbols for dyadic functions defined to yield the value 1 if the indicated relation actually holds, and the value zero if it does not. Thus 3≤4 yields the value 1, and 5+(3≤4) yields the value 6.

<u>Arrays</u>. The ability to refer to collections or arrays of items is an important element in any natural language and is equally important in mathematics. The notation of vector algebra embodies the use of arrays (vectors, matrices, 3-dimensional arrays, etc.) but in a manner which is difficult to learn and limited primarily to the treatment of linear functions. Arrays are not normally included in elementary algebra, probably because they are thought to be difficult to learn and not relevant to elementary topics.

A vector (that is, a 1-dimensional array) can be represented by a list of its elements (e.g., 1 3 5 7) and all functions can be assumed to be applied element-by-element. For example:

```
      1 2 3 4 × 4 3 2 1 produces
4 6 6 4
```

Similarly:

```
      1 2 3 4 + 4 3 2 1
5 5 5 5
      ! 1 2 3 4
1 2 6 24
```

```
      1  2  3  4  *  2
1  4  9  16
      2  *  1  2  3  4
2  4  8  16
```

In addition to applying a function to each element of an array, it is also necessary to be able to apply some specified function to the collection itself. For example, "Take the sum of all elements", or "Take the product of all elements", or "Take the maximum of all elements". This can be denoted as follows:

```
      +/2 5 3 2
12
      ×/2 5 3 2
60
      ⌈/2 5 3 2
5
```

The rules for using such vectors are simple and obvious from the foregoing examples. Vectors are relevant to elementary mathematics in a variety of ways. For example:

1. They can be used (as in the foregoing examples) to display the patterns produced by various functions when applied to certain patterns of arguments.

2. They can be used to represent points in coordinate geometry. Thus `5 7 19` and `2 3 7` represent two points, `5 7 19 - 2 3 7` yields `3 4 12`, the displacement between them, and `(+/(5 7 19 - 2 3 7)*2)*.5` yields `13`, the distance between them.

3. They can be used to represent rational numbers. Thus if `3 4` represents the fraction three-fourths, then `3 4×5 6` yields `15 24`, the product of the fractions represented by `3 4` and `5 6`. Moreover, `÷/3 4` and `÷/5 6` and `÷/15 24` yield the actual numbers represented.

4. A polynomial can be represented by its vector of coefficients and vector of exponents. For example, the polynomial with coefficients `3 1 2 4` and exponents `0 1 2 3` can be evaluated for the argument `5` by the following expression:

```
      +/3 1 2 4 × 5 * 0 1 2 3
558
```

Constants. Conventional notation provides means for writing any positive constant (e.g., 17 or 3.14) but there is no distinct notation for negative constants, since the symbol - occurring in a number like -35 is indistinguishable from the symbol for the negation function. Thus negative thirty-five is written as an expression, which is much as if we neglected to have symbols for five and zero because expressions for them could be written in a variety of ways such as 8-3 and 8-8.

It seems advisable to follow Beberman [1] in using a raised minus sign to denote negative numbers. For example:

```
      3 - 5 4 3 2 1
¯2 ¯1  0  1  2
```

Conventional notation also provides no convenient way to represent numbers which are easily expressed in expressions of the form 2.14×10^{8} or $3.265\times10^{\bar{}9}$. A useful practice widely used in computer languages is to replace the symbols ×10 by the symbol *E* (for <u>exponent</u>) as follows: 2.14*E*8 and 3.265*E*¯9.

<u>Order of execution</u>. The order of execution in an algebraic expression is commonly specified by parentheses. The rules for parentheses are very simple, but the rules which apply in the absence of parentheses are complex and chaotic. They are based primarily on a hierarchy of functions (e.g., the power function is executed before multiplication, which is executed before addition) which has apparently arisen because of its convenience in writing polynomials.

Viewed as a matter of language, the only purpose of such rules is the potential economy in the use of parentheses and the consequent gain in readability of complex expressions. Economy and simplicity can be achieved by the following rule: parentheses are obeyed as usual and otherwise expressions are evaluated from right to left with all functions being treated equally. The advantages of this rule and the complexity and ambiguity of conventional rules are discussed in Berry [2], page 27 and in Iverson [3], Appendix A. Even polynomials can be conveniently written without parentheses if use is made of vectors. For example, the polynomial in *X* with coefficients 3 1 2 4 can be written without parentheses as +/3 1 2 4 × *X* ⋆ 0 1 2 3. Moreover, Horner's expression for the efficient evaluation of this same polynomial can also be written without parentheses as follows:

3+*X*×1+*X*×2+*X*×4

<u>Analogies with natural language</u>. The arithmetic expression 3×4 can be viewed as an order to <u>do</u> something, that is, multiply the arguments 3 and 4. Similarly, a more complex expression can be viewed as an order to perform a number of operations in a specified order. In this sense, an arithmetic expression is an imperative sentence, and a function corresponds to an imperative verb in natural language. Indeed, the word "function" derives from the latin verb "fungi" meaning "to perform".

This view of a function does not conflict with the usual mathematical definition as a specified correspondence between the elements of domain and range, but rather supplements this static view with a dynamic view of a function as that which <u>produces</u> the corresponding value for any specified element of the domain.

If functions correspond to imperative verbs, then their arguments (the things upon which they act) correspond to nouns. In fact, the word "argument" has (or at least had) the meaning topic, theme, or subject. Moreover, the positive integers, being the most concrete of arithmetical objects, may be said to correspond to proper nouns.

What are the roles of negative numbers, rational numbers, irrational numbers, and complex numbers? The subtraction function, introduced as an inverse to addition, yields positive integers in some cases but not in others, and negative numbers are introduced to refer to the results in these cases. In other words, a negative number refers to a process or the result of a process, and is therefore analogous to an abstract noun. For example, the abstract noun "justice" refers not to some concrete object (examples of which one may point to) but to a process or result of a process. Similarly, rational and complex numbers refer to the results of processes; division, and finding the zeros of polynomials, respectively.

A.3 ALGEBRAIC NOTATION

Names. An expression such as 3×*X* can be evaluated only if the variable *X* has been assigned an actual value. In one sense, therefore, a variable corresponds to a pronoun whose referent must be made clear before any sentence including it can be fully understood. In English the referent may be made clear by an explicit statement, but is more often made clear by indirection (e.g., "See the door. Close it."), or by context.

In conventional algebra, the value assigned to a variable name is usually made clear informally by some statement such as "Let *X* have the value 6" or "Let *X*=6". Since the equal symbol (that is, '=') is also used in other ways, it is better to avoid its use for this purpose and to use a distinct symbol as follows:

```
      X←6
      Y←3×4
      X+Y
18
      (X-3)×(X-5)
3
```

Assigning names to expressions. In the foregoing example, the expression (*X*-3)×(*X*-5) was written as an instruction to evaluate the expression for a particular value already assigned to *X*. One also writes the same expression for the quite different notion "Consider the expression (*X*-3)×(*X*-5) for any value which might later be assigned to the argument *X*." This is a distinct notion which should be represented by distinct notation. The idea is to be able to refer to the expression and this can be done by assigning a name to it. The following notation serves:

```
      ∇ Z ← G X
      Z←(X-3)×(X-5)∇
```

The ∇'s indicate that the symbols between them define a function; the first line shows that the name of the function is *G*. The names *X* and *Z* are dummy names standing for the argument and result, and the second line shows how they are related.

Following this definition, the name *G* may be used as a function. For example:

```
      G 6
3
      G 1 2 3 4 5 6 7
8 3 0 ¯1 0 3 8
```

Iterative functions can be defined with equal ease as shown in Chapter 12.

Form of names. If the variables occurring in algebraic sentences are viewed simply as names, it seems reasonable to employ names with some mnemonic significance as illustrated by the following sequence:

```
LENGTH←6
WIDTH←5
AREA←LENGTH×WIDTH
HEIGHT←4
VOLUME←AREA×HEIGHT
```

This is not done in conventional notation, apparently because it is ruled out by the convention that the multiplication sign may be elided; that is, *AREA* cannot be used as a name because it would be interpreted as *A×R×E×A*.

This same convention leads to other anomalies as well, some of which were discussed in the section on arithmetic notation. The proposal made there (i.e., that the multiplication sign cannot be elided) will permit variable names of any length.

A.4 ANALOGIES WITH THE TEACHING OF NATURAL LANGUAGE

If one views the teaching of algebra as the teaching of a language, it appears remarkable how little attention is given to the reading and writing of algebraic sentences, and how much attention is given to identities, that is, to the analysis of sentences with a view to determining other equivalent sentences; e.g., "Simplify the expression (*X*-4) × (*X*+4) ." It is possible that this emphasis accounts for much of the difficulty in teaching algebra, and that the teaching and learning processes in natural languages may suggest a more effective approach.

In the learning of a native language one can distinguish the following major phases:

1. An informal phase, in which the child learns to communicate in a combination of gestures, single words, etc., but with no attempt to form grammatical sentences.

2. A formal phase, in which the child learns to communicate in formal sentences. This phase is essential because it is difficult or impossible to communicate complex matters with precision without imposing some formal structure on the language.

3. An analytic phase, in which one learns to analyze sentences with a view to determining equivalent (and perhaps "simpler" or "more effective") sentences. The extreme case of such analysis is Aristotelian Logic, which attempts a formal analysis of certain classes of sentences. More practical everyday cases occur every time one carefully reads a composition and suggests alternative sentences which convey the same meaning in a briefer or simpler form.

The same phases can be distinguished in the teaching of algebraic notation:

1. An informal phase in which one issues an instruction to add 2 and 3 in any way which will be understood. For example:

   2+3 Add 2 and 3

   $\begin{array}{r}2\\ \underline{3}\end{array}$ $\begin{array}{r}2\\ \underline{+3}\end{array}$

   Add two and three

   Add // and ///

   The form of the expression is unimportant, provided that the instruction is understood.

2. A formal phase in which one emphasizes proper sentence structure and would not accept expressions such as $6 \times \begin{array}{c}2\\ \underline{3}\end{array}$ or 6×(add two and three) in lieu of 6×(2+3). Again, adherence to certain structural rules is necessary to permit the precise communication of complex matters.

3. An analytic phase in which one learns to analyze sentences with a view to establishing certain relations (usually identity) among them. Thus one learns not only that 3+4 is equal to 4+3 but that the sentences $X+Y$ and $Y+X$ are equivalent, that is, yield the same result whatever the meanings assigned to the pronouns X and Y.

In learning a native language, a child spends many years in the informal and formal phases (both in and out of school) before facing the analytic phase. By this time she has easy familiarity with the purposes of a language and the meanings of sentences which might be analyzed and transformed. The situation is quite different in most conventional courses in algebra - very little time is spent in the formal phase (reading, writing and "understanding" formal algebraic sentences) before attacking identities (such as commutativity, associativity, distributivity, etc.). Indeed, students often do not realize that they might quickly check their work in "simplification" by substituting certain values for the variables occurring in the original and derived expressions and comparing the evaluated results to see if the expressions have the same "meaning", at least for the chosen values of the variables.

It is interesting to speculate on what would happen if a native language were taught in an analogous way, that is, if children were forced to analyze sentences at a stage in their development when their grasp of the purpose and meaning of sentences were as shaky as the algebra student's grasp of the purpose and meaning of algebraic sentences. Perhaps they would fail to learn to converse, just as many students fail to learn the much simpler task of reading.

Another interesting aspect of learning the non-analytic aspects of a native language is that much (if not most) of the motivation comes not from an interest in language, but from the intrinsic interest of the material (in children's stories, everyday dialogue, etc.) for which it is used. It is doubtful that the same is true in algebra - ruling out statements of an analytic nature (identities, etc.), how many "interesting" algebraic sentences does a student encounter?

The use of arrays can open up the possibility of much more interesting algebraic sentences. This can apply both to sentences to be read (that is, evaluated) and written by students. For example, the statements:

```
2*1 2 3 4 5
2×1 2 3 4 5
2÷1 2 3 4 5
1 2 3 4 5÷2
1 2 3 4 5*2
1 2 3 4 5×5 4 3 2 1
```

produce interesting patterns and therefore have more intrinsic interest than similar expressions involving only single quantities. For example, the last expression can be construed as yielding a set of possible areas for a rectangle having a fixed perimeter of 12.

More interesting possibilities are opened up by certain simple extensions of the use of arrays. One example of such extensions will be treated here. This extension allows one to apply any dyadic function to two vectors *A* and *B* so as to obtain not simply the element-by-element product produced by the expression *A*×*B*, but a table of all products produced by pairing each element of *A* with each element of *B*. For example:

```
A←1 2 3
B←2 3 5 7

A∘.×B

2   3   5   7
4   6  10  14
6   9  15  21

A∘.+B

3   4   6   8
4   5   7   9
5   6   8  10

A∘.*B

1   1    1     1
4   8   32   128
9  27  243  2187
```

If *S*←1 2 3 4 5 6 7, then the following expressions yield an addition table, a multiplication table, a subtraction table, a maximum table, an "equal" table, and a "greater than or equal" table:

```
S∘.+S
2   3   4   5   6   7   8
3   4   5   6   7   8   9
4   5   6   7   8   9  10
5   6   7   8   9  10  11
6   7   8   9  10  11  12
7   8   9  10  11  12  13
8   9  10  11  12  13  14

S∘.⌈S
1  2  3  4  5  6  7
2  2  3  4  5  6  7
3  3  3  4  5  6  7
4  4  4  4  5  6  7
5  5  5  5  5  6  7
6  6  6  6  6  6  7
7  7  7  7  7  7  7

S∘.×X
1   2   3   4   5   6   7
2   4   6   8  10  12  14
3   6   9  12  15  18  21
4   8  12  16  20  24  28
5  10  15  20  25  30  35
6  12  18  24  30  36  42
7  14  21  28  35  42  49

S∘.=S
1 0 0 0 0 0 0
0 1 0 0 0 0 0
0 0 1 0 0 0 0
0 0 0 1 0 0 0
0 0 0 0 1 0 0
0 0 0 0 0 1 0
0 0 0 0 0 0 1

S∘.-S
0  ¯1  ¯2  ¯3  ¯4  ¯5  ¯6
1   0  ¯1  ¯2  ¯3  ¯4  ¯5
2   1   0  ¯1  ¯2  ¯3  ¯4
3   2   1   0  ¯1  ¯2  ¯3
4   3   2   1   0  ¯1  ¯2
5   4   3   2   1   0  ¯1
6   5   4   3   2   1   0

S∘.≥S
1 0 0 0 0 0 0
1 1 0 0 0 0 0
1 1 1 0 0 0 0
1 1 1 1 0 0 0
1 1 1 1 1 0 0
1 1 1 1 1 1 0
1 1 1 1 1 1 1
```

Moreover, the graph of a function can be produced as an "equal" table as follows. First recall the function *G* defined earlier:

```
     ∇Z←G X
      Z←(X-3)×(X-5)∇

     G S
8 3 0 ¯1 0 3 8
```

The range of the function for this set of arguments is from 8 down to ¯1, and the elements of this range are all contained in the following vector:

```
     R←8 7 6 5 4 3 2 1 0 ¯1
```

Consequently, the "equal" table *R∘.=G S* produces a rough graph of the function (represented by 1's) as follows:

```
     R∘.=G S
1 0 0 0 0 0 1
0 0 0 0 0 0 0
0 0 0 0 0 0 0
0 0 0 0 0 0 0
0 0 0 0 0 0 0
0 1 0 0 0 1 0
0 0 0 0 0 0 0
0 0 0 0 0 0 0
0 0 1 0 1 0 0
0 0 0 1 0 0 0
```

A.5 A PROGRAM FOR ELEMENTARY ALGEBRA

The foregoing analysis suggests the development of an algebra curriculum with the following characteristics:

1. The notation used is unambiguous, with simple and consistent rules of syntax, and with provision for the simple and direct use of arrays. Moreover, the notation is not taught as a separate matter, but is introduced as needed in conjunction with the concepts represented.

2. Heavy use is made of arrays to display mathematical properties of functions in terms of patterns observed in vectors and matrices (tables), and to make possible the reading, writing, and evaluation of a host of interesting algebraic sentences before approaching the analysis of sentences and the concomitant development of identities.

Such an approach has been adopted in the present text, where it has been carried through as far as the treatment of polynomials and of linear functions and linear equations. The extension to further work in polynomials, to slopes and derivatives, and to the circular and hyperbolic functions is carried forward in Iverson [9] and in Orth [10] .

It must be emphasized that the proposed notation, though simple, is not limited in application to elementary algebra. A glance at the bibliography of Rault and Demars [4] will give some idea of the wide range of applicability.

The role of the computer. Because the proposed notation is simple and systematic it can be executed by automatic computers and has been made available on a number of time-shared terminal systems. The most widely used of these is described in Falkoff and Iverson [5]. It is important to note that the notation is executed directly, and the user need learn nothing about the computer itself. In fact, each of the examples in this appendix are shown exactly as they would be typed on a computer terminal keyboard.

The computer can obviously be useful in cases where a good deal of tedious computation is required, but it can be useful in other ways as well. For example, it can be used by a student to explore the behavior of functions and discover their properties. To do this a student will simply enter expressions which apply the functions to various arguments. If the terminal is equipped with a display device, then such exploration can even be done collectively by an entire class. This and other ways of using the computer are discussed in Berry et al [6] and in Appendix C.

REFERENCES

1. Beberman, M., and H. E. Vaughan, High School Mathematics Course 1, Heath, 1964.

2. Berry, P. C., APL\360 Primer, IBM Corp., 1969.

3. Iverson, K. E., Elementary Functions: an algorithmic treatment, Science Research Associates, 1966.

4. Rault, J. C., and G. Demars,"Is APL Epidemic? Or a study of its growth through an extended bibliography", Fourth International APL User's Conference, Board of Education of the City of Atlanta, Georgia, 1972.

5. Falkoff, A. D., and K. E. Iverson, APL Language, Form Number GC26-3847, IBM Corp.

6. Berry, P. C., A. D. Falkoff, and K. E. Iverson, "Using the Computer to Compute: A Direct but Neglected Approach to Teaching Mathematics", IFIP World Conference on Computer Education, Amsterdam, August 24-28, 1970.

7. Iverson, K. E. (APL Press, 1976):

    Introducing APL to Teachers

    APL in Exposition

    An Introduction to APL for Scientists and Engineers

8. Berry, P. C., G. Bartoli, C. Dell'Aquila and V. Spadavecchia, APL and Insight: Using Functions to Represent Concepts in Teaching, IBM Philadelphia Scientific Center Technical Report No. 320-3009, December, 1971.

9. Iverson, K. E., Elementary Analysis, APL Press, 1976.

10. Orth, D. L., Calculus in a new key, APL Press, 1976.

4 The Design of APL

A. D. Falkoff
K. E. Iverson

The Design of APL

Abstract: This paper discusses the development of APL, emphasizing and illustrating the principles underlying its design. The principle of simplicity appears most strongly in the minimization of rules governing the behavior of APL objects, while the principle of practicality is served by the design process itself, which relies heavily on experimentation. The paper gives the rationale for many specific design choices, including the necessary adjuncts for system management.

Introduction

This paper attempts to identify the general principles that guided the development of APL and its computer realizations, and to show the role these principles played in the evolution of the language. The reader will be assumed to be familiar with the current definition of APL [1]. A brief chronology of the development of APL is presented in an appendix.

Different people claiming to follow the same broad principles may well arrive at radically different designs; an appreciation of the actual role of the principles in design can therefore be communicated only by illustrating their application in a variety of specific instances. It must be remembered, of course, that in the heat of battle principles are not applied as consciously or systematically as may appear in the telling. Some notion of the evolution of the ideas may be gained from consulting earlier discussions, particularly Refs. 2–4.

The actual operative principles guiding the design of any complex system must be few and broad. In the present instance we believe these principles to be simplicity and practicality. Simplicity enters in four guises: *uniformity* (rules are few and simple), *generality* (a small number of general functions provide as special cases a host of more specialized functions), *familiarity* (familiar symbols and usages are adopted whenever possible), and *brevity* (economy of expression is sought). Practicality is manifested in two respects: concern with actual application of the language, and concern with the practical limitations imposed by existing equipment.

We believe that the design of APL was also affected in important respects by a number of procedures and circumstances. Firstly, from its inception APL has been developed by *using* it in a succession of areas. This emphasis on application clearly favors practicality and simplicity. The treatment of many different areas fostered generalization; for example, the general inner product was developed in attempting to obtain the advantages of ordinary matrix algebra in the treatment of symbolic logic.

Secondly, the lack of any machine realization of the language during the first seven or eight years of its development allowed the designers the freedom to make radical changes, a freedom not normally enjoyed by designers who must observe the needs of a large working population dependent on the language for their daily computing needs. This circumstance was due more to the dearth of interest in the language than to foresight.

Thirdly, at every stage the design of the language was controlled by a small group of not more than five people. In particular, the men who designed (and coded) the implementation were part of the language design group, and all members of the design group were involved in broad decisions affecting the implementation. On the other hand, many ideas were received and accepted from people outside the design group, particularly from active users of some implementation of APL.

Finally, design decisions were made by Quaker consensus; controversial innovations were deferred until they could be revised or reevaluated so as to obtain unanimous agreement. Unanimity was not achieved without cost in time and effort, and many divergent paths were explored and assessed. For example, many different notations for the circular and hyperbolic functions were entertained over a period of more than a year before the present scheme was proposed, whereupon it was quickly adopted. As the language grows, more effort is needed to explore the ramifications of any major innovation. Moreover, greater care is needed in introducing new facilities, to avoid the possibility of later retraction that would inconvenience thousands of users. An example of the degree of preliminary exploration that may be involved is furnished by the depth and diversity of the investigations reported in the papers by Ghandour and Mezei [5] and by More [6].

The character set

The typography of a language to be entered at a simple keyboard is subject to two major practical restrictions: it must be linear, rather than two-dimensional, and it must be printable by a limited number of distinct symbols.

When one is not concerned with an immediate machine realization of a language, there is no strong reason to so limit the typography and for this reason the language may develop in a freer *publication form.* Before the design of a machine realization of APL, the restrictions appropriate to a keyboard form were not observed. In particular, different fonts were used to indicate the rank of a variable. In the keyboard form, such distinctions can be made, if desired, by adopting classes of names for certain classes of things.

The practical objective of linearizing the typography also led to increased uniformity and generality. It led to the present bracketed form of indexing, which removes the rank limitation on arrays imposed by use of superscripts and subscripts. It also led to the regularization of the form of dyadic functions such as *N*⍺*J* and *N*⍵*J* (later eliminated from the language). Finally, it led to writing inner and outer products in the linear form +.× and ∘.× and eventually to the recognition of such expressions as instances of the use of *operators*.

The use of arrays and of operators greatly reduced the demand for distinct characters in APL, but the limitations imposed by the normal 88-symbol typewriter keyboard fostered two innovations which greatly increased the utility of the 88 symbols: the systematic use of most function symbols to represent both a dyadic and a monadic function, as suggested in conventional notation by the double use of the minus sign to represent both subtraction (a *dyadic* function) and negation (a *monadic* function); and the use of composite characters formed by typing one symbol over another (through the use of a backspace), as in ⌽ and ! and ⍟.

It was necessary to restrict the alphabetic characters to a single font and capitals were chosen for readability. Italics were initially favored because of their common use for denoting variables in mathematics, but were finally chosen primarily because they distinguished the letter *O* from the digit 0 and letters like *L* and *T* from the graphic symbols ⌊ and ⊤.

To allow the possibility of adding complete alphabetic fonts by overstriking, the underscore (_), diaeresis (¨), overbar (¯), and quad (⎕) were provided. In the APL\360 realization, only the underscore is used in this way. The inclusion of the overbar on the typeball fortunately filled a need we had not anticipated—a symbol for negative constants, distinct from the symbol for the negation function. The quad proved a useful symbol alone and in combination (as in ⌹), and the diaeresis still remains unassigned.

The SELECTRIC® typewriter imposed certain practical limitations on the placement of symbols on the keyboard, e.g., only narrow characters can appear in the upper row of the typing element. Within these limitations we attempted to make the keyboard easy to learn by grouping related symbols (such as the relations) in a rational order and by making mnemonic associations between letters and the functions associated with them in the shifted case (such as the *magnitude* function | with *M*, and the membership symbol ∊ with *E*).

Valence and order of execution

The *valence* of a function is the number of arguments it takes; APL primitives have valences of 1 (monadic functions) and 2 (dyadic functions), and user-defined functions may have a valence of 0 as well. The form for all APL primitives follows the familiar model of arithmetic, that is, the symbol for a dyadic function occurs between its arguments (as in 3+4) and the symbol for a monadic function occurs before its argument (as in -4).

A function *f* of valence greater than two is conventionally written in the form *f*(*a*,*b*,*c*,*d*). This can be construed as a monadic function *F* applied to the vector argument *a*,*b*,*c*,*d*, and this interpretation is used in APL. In the APL\360 realization, the arguments *a*,*b*,*c*, and *d* must share a common structure. The definition and implementation of generalized arrays, whose elements include *enclosed* arrays, will, of course, remove this restriction.

The result of any primitive APL function depends only on its immediate arguments, and the interpretation of each part of an APL statement is therefore localized. Likewise, the interpretation of each statement is independent of other statements in a program. This independence of context contributes significantly to the readability and ease of implementation of the language.

The order of execution of an APL expression is controlled by parentheses in the familiar way, and parentheses are used for no other purpose. The order is otherwise determined by one simple rule: the right argument of any function is the value of the entire expression following it. In particular, there is no precedence among functions; all functions, user-defined as well as primitive, are treated alike.

This simple rule has several consequences of practical advantage to the user:

a) An unparenthesized expression is easy to read from left to right because the first function encountered is the major function, the next is the major function in its right argument, etc.
b) An unparenthesized expression is also easy to read from right to left because this is the order in which it is executed.
c) If T is any vector of numerical terms, then the present rule makes the expressions `-/T` and `÷/T` very useful: the former is the alternating sum of T and the latter is the alternating product. Moreover, a continued fraction may be written without parentheses in the form `3+÷4+÷5+÷6`, and the efficient evaluation of a polynomial can be written without parentheses in the form `3+X×4+X×5+X×6`.

The rule that multiplication is executed before addition and that the power function is executed before multiplication has been long accepted in mathematics. In discarding any established rule it is wise to speculate on the reasons for its adoption and on whether they still apply. This rule makes parentheses unnecessary in the writing of polynomials, and this alone appears to be a sufficient reason for its original adoption. However, in APL a polynomial can be written more perspicuously in the form `+/C×X*E`, which also requires no parentheses. The question of the order of execution has been discussed in several places: Falkoff et al. [2,3], Berry [7], and Appendix A of Iverson [8].

The order in which isolated parts of a statement, such as the parts `(X+4)` and `(Y-2)` in the statement `(Y+4)×(Y-2)`, are executed is normally immaterial, but does matter when repeated specifications are permitted in a statement as in `(A←2)+A`. Although the use of such expressions is poor practice, it is desirable to make the interpretation unequivocal: the rule adopted (as given in Lathwell and Mezei [9]) is that the rightmost function or specification which can be performed is performed first.

It is interesting to note that the use of embedded assignment was first suggested during the course of the implementation when it was realized that special steps were needed to prevent it. The order of executing isolated parts of a statement was at first left unspecified (as stated in Falkoff and Iverson [1]) to allow freedom in implementation, since isolated parts could then be executed in parallel on any machine offering parallel processing. However, embedded assignment found such wide use that an unambiguous definition became essential to fix the behavior of programs moving from system to system.

Another aspect of the order of execution is the order among statements, which is normally taken as the order of appearance, except as modified by explicit *branches*. In the publication form of the language branches were denoted by arrows drawn from a branch point to the set of possible destinations, and the drawing of branch arrows is still to be recommended as an adjunct for clarifying the structure of a program (Iverson [10], page 3).

In formalizing branching it was necessary to introduce only one new concept (denoted by →) and three simple conventions: 1) continuing with the statement indicated by the first element of a vector argument of →, or with the next statement in sequence if the argument is an empty vector, 2) terminating the function if the indicated continuation is not the index of a statement in the program, and 3) the use of *labels*, local names defined by the indices of juxtaposed statements. At first labels were treated as local variables, but it was found to be more convenient in both use and implementation to treat them as local constants.

Since the branch arrow can be followed by any valid expression it provides convenient multi-way conditional branches. For example, if L is a Boolean vector and S is a corresponding set of statement numbers (often formed as the catenation of a set of labels), then `→L/S` provides a `(1+ρL)`-way branch (to one of the elements of S or falling through if every element of L is zero); if I is an empty vector or an index to the vector S, then `→S[I]` provides a similar `(1+ρL)`-way branch.

Programming languages commonly incorporate special forms of sequence control, typified by the DO statement of FORTRAN. These forms are excluded from APL because their cost in complication of the language outweighs their utility. The array operations in APL obviate many instances of iteration, and those which remain can be represented in a variety of ways. For example, grouping the initialization, modification, and testing of the control variable at the head of the iterated segment provides a particularly perspicuous arrangement. Moreover, specialized sequence control statements are usually context dependent and necessarily introduce new rules.

Conditional statements of the IF THEN ELSE type are not only context dependent, but their inherent limitation to a sequence of binary choices often leads to awkward constructions. These, and other, special sequence control forms can usually be modeled readily in APL and provided as application packages if desired.

Scalar functions

The emphasis on generality is illustrated in the definitions of many of the scalar functions. For example, the definition of the factorial is not limited to non-negative integers but is extended in the manner of the gamma function. Similarly, the residue is extended to all numbers in a simple and useful way: M|N is defined as the smallest (in magnitude) among the quantities N-M×I (where I is an integer) which lie in the range from 0 to M. If no such quantity exists (as in the case where M is zero) then the restriction to the range 0 to M is discarded, that is, 0|X is X. As another example, 0*0 is defined as 1 because that is the limiting value of X*Y when the point 0 0 is approached along any path other than the X axis, and because this definition is needed to make the common general form of writing a polynomial (in which the constant term C is written as C×X*0) applicable when the value of the argument X is zero.

The urge to generality must be tempered to avoid setting traps for the unwary, and compromise is sometimes necessary. For example, X÷0 could be defined as infinity (i.e., the largest representable number in an implementation) so as to obviate special treatment of the case Y=0 when computing the arc tangent of X÷Y, but is instead defined to yield a domain error. Nevertheless, 0÷0 is given the value 1, in spite of the fact that the mathematical argument for it is much weaker than that for 0*0, because it was deemed desirable to avoid an error stop in this case.

Eventually it will be desirable to be able to set separate limits on domains to suit various classes of users. For example, an implementation that incorporates complex numbers must yield a result for the expression ¯1*.5 but should admit of being set to yield a domain error for a user studying elementary arithmetic. The experienced user should be permitted to use an implementation in a mode that gives him complete control of domain and other errors, i.e., an error should not stop execution but should give necessary information about the error in a form which can be used by the program in which it occurs. Such a facility has not yet been incorporated in APL implementations.

A very general and useful set of functions was introduced by adopting the relation symbols < ≤ = ≥ > ≠ to represent functions (i.e., propositions) rather than assertions. The result of any proposition was defined to be 0 or 1 (rather than, say, *true* or *false*) so that it would lie in the domain of other arithmetic functions. Thus X=Y and X≠Y represent general comparisons, but if X and Y are integers then X=Y is the Kronecker delta and X≠Y is its inverse; if X and Y are Boolean variables, then X≠Y is the *exclusive-or* and X≤Y is material implication. This definition also allows expressions that incorporate both relational and arithmetic functions (such as (2=+/[1]0=S∘.|S)/S←⍳N, which yields the primes up to integer N). Moreover, identities among Boolean functions are more evident when expressed in these terms than when expressed in more conventional symbols.

The adoption of the relation symbols as functions does not preclude their use as *assertions* in informal sentences. For example, although one might feel compelled to substitute "X≤Y is true" for "X≤Y" in the sentence "If X≤Y then (X<Y)∨(X=Y)", there is no more reason to do so than to substitute "Bob is there is true" for "Bob is there" in the sentence which begins "If Bob is there then . . ."

Although we strove to adopt familiar symbols and usage, any clash with the principle of uniformity was invariably resolved in favor of uniformity. For example, familiar symbols (such as + - × ÷) are used where possible, but anomalies such as |X| for magnitude and N! for factorial are regularized to |X and !N. Notation such as X^N for power and $\binom{M}{N}$ for the binomial coefficient are replaced by regular dyadic forms X*N and M!N. Elision of the times sign is not permitted; this allows the use of multiple-character names and avoids confusion between multiplication, as in X(X+3), and the application of a function, as in F(X+3).

Moreover, each of the primitive scalar functions in APL is extended to arrays in exactly the same way. In particular, if V and W are vectors the expressions V×W and 3+V are permitted as well as the expressions V+W and 3×V, although only the latter pair would be permitted (in the sense used in APL) in conventional vector algebra.

One view of simplicity might exclude as redundant those functions which are easily expressed in terms of others. For example, ⌈X may be written as -⌊-X, and ⌈/X may be written as -⌊/-X, and ∧/L may be written as ~∨/~L. From another viewpoint it is simpler to use a more complete or symmetric set of primitives, since one need not remember which of a pair is provided and how to express the other in terms of it. In APL, completeness has been favored. For example, symbols are provided for all of the nontrivial logical functions although all are easily expressed in terms of a small subset of them.

The use of the circle to denote the whole family of functions related to the circular functions is a practical technique for conserving symbols as well as a useful generalization. It leads to many convenient expressions involving reduction and inner and outer products (such as 1 2 3∘.○X for a table of sines, cosines and tangents). Moreover, anyone wishing to use the symbol SIN for the sine function can define the function SIN as either 1○X (for radian arguments) or 1○X×180÷○1 (for degree arguments). The notational scheme employed for the circular functions must clearly be used with discretion; it could be used to replace all monadic functions by a single dyadic function with an integer left argument to encode each monadic function.

Operators

The dot in the expression M+.×N is an example of an *operator*; it takes functions (in this case + and ×) as arguments and produces a new function called an *inner product*. (In elementary mathematics the term *operator* is also used as a synonym for *function*, but in APL we eschew this usage.) The evolution of operators in APL furnishes an example of growing generality which has as yet been neither fully exploited nor fully regularized.

The operators now in APL were introduced one by one (reduction, then inner product, then outer product, then axis operators such as `⌽[I]`) without being recognized as members of a class. When this class property was recognized it was apparent that the operators had not been given a consistent syntax and that the notation should eventually be regularized to give operators the same syntax as functions, i.e., an operator taking two arguments occurs between its (function) arguments (as in `+.×`) and an operator taking one argument appears in front of it. It also became evident that our treatment of operators had introduced a useful heirarchy into the order of execution, operators being executed before functions.

The recognition of operators as such has also made clear the much broader role they might be expected to play—derivative and integral operators are only two of many useful operators that must be added to the language.

The use of the outer product operator furnishes a clear example of a significant process in the evolution of the language: when a new facility is introduced it takes considerable time to recognize the many ways in which it can be used and therefore to appreciate its role in the further development of the language. The notation $\alpha^j(n)$ (later regularized to `N⍺J`) had been introduced early to represent a *prefix* vector, i.e., a Boolean vector of `N` elements with `J` leading 1's. Some thought had been given to extending the definition to a *vector* `J` (perhaps to yield an `N`=column matrix whose rows were prefix vectors determined by the elements of `J`) but no decision had been taken. When considering such an extension we normally communicate by defining any proposed notation in terms of existing primitives. After the outer product was introduced the proposed extension was written simply as `J∘.≥⍳N`, and it became clear that the function α was now redundant.

One should not conclude from this example that every function or set of functions easily expressed in terms of another is discarded as redundant; judgment must be exercised. In the present instance the ⍺ was discarded partly because it was too restrictive, i.e., the outer product form could be applied to yield a host of related functions (such as `J∘.<⍳N` and `J∘.<⌽⍳N`) not all of which were expressible in terms of the prefix and suffix functions ⍺ and ⍵. As mentioned in the discussion of scalar functions, the completeness of an obvious family of functions is also a factor to be considered.

Operators are attractive from several points of view. Because they provide a scheme for denoting whole classes of related functions, they offer uniformity of expression and great economy of symbols. The conciseness of expression that they allow can also be directly related to efficiency of implementation. Moreover, they introduce a new level of generality which plays an important role in the formal manipulability of the language.

Formal manipulation

APL is rich in identities and is therefore amenable to a great deal of fruitful formal manipulation. For example, many of the familiar identities of ordinary matrix algebra extend to inner products other than `+.×`, and de Morgan's law and other dualities extend to inner and outer products on arrays. The emphasis on generality, uniformity, and simplicity is likely to lead to a language rich in identities, but our emphasis on identities has been such that it should perhaps be enunciated as a separate and important guiding principle. Indeed, the preface to Iverson [10] cites one chapter (on the logical calculus) as illustration of "the formal manipulability of the language and its utility in theoretical work". A variety of identities is treated in [10] and [11], and a schema for proofs in APL is presented in [12].

Two examples will be used to illustrate the role of identities in the development of the language. The identity

```
(+/X)=(+/U/X)++/(~U)/X
```

applies for any numerical vector `X` and logical vector `U`. Maintaining this identity for the case where `U` is a vector of zeros forces one to define the sum over an empty vector as zero. A similar identity holds for reduction by any associative and commutative function and leads one to define the reduction of an empty array by any function as the identity element of that function.

The dyadic transpose `I⍉A` performs a general permutation on the coordinates of `A` as specified by the argument `I`. The monadic transpose is a special case which, in order to yield ordinary matrix transpose for an array of rank two, was initially defined to interchange the last two coordinates. It was later realized that the identity

```
∧/,(M+.×N)=⍉(⍉N)+.×⍉M
```

expected to hold for matrices would not hold for higher rank arrays. To make the identity true in general, the monadic transpose was defined to reverse the order of the coordinates as follows:

```
∧/,(⍉A)=(⌽⍳⍴⍴A)⍉A.
```

Moreover, the form chosen for the left argument of the dyadic transpose led to the following important identity:

```
∧/,(I⍉J⍉A)=I[J]⍉A.
```

Execute and format

In designing an executable language there is a fundamental choice to be made: Is the statement of an expression to be taken as an order to evaluate it, or must the evaluation be indicated by an explicit function in the language? This decision was made very early in the development of APL, albeit with little deliberation. Nevertheless, once the choice became manifest, early in the development of the implementation, it was applied uniformly in all situations.

There were some arguments against this, of course, particularly in the application of a function to its arguments, where it is often useful to be able to "call by name," which requires that the evaluation of the argument be deferred. But if implemented literally (i.e., if functions could be defined with this as an option) then names per se would have to be known to the language and would constitute an additional object type with its own rules of behavior and specialized primitive functions. A deliberate effort had been made to eliminate unnecessary type distinctions, as in the uniform language treatment of numbers regardless of their internal representation, and this point of view prevailed. In the interest of keeping the semantic rules simple, the idea of "call by name" was rejected as a primitive concept in APL.

Nevertheless, there are important cases where the formal argument of a function should not be evaluated at the time of invocation—as in the application of a generalized root finder to an arbitrary function. There are also situations where it is useful to inhibit evaluation of an expression, as in certain conditional forms, and the need for some treatment of the problem was clear. The basis for a solution was at hand in the form of character arrays, which were already objects of the language. Effectively, putting quotes around a statement inhibits its execution by making it a data item, a character array subject to the normal language functions. To get the effect of working with names, or with expressions to be conditionally evaluated, it was only necessary to introduce the notion of "unquote," or more properly "execute," as a function that would cause a character array to be evaluated as if it were the same expression without the inhibition.

The actual introduction of the execute function did not come for some time after its recognition as the likely solution. The development that preceded its final acceptance into APL illustrates several design principles.

The concept of an execute function is a very powerful one. In a sense, it makes the language "self-conscious," and introduces endless possibilities for obscurity in programs. This might have been a reason for not allowing it, but we had long since realized that a general-purpose language cannot be made foolproof and remain effective. Furthermore, APL is easily partitioned, and beginning users, or users of application packages, need not know about more sophisticated aspects of the language. The real issues were whether the function was of sufficiently broad utility, whether it could be defined simply, and whether it was perhaps a special case of a more general capability that should be implemented instead. There was also the need to establish a symbol for it.

The case for general utility was easily made. The execute function does allow names to be used as arguments to functions without the need for a new data type; it provides the means for generating variables under program control, which can be useful, for example, in managing data that do not conveniently fit into rectangular arrays; it allows the construction and execution of statements under program control; and in interpretive implementations it provides conversion from characters to numbers at machine speeds.

The behavior of the execute function is simply described: it treats a character array argument as a representation of an APL statement and attempts to evaluate or execute the statement so represented. System commands and attempts to enter function definition mode are not valid APL statements and are excluded from the domain of execute. It can be said that, except for these exclusions, execute acts upon a character array as if the elements of the array were entered at a terminal in the immediate execution mode.

Incidentally, there was pressure to arbitrarily include system commands in the domain of execute as a means of providing access to other workspaces under program control in order to facilitate work with large collections of data. This was resisted on the basis that the execute function should not allow by subterfuge what was otherwise disallowed. Indeed, consideration of this aspect of the behavior of execute led to the removal of certain anomalies in function definition and a clarification of the role of the escape characters) and ∇.

The question of generality has not been finally settled. Certainly, the execute function could be considered a member of a class that includes constructs like those of the lambda calculus. But it is not necessary to have the ultimate answer in order to proceed, and the simplicity of the definition adopted gives some assurance that generalizations are not being foreclosed.

For some time during its experimental implementation the symbol for execute was the epsilon. This was chosen for obvious mnemonic reasons and because no other monadic use was made of this symbol. As thought was being given to another new function—format—it was observed that over some part of each of their domains format and execute were inverses. Furthermore, over these parts of their domains they were strongly related to the functions encode and decode, and we therefore adopted their symbols overstruck by the symbol ∘.

The format function furnishes another example of a primitive whose behavior was first defined and long experimented with by means of APL defined functions. These defined functions were the *DFT* (Decimal Format) and *EFT* (Exponential Format) familiar to most users of the APL system. The main advantage of the primitive format function over these definitions is its much more efficient use of computer time.

The format function has both a dyadic and a monadic definition, but the execute function is monadic only. This leaves the way open for a related dyadic function, for which there has been no dearth of suggestions, but none will be adopted until more experience has been gained in the use of what we already have.

System commands and other environmental facilities

The definition of APL is purely abstract: the objects of the language, arrays of numbers and characters, are acted upon by the primitive functions in a manner independent of their representation and independent of any practical interpretation placed upon them. The advantages of such an abstract definition are that it makes the language truly machine independent, and avoids bias in favor of particular application areas. But not everything in a computing system is abstract, and provision must be made to manage system resources and otherwise communicate with the environment in which the language functions operate.

Maintaining the abstract nature of the language in a real computing system therefore seemed to imply a need for language-like facilities in some sense outside of APL. The need was first met by the use of system commands, which are syntactically not part of APL, and are also excluded from dynamic use within APL programs. They provided a simple and, in some ways, convenient answer to the problem of system management, but proved insufficient because the actions and information provided by them are often required dynamically.

The exclusion of system commands from programs was based more strongly on engineering considerations than on a theoretic compulsion, since the syntactic distinction alone sets them apart from the language, but there remained a reluctance to allow such syntactic anomalies in a program. The real issue, which was whether the functions provided by the system commands were properly the province of APL, was tabled for the time being, and defined functions that mimic the actions of certain of them were introduced to allow dynamic execution. The functions so provided were those affecting only the environment within a workspace, such as width and origin, while those that would have affected major physical resources of the system were still excluded for engineering reasons.

These environmental defined functions were based on the use of still another class of functions—called "I-beams" because of the shape of the symbol used for them—which provide a more general facility for communication between APL programs and the less abstract parts of the system. The I-beam functions were first introduced by the system programmers to allow them to execute System/360 instructions from within APL programs, and thus use APL as a direct aid in their programming activity. The obvious convenience of functions of this kind, which appeared to be part of the language, led to the introduction of the monadic I-beam function for direct use by anyone. Various arguments to this function yielded information about the environment such as available space and time of day.

Though clearly an ad hoc facility, the I-beam functions appear to be part of the language because they obey APL syntax and can be executed from within an APL program. They were too useful to do without in the absence of a more rational solution to the problem, and so were graced with the designation "system-dependent functions," while we continued to use the system and think about the general problem of communication among the subsystems composing it.

Shared variables

The logical basis for a generalized communication facility in APL\360 was laid in 1964 with the publication of the formal description of System/360 [2]. It was then observed that the interaction between concurrent "asynchronous" processes (programs) could be completely comprehended by an interface comprising variables that were shared by the cooperating processes. (Another facility was also used, where one program forced a branch in another, but this can be regarded as a derivative representation based on variables shared between one program and a processor that drives the other.) It was not until six or seven years later, however, that the full force of this observation was brought to bear on the practical problem of controlling in an organic way the environment in which APL programs run.

Three processors can be identified during the execution of an APL program: APL, or the processor that actually executes the program; the *system*, or host that manages libraries and other environmental factors, which in APL\360 is the System/360 processor; and the user, who may be observing and processing output or providing input to the program. The link between APL and system is the set of I-beam functions, that between user and system is the set of system commands, and between user and APL, the quad and quote-quad. With the exception of the quote-quad, which is a true variable, all these links are constructs on the interfaces rather than the interfaces themselves.

It can be seen that the quote-quad is shared by the user and APL. Characteristically, a value assigned to it in a program is presented to the user at the terminal, who utilizes this information as he sees fit. If later read by the program, the value of the quote-quad then has no fixed relationship to what was earlier specified by the program. The values written and read by the program are *a fortiori* APL objects—abstract arrays—but they may have practical significance to the user-processor, suggesting, for example, that an experimental observation be made and the results entered at the keyboard.

Using the quote-quad as the paradigm for their behavior, a general facility for shared variables was designed and implemented starting in late 1969 (see Lathwell [13]). The underlying concept was to provide communication across the boundary between independent processors by explicitly establishing certain variables as being shared between them. A shared variable is syntactically indistinguishable from others and may be used normally either on the right or left of an assignment arrow.

Although motivated most strongly at the time by a need to provide a "file and I/O" capability for APL\360, the shared variable facility satisfied other needs as well, a significant criterion for the inclusion of a new feature in the language. It provides for general communication, not only between APL and the host system, but also between APL programs running concurrently at different terminals, which is in a sense a more fundamental use of the idea.

Perhaps as important as the practical use of the facility is the potency that an implementation lends to the concept of shared variables as a basis for understanding communication in any system. With respect to APL\360, for example, we had long used the term "distinguished variable" in discussing the interface between APL and system, meaning thereby variables, like trace and stop vectors, which hold control or state information. It is now clear that "distinguished variables" are shared variables, distinguished from ordinary variables by the fact of their being shared, and further qualified by their membership in a particular interface. In principle, the environment and resources of APL\360 could be completely controlled through the use of an appropriate set of such distinguished variables.

System functions

In a given application area it is usually easier to work with APL augmented by defined functions, designed to embody the significant concepts of the area, than with the primitive functions of the language alone. Such defined functions, together with the relevant variables or data objects, constitute an application language, or application extension. Managing the resources or environment of an APL computing system is a particular application, in which the data objects are the distinguished variables that define the interface between APL and system.

For convenience, the defined functions constituting an application extension for system management should behave differently from other defined functions, at least to the extent of being available at all times, like the primitives, without having to be copied from workspace to workspace. Such ubiquity requires that the names of these functions be distinguished from those a user might invent. This distinction can only be made, if APL is to remain essentially context independent, by the establishment of a class of reserved names. This class has been defined as names starting with the quad character, and functions having such names are called *system functions*. A similar naming convention applies to distinguished variables, or *system variables*, as they are now called.

In principle, system functions work with system variables that are independently identifiable. In practice, the system variables in a particular situation may not be available explicitly, and the system functions may be locked. This can come about because direct access to the interface by the user is deemed undesirable for technical reasons, or because of economic considerations such as efficiency or protection of proprietary rights. In such situations system functions are superficially distinguishable from primitive functions only by virtue of the naming convention.

The present I-beam functions behave like system functions. Fortunately, there are only two of them: the monadic function that is familiar to all users of APL, and the dyadic function that is still known mostly to system programmers. Despite their usefulness, these functions are hardly to be taken as examples of good application language design, depending as they do on arbitrary numerical arguments to give them meaning, and having no meaningful relationships with each other. The monadic I-beams are more like read-only variables—changeable constants, as it were—than functions. Indeed, except for their syntax, they behave precisely like shared variables where the processor on the other side replaces the value between each reference on the APL side.

The shared variable facility itself requires communication between APL and system in order to establish a desired interface between APL and cooperating processors. The prospect of inventing new system commands for this, or otherwise providing an ad hoc facility, was most distasteful, and consideration of this problem was a major factor in leading toward the system function concept. It was taken as an indication of the validity of the shared variable approach to communication when the solution to the problem it engendered was found within the conceptual framework it provided, and this solution also proved to be a basis for clarifying the role of facilities already present.

In due course a set of system functions must be designed to parallel the facilities now provided by system commands and go beyond them. Aside from the obvious advantage of being dynamically executable, such a set of system functions will have other advantages and some disadvantages. The major operational advantage is that the system functions will be able to use the full power of APL to generate their arguments and exploit their results. Countering this, there is the fact that this power has a price: the automatic name isolation provided by the extralingual system commands will not be available to the system functions. Names used as arguments will have to be presented as character arrays, which is not a disadvantage in programs, although it is less convenient for casual keyboard entry than is the use of unadorned names in system commands.

A more profound advantage of system functions over system commands lies in the possibility of designing the former to work together constructively. System commands are foreclosed from this by the rudimentary nature of their syntax; they do constitute a language, but one having no constructive potential.

Workspaces, files, and input-output

The workspace organization of APL\360 libraries serves to group together functions and variables intended to work together, and to render them active or inactive as a group, preserving the state of the computation during periods of inactivity. Workspaces also implicitly qualify the names of objects within them, so that the same name may be used independently in a multiplicity of workspaces in a given system. These are useful attributes; the grouping feature, for example, contributes strongly to the convenience of using APL by obviating the linkage problems found in other library systems.

On the other hand, engineering decisions made early in the development of APL\360 determined that the workspaces be of fixed size. This limits the size of objects that can be managed within them and often becomes an inconvenience. Consequently, as usage of APL\360 developed, a demand arose for a "file" facility, at first to work with large volumes of data under program control, and later to utilize data generated by other systems. There was also a demand to make use of high-speed input and output equipment. As noted in an earlier section, these demands led in time to the development of the shared variable facility. Three considerations were paramount in arriving at this solution.

One consideration was the determination to maintain the abstract nature of APL. In particular, the use of primitive functions whose definitions depend on the representation of their arguments was to be avoided. This alone was sufficient to rule out the notion of a file as a formal concept in the language. APL has primitive array structures that either encompass the logical structure of files or can be extended to do so by relatively simple functions defined on them. The user of APL may regard any array or collection of arrays as a file, and in principle should be able to use the data so organized without regard to the medium on which these arrays may be stored.

The second consideration was the not uncommon observation that files are used in two ways, as a medium for exchange of information and as a dynamic extension of working storage during computation (see Falkoff [14]). In keeping with the principle just noted, the proper solution to the second problem must ultimately be the removal of workspace size limitations, and this will probably be achieved in the course of general developments in the industry. We saw no prospect of a satisfactory direct solution being achieved locally in a reasonable time, so attention was concentrated on the first problem in the expectation that, with a good general communication facility, on-line storage devices could be used for workspace extension at least as effectively as they are so used in other systems.

The third consideration was one of generality. One possible approach to the communication problem would have been to increase the roster of system commands and make them dynamically executable, or add variations to the I-beam functions to manage specific storage media and I/O equipment or access methods. But in addition to being unpleasant because of its ad hoc nature, this approach did not promise to be general enough. In working interactively with large collections of data, for example, the possible functional variations are almost limitless. Various classes of users may be allowed access for different purposes under a variety of controls, and unless it is intended to impose restrictive constraints ahead of time, it is futile to try to anticipate the solutions to particular problems. Thus, to provide a communication facility by accretion appeared to be an endless task.

The shared variable approach is general enough because, by making the interface explicitly available with primitive controls on the behavior of the shared variable, it provides only the basic communication mechanism. It then remains for the specific problem to be managed by bringing to bear on it the full power of APL on one side, and that of the host system on the other. The only remaining question is one of performance: does the shared variable concept provide the basis for an effective implementation? This question has been answered affirmatively as a result of direct experimentation.

The net effect of this approach has been to provide for APL an application extension comprising the few system functions necessary to manage shared variables. Actual file or I/O applications are managed, as required, by user-defined functions. The system functions are used only to establish sharing, and the shared variables are then used for the actual transfer of information between APL workspaces and file or I/O processors.

Appendix. Chronology of APL development

The development of APL was begun in 1957 as a necessary tool for writing clearly about various topics of interest in data processing. The early development is described in the preface of Iverson [10] and Brooks and Iverson [15]. Falkoff became interested in the work shortly after Iverson joined IBM in 1960, and used the language in his work on parallel search memories [16]. In early 1963 Falkoff began work on a formal description of System/360 in APL and was later joined in this work by Iverson and Sussenguth [2].

Throughout this early period the language was used by both Falkoff and Iverson in the teaching of various topics at various universities and at the IBM Systems Research Institute. Early in 1964 Iverson began using it in a course in elementary functions at the Fox Lane High School in Bedford, New York, and in 1966 published a text that grew out of this work [8]. John L. Lawrence (who, as editor of the *IBM Systems Journal*, procured and assisted in the publication of the formal description of System/360) became interested in the use of APL at high school and college level and invited the authors to consult with him in the development of curriculum material based on the use of computers. This work led to the preparation of curriculum material in a number of areas and to the publication of an APL\360 Reference Manual by Sandra Pakin [17].

Although our work through 1964 had been focused on the language as a tool for communication among *people*, we never doubted that the same characteristics which make the language good for this purpose would make it good for communication with a machine. In 1963 Herbert Hellerman implemented a portion of the language on an IBM/1620 as reported in [18]. Hellerman's system was used by students in the high school course with encouraging results. This, together with our earlier work in education, heightened our interest in a full-scale implementation.

When the work on the formal description of System/360 was finished in 1964 we turned our attention to the problem of implementation. This work was brought to rapid fruition in 1965 when Lawrence M. Breed joined the project and, together with Philip S. Abrams, produced an implementation on the 7090 by the end of 1965. Influenced by Hellerman's interest in time-sharing we had already developed an APL typing element for the IBM 1050 computer terminal. This was used in early 1966 when Breed adapted the 7090 system to an experimental time-sharing system developed under Andrew Kinslow, allowing us the first use of APL in the manner familiar today. By November 1966, the system had been reprogrammed for System/360 and APL service has been available within IBM since that date. The system became available outside IBM in 1968.

A paper by Falkoff and Iverson [3] provided the first published description of the APL\360 system, and a companion paper by Breed and Lathwell [19] treated the implementation. R. H. Lathwell joined the design group in 1966 and has since been concerned primarily with the implementations of APL and with the use of APL itself in the design process. In 1971 he published, together with Jorge Mezei, a formal definition of APL in APL [9].

The APL\360 System benefited from the contributions of many outside of the central design group. The preface to the User's Manual [1] acknowledges many of these contributions.

References

1. A. D. Falkoff and K. E. Iverson, *APL\360 User's Manual*, IBM Corporation, (GH20-0683-1) 1970.
2. A. D. Falkoff, K. E. Iverson, and E. H. Sussenguth, "A Formal Description of System/360," *IBM Systems Journal*, **3**, 198 (1964).
3. A. D. Falkoff and K. E. Iverson, "The APL\360 Terminal System", *Symposium on Interactive Systems for Experimental Applied Mathematics*, eds., M. Klerer and J. Reinfelds, Academic Press, New York, 1968.
4. A. D. Falkoff, "Criteria for a System Design Language," *Report on NATO Science Committee Conference on Software Engineering Techniques*, April 1970.
5. Z. Ghandour and J. Mezei, "General Arrays, Operators and Functions," *IBM J. Res. Develop.* **17**, 335 (1973, this issue).
6. T. More, "Axioms and Theorems for a Theory of Arrays—Part I," *IBM J. Res. Develop.* **17**, 135 (1973).
7. P. C. Berry, *APL\360 Primer*, IBM Corporation, (GH-20-0689-2) 1971.
8. K. E. Iverson, *Elementary Functions: An Algorithmic Treatment*, Science Research Associates, Chicago, 1966.
9. R. H. Lathwell and J. E. Mezei, "A Formal Description of APL," *Colloque APL*, Institut de Recherche d'Informatique et d'Automatique, Rocquencourt, France, 1971.
10. K. E. Iverson, *A Programming Language*, Wiley, New York, 1962.
11. K. E. Iverson, "Formalism in Programming Languages," *Communications of the ACM*, **7**, 80 (February, 1964).
12. K. E. Iverson, *Algebra: an algorithmic treatment*, Addison-Wesley Publishing Co., Reading, Mass., 1972.
13. R. H. Lathwell, "System Formulation and APL Shared Variables," *IBM J. Res. Develop.* **17**, 353 (1973, this issue).
14. A. D. Falkoff, "A Survey of Experimental APL File and I/O Systems in IBM", *Colloque APL*, Institut de Recherche d'Informatique et D'Automatique, Rocquencourt, France, 1971.
15. F. P. Brooks and K. E. Iverson, *Automatic Data Processing*, Wiley, New York, 1963.
16. A. D. Falkoff, "Algorithms for Parallel Search Memories," *Journal of the ACM*, 488 (1962).
17. S., Pakin, *APL\360 Reference Manual*, Science Research Associates, Inc., Chicago, 1968.

18. H. Hellerman, "Experimental Personalized Array Translator System," *Communications of the ACM* 7, 433 (July, 1964).
19. L. M. Breed and R. H. Lathwell, "Implementation of APL/360," *Symposium on Interactive Systems for Experimental Applied Mathematics*, eds., M. Klerer and J. Reinfelds, Academic Press, New York, 1968.

Received May 16, 1972

The authors are located at the IBM Data Processing Division Scientific Center, 3401 Market Street, Philadelphia, Pennsylvania 19104.

5 The Evolution of APL

THE EVOLUTION OF APL

Adin D. Falkoff
Kenneth E. Iverson

Research Division
IBM Corporation

This paper is a discussion of the evolution of the APL language, and it treats implementations and applications only to the extent that they appear to have exercised a major influence on that evolution. Other sources of historical information are cited in References 1-3; in particular, The Design of APL [1] provides supplementary detail on the reasons behind many of the design decisions made in the development of the language. Readers requiring background on the current definition of the language should consult APL Language [4].

Although we have attempted to confirm our recollections by reference to written documents and to the memories of our colleagues, this remains a personal view which the reader should perhaps supplement by consulting the references provided. In particular, much information about individual contributions will be found in the Appendix to The Design of APL [1], and in the Acknowledgements in A Programming Language [10] and in APL\360 User's Manual [23]. Because Reference 23 may no longer be readily available, the acknowledgements from it are reprinted in Appendix A.

McDonnell's recent paper on the development of the notation for the circular functions [5] shows that the detailed evolution of any one facet of the language can be both interesting and illuminating. Too much detail in the present paper would, however, tend to obscure the main points, and we have therefore limited ourselves to one such example. We can only hope that other contributors will publish their views on the detailed developments of other facets of the language, and on the development of various applications of it.

The development of the language was first begun by Iverson as a tool for describing and analyzing various topics in data processing, for use in teaching classes, and in writing a book, Automatic Data Processing [6], undertaken together with Frederick P. Brooks, Jr., then a graduate student at Harvard. Because the work began as incidental to other work, it is difficult to pinpoint the beginning, but it was probably early 1956; the first explicit use of the language to provide communication between the designers and programmers of a complex system occurred during a leave from Harvard spent with the management consulting firm of McKinsey and Company in 1957. Even after others were drawn into the development of the language, this development remained largely incidental to the work in which it was used. For example, Falkoff was first attracted to it (shortly after Iverson joined IBM in 1960) by its use as a tool in his work in parallel search memories [7], and in 1964 we began to plan an implementation of the language to enhance its utility as a design tool, work which came to fruition when we were joined by Lawrence M. Breed in 1965.

The most important influences in the early phase appear to be Iverson's background in mathematics, his thesis work in the machine solutions of linear differential equations [8] for an economic input-output model proposed by Professor Wassily Leontief (who, with Professor Howard Aiken, served as thesis adviser), and Professor Aiken's interest in the newly-developing field of commercial applications of computers. Falkoff brought to the work a background in engineering and technical development, with experience in a number of disciplines, which had left him convinced of the overriding importance of simplicity, particularly in a field as subject to complication as data processing.

Although the evolution has been continuous, it will be helpful to distinguish four phases according to the major use or preoccupation of the period: academic use (to 1960), machine description (1961-1963), implementation (1964-1968), and systems (after 1968).

1. ACADEMIC USE

The machine programming required in Iverson's thesis work was directed at the development of a set of subroutines designed to permit convenient experimentation with a variety of mathematical methods. This implementation experience led to an emphasis on implementable language constructs, and to an understanding of the role of the representation of data.

The mathematical background shows itself in a variety of ways, notably:

1. In the use of functions with explicit arguments and explicit results; even the relations ($< \le = \ge > \ne$) are treated as such functions.

2. In the use of logical functions and logical variables. For example, the compression function (denoted by /) uses as one argument a logical vector which is, in effect, the characteristic vector of the subset selected by compression.

3. In the use of concepts and terminology from tensor analysis, as in *inner product* and *outer product* and in *the use of rank* for the "dimensionality" of an array, and in the treatment of a scalar as an array of rank zero.

4. In the emphasis on generality. For example, the generalizations of summation (by $F/$), of inner product (by $F.G$), and of outer product (by $\circ.F$) extended the utility of these functions far beyond their original area of application.

5. In the emphasis on identities (already evident in [9]) which makes the language more useful for analytic purposes, and which leads to a uniform treatment of special cases as, for example, the definition of the reduction of an empty vector, first given in *A Programming Language* [10].

In 1954 Harvard University published an announcement [11] of a new graduate program in Automatic Data Processing organized by Professor Aiken. (The program was also reported in a conference on computer education [12]). Iverson was one of the new faculty appointed to prosecute the program; working under the guidance of Professor Aiken in the development of new courses provided a stimulus to his interest in developing notation, and the diversity of interests embraced by the program promoted a broad view of applications.

The state of the language at the end of the academic period is best represented by the presentation in *A Programming Language* [10], submitted for publication in early 1961. The evolution in the latter part of the period is best seen by comparing references 9 and 10. This comparison shows that *reduction* and *inner* and *outer product* were all introduced in that period, although not then recognized as a class later called *operators*. It also shows that specification was originally (in Reference 9) denoted by placing the specified name at the right, as in $P+Q\rightarrow Z$. The arguments (due in part to F.P. Brooks, Jr.) which led to the present form ($Z\leftarrow P+Q$) were that it better conformed to the mathematical form $Z=P+Q$, and that in reading a program, any backward reference to determine how a given variable was specified would be facilitated if the specified variables were aligned at the left margin. What this comparison does not show is the removal of a number of special comparison functions (such as the comparison of a vector with each row of a matrix) which were seen to be unnecessary when the power of the inner product began to be appreciated, as in the expression $M\wedge.=V$. This removal provides one example of the simplification of the language produced by generalizations.

2. MACHINE DESCRIPTION

The machine description phase was marked by the complete or partial description of a number of computer systems. The first use of the language to describe a complete computing system was begun in early 1962 when Falkoff discussed with Dr. W.C. Carter his work in the standardization of the instruction set for the machines that were to become the IBM System/360 family. Falkoff agreed to undertake a formal description of the machine language, largely as a vehicle for demonstrating how parallel processes could be rigorously represented. He was later joined in this work by Iverson when he returned from a short leave at Harvard, and still later by E.H. Sussenguth. This work was published as "A Formal Description of System/360" [13].

This phase was also marked by a consolidation and regularization of many aspects which had little to do with machine description. For example, the cumbersome definition of maximum and minimum (denoted in Reference 10 by $U\lceil V$ and $U\lfloor V$ and equivalent to what would now be written as $\lceil/U/V$ and $\lfloor/U/V$) was replaced, at the suggestion of Herbert Hellerman, by the present simple scalar functions. This simplification was deemed practical because of our increased understanding of the potential of reduction and inner and outer product.

The best picture of the evolution in this period is given by a comparison of *A Programming Language* [10] on the one hand,

and "A Formal Description of System/360" [13] and "Formalism in Programming Languages" [14] on the other. Using explicit page references to Reference 10, we will now give some further examples of regularization during this period:

1. The elimination of embracing symbols (such as $|X|$ for absolute value, $\lfloor X \rfloor$ for floor, and $\lceil X \rceil$ for ceiling) and replacement by the leading symbol only, thus unifying the syntax for monadic functions.

2. The conscious use of a single function symbol to represent both a monadic and a dyadic function (still referred to in Reference 10 as unary and binary).

3. The adoption of multi-character names which, because of the failure (page 11) to insist on no elision of the times sign, had been permitted (page 10) only with a special indicator.

4. The rigorous adoption of a right-to-left order of execution which, although stated (page 8) had been violated by the unconscious application of the familiar precedence rules of mathematics. Reasons for this choice are presented in *Elementary Functions* [15], in Berry's *APL\360 Primer* [16], and in *The Design of APL* [1].

5. The concomitant definition of reduction based on a right-to-left order of execution as opposed to the opposite convention defined on page 16.

6. Elimination of the requirement for parentheses surrounding an expression involving a relation (page 11). An example of the use without parentheses occurs near the bottom of page 241 of Reference 13.

7. The elimination of implicit specification of a variable (that is, the specification of some function of it, as in the expression ⍳S←2 on page 81), and its replacement by an explicit inverse function (⊤ in the cited example).

Perhaps the most important developments of this period were in the use of a collection of concurrent autonomous programs to describe a system, and the formalization of shared variables as the means of communication among the programs. Again, comparisons may be made between the system of programs of Reference 13, and the more informal use of concurrent programs introduced on page 88 of Reference 10.

It is interesting to note that the need for a random function (denoted by the question mark) was first felt in describing the operation of the computer itself. The architects of the IBM System/360 wished to leave to the discretion of the designers of the individual machines of the 360 family the decision as to what was to be found in certain registers after the occurrence of certain errors, and this was done by stating that the result was to be random. Recognizing more general use for the function than the generation of random logical vectors, we subsequently defined the monadic question mark function as a scalar function whose argument specified the population from which the random elements were to be chosen.

3. IMPLEMENTATION

In 1964 a number of factors conspired to turn our attention seriously to the problem of implementation. One was the fact that the language was by now sufficiently well-defined to give us some confidence in its suitability for implementation. The second was the interest of Mr. John L. Lawrence who, after managing the publication of our description of System/360, asked for our consultation in utilizing the language as a tool in his new responsibility (with Science Research Associates) for developing the use of computers in education. We quickly agreed with Mr. Lawrence on the necessity for a machine implementation in this work. The third was the interest of our then manager, Dr. Herbert Hellerman, who, after initiating some implementation work which did not see completion, himself undertook an implementation of an array-based language which he reported in the *Communications of the ACM* [17]. Although this work was limited in certain important respects, it did prove useful as a teaching tool and tended to confirm the feasibility of implementation.

Our first step was to define a character set for APL. Influenced by Dr. Hellerman's interest in time-sharing systems, we decided to base the design on an 88-character set for the IBM 1050 terminal, which utilized the easily-interchanged Selectric® typing element. The design of this character-set exercised a surprising degree of influence on the development of the language.

As a practical matter it was clear that we would have to accept a linearization of the language (with no superscripts or subscripts) as well as a strict limit on the size of the primary character set. Although we expected these limitations to have a deleterious effect, and at first found unpleasant some of the linearity forced upon us, we now feel that the changes were beneficial, and that many led to important generalizations. For example:

1. On linearizing indexing we realized that the sub- and super-script form had inhibited the use of arrays of rank greater than 2, and had also inhibited the use of several levels of indexing; both inhibitions were relieved by the linear form $A[I;J;K]$.

2. The linearization of the inner and outer product notation (from $M\overset{+}{\times}N$ and $M\overset{\circ}{\times}N$ to $M+.\times N$ and $M\circ.\times N$) led eventually to the recognition of the operator (which was now represented by an explicit symbol, the period) as a separate and important component of the language.

3. Linearization led to a regularization of many functions of two arguments (such as $N\alpha J$ for $\alpha^j(n)$ and $A\star B$ for a^b) and to the redefinition of certain functions of two or three arguments so as to eliminate one of the arguments. For example, $\iota^j(n)$ was replaced by ιN, with the simple expression $J+\iota N$ replacing the original definition. Moreover, the simple form ιN led to the recognition that $J\geq\iota N$ could replace $N\alpha J$ (for J a scalar) and that $J\circ.\geq\iota N$ could generalize $N\alpha J$ in a useful manner; as a result the functions α and ω were eventually withdrawn.

4. The limitation of the character set led to a more systematic exploitation of the notion of ambiguous valence, the representation of both a monadic and a dyadic function by the same symbol.

5. The limitation of the character set led to the replacement of the two functions for the number of rows and the number of columns of an array, by the single function (denoted by ρ) which gave the dimension vector of the array. This provided the necessary extension to arrays of arbitrary rank, and led to the simple expression $\rho\rho A$ for the rank of A. The resulting notion of the dimension vector also led to the definition of the dyadic reshape function $D\rho X$.

6. The limitation to 88 primary characters led to the important notion of composite characters formed by striking one of the basic characters over another. This scheme has provided a supply of easily-read and easily-written symbols which were needed as the language developed further. For example, the quad, overbar, and circle were included not for specific purposes but because they could be used to overstrike many characters. The overbar by itself also proved valuable for the representation of negative numbers, and the circle proved convenient in carrying out the idea, proposed by E.E. McDonnell, of representing the entire family of (monadic) circular functions by a single dyadic function.

7. The use of multiple fonts had to be re-examined, and this led to the realization that certain functions were defined not in terms of the value of the argument alone, but also in terms of the form of the name of the argument. Such dependence on the forms of names was removed.

We did, however, include characters which could print above and below alphabetics to provide for possible font distinctions. The original typing element included both the present flat underscore, and a saw-tooth one (the pralltriller as shown, for example, in Webster's Second), and a hyphen. In practice, we found the two underscores somewhat difficult to distinguish, and the hyphen very difficult to distinguish from the minus, from which it differed only in length. We therefore made the rather costly change of two characters, substituting the present delta and del (inverted delta) for the pralltriller and the hyphen.

In the placement of the character set on the keyboard we were subject to a number of constraints imposed by the two forms of the IBM 2741 terminal (which differed in the encoding from keyboard-position to element-position), but were able to devise a grouping of symbols which most users find easy to learn. One pleasant surprise has been the discovery that numbers of people who do not use APL have adopted the type element for use in mathematical typing. The first publication of the character set appears to be in Elementary Functions [15].

Implementation led to a new class of questions, including the formal definition of functions, the localization and scope of names, and the use of tolerances in comparisons and in printing output. It also led to systems questions concerning the environment and its management, including the matter of libraries and certain parameters such as index origin, printing precision, and printing width.

Two early decisions set the tone of the implementation work: 1) The implementation was to be experimental, with primary emphasis on flexibility to permit experimentation with language concepts, and with questions of execution efficiency subordinated, and 2) The language was to be compromised as little as possible by machine considerations.

These considerations led Breed and P.S. Abrams (both of whom had been attracted to our work by Reference 13) to propose and build an *interpretive* implementation in the summer of 1965. This was a batch system with punched card input, using a multi-character encoding of the primitive function symbols. It ran on the IBM 7090 machine and we were later able to experiment with it interactively, using the typeball previously designed, by placing the interpreter under an experimental time sharing monitor (TSM) available on a machine in a nearby IBM facility.

TSM was available to us for only a very short time, and in early 1966 we began to consider an implementation on System/360, work that started in earnest in July and culminated in a running system in the fall. The fact that this interpretive and experimental implementation also proved to be remarkably practical and efficient is a tribute to the skill of the implementers, recognized in 1973 by the award to the principals (L.M. Breed, R.H. Lathwell, and R.D. Moore) of ACM's Grace Murray Hopper Award. The fact that the many APL implementations continue to be largely interpretive may be attributed to the array character of the language which makes possible efficient interpretive execution.

We chose to treat the occurrence of a statement as an order to evaluate it, and rejected the notion of an explicit function to indicate evaluation. In order to avoid the introduction of "names" as a distinct object class, we also rejected the notion of "call by name". The constraints imposed by this decision were eventually removed in a simple and general way by the introduction of the *execute* function, which served to execute its character string argument as an APL expression. The evolution of these notions is discussed at length in the section on "Execute and Format" in *The Design of APL* [1].

In earlier discussions with a number of colleagues, the introduction of declarations into the language was urged upon us as a requisite for implementation. We resisted this on the general basis of simplicity, but also on the basis that information in declarations would be redundant, or perhaps conflicting, in a language in which arrays are primitive. The choice of an interpretive implementation made the exclusion of declarations feasible, and this, coupled with the determination to minimize the influence of machine considerations such as the internal representations of numbers on the design of the language, led to an early decision to exclude them.

In providing a mechanism by which a user could define a new function, we wished to provide six forms in all: functions with 0, 1, or 2 explicit arguments, and functions with 0 or 1 explicit results. This led to the adoption of a *header* for the function definition which was, in effect, a paradigm for the way in which a function was used. For example, a function *F* of two arguments having an explicit result would typically be used in an expression such as *Z←A F B*, and this was the form used for the header.

The names for arguments and results in the header were of course made local to the function definition, but at the outset no thought was given to the localization of other names. Fortunately, the design of the interpreter made it relatively easy to localize the names by adding them to the header (separated by semicolons), and this was soon done. Names so localized were strictly local to the defined function, and their scope did not extend to any other functions used within it. It was not until the spring of 1968 when Breed returned from a talk by Professor Alan Perlis on what he called "dynamic localization" that the present scheme was adopted, in which name scopes extend to functions called within a function.

We recognized that the finite limits on the representation of numbers imposed by an implementation would raise problems which might require some compromise in the definition of the language, and we tried to keep these compromises to a minimum. For example, it was clear that we would have to provide both integer and floating point representations of numbers and, because we anticipated use of the system in logical design, we wished to provide an efficient (one bit per element) representation of logical arrays as well. However, at the cost of considerable effort and some loss of efficiency, both well worthwhile, the transitions between representations were made to be imperceptible to the user, except for secondary effects such as storage requirements.

Problems such as overflow (i.e., a result outside the range of the representations available) were treated as domain errors, the term *domain* being understood as the domain of the machine function provided, rather than as the domain of the abstract mathematical function on which it was based.

One difficulty we had not anticipated was the provision of sensible results for the comparison of quantities represented to a limited precision. For example, if *X* and *Y* were specified by *Y←2÷3* and *X←3×Y*, then we wished to have the comparison 2=*X* yield 1 (representing *true*) even though the representation of the quantity *X* would differ slightly from 2.

This was solved by introducing a comparison tolerance (christened fuzz by L.M. Breed, who knew of its use in the Bell Interpreter [18]) which was multiplied by the larger in magnitude of the arguments to give a tolerance to be applied in the comparison. This tolerance was at first fixed (at 1E¯13) and was later made specifiable by the user. The matter has proven more difficult than we first expected, and discussion of it still continues [19, 20].

A related, but less serious, question was what to do with the rational root of a negative number, a question which arose because the exponent (as in the expression ¯8*2÷3) would normally be presented as an approximation to a rational. Since we wished to make the mathematics behave "as you thought it did in high school" we wished to treat such cases properly at least for rationals with denominators of reasonable size. This was achieved by determining the result sign by a continued fraction expansion of the right argument (but only for negative left arguments) and worked for all denominators up to 80 and "most" above.

Most of the mathematical functions required were provided by programs taken from the work of the late Hirondo Kuki in the FORTRAN IV Subroutine Library. Certain functions (such as the inverse hyperbolics) were, however, not available and were developed, during the summers of 1967 and 1968, by K. M. Brown, then on the faculty of Cornell University.

The fundamental decision concerning the systems environment was the adoption of the concept of a workspace. As defined in "The APL\360 Terminal System" [21]:

> APL\360 is built around the idea of a workspace, analogous to a notebook, in which one keeps work in progress. The workspace holds both defined functions and variables (data), and it may be stored into and retrieved from a library holding many such workspaces. When retrieved from a library by an appropriate command from a terminal, a copy of the stored workspace becomes active at that terminal, and the functions defined in it, together with all the APL primitives, become available to the user.
>
> The three commands required for managing a library are "save", "load", and "drop", which respectively store a copy of an active workspace into a library, make a copy of a stored workspace active, and destroy the library copy of a workspace. Each user of the system has a private library into which only he can store. However, he may load a workspace from any of a number of common libraries, or if he is privy to the necessary information, from another user's private library. Functions or variables in different workspaces can be combined, either item by item or all at once, by a fourth command, called "copy". By means of three cataloging commands, a user may get the names of workspaces in his own or a common library, or get a listing of functions or variables in his active workspace.

The language used to control the system functions of loading and storing workspaces was not APL, but comprised a set of system commands. The first character of each system command is a right parenthesis, which cannot occur at the left of a valid APL expression, and therefore acts as an "escape character", freeing the syntax of what follows. System commands were used for other aspects such as sign-on and sign-off, messages to other users, and for the setting and sensing of various system parameters such as the index origin, the printing precision, the print width, and the random link used in generating the pseudo-random sequence for the random function.

When it first became necessary to name the implementation we chose the acronym formed from the book title A Programming Language [10] and, to allow a clear distinction between the language and any particular implementation of it, initiated the use of the machine name as part of the name of the implementation (as in APL\1130 and APL\360). Within the design group we had until that time simply referred to "the language".

A brief working manual of the APL\360 system was first published in November 1966 [22], and a full manual appeared in 1968 [23]. The initial implementation (in FORTRAN on an IBM 7090) was discussed by Abrams [24], and the time-shared implementation on System/360 was discussed by Breed and Lathwell [25].

3. SYSTEMS

Use of the APL system by others in IBM began long before it had been completed to the point described in APL\360 User's Manual [23]. We quickly learned the difficulties associated with changing the specifications of a system already in use, and the impact of changes on established users and programs. As a result we learned to appreciate the importance of the relatively long period of development of the language which preceded the implementation; early implementation of languages tends to stifle radical change, limiting further development to the addition of features and frills.

On the other hand, we also learned the advantages of a running model of the language in exposing anomalies and, in particular, the advantage of input from a large population of users concerned with a broad range of applications. This use quickly exposed the major deficiencies of the system.

Some of these deficiencies were rectified by the generalization of certain functions and the addition of others in a process of gradual evolution. Examples include the extension of the catenation function to apply to arrays other than vectors and to permit lamination, and the addition of a generalized matrix inverse function discussed by M.A. Jenkins [26].

Other deficiencies were of a systems nature, concerning the need to communicate between concurrent APL programs (as in our description of System/360), to communicate with the APL system itself within APL rather than by the ad hoc device of system commands, to communicate with alien systems and devices (as in the use of file devices), and the need to define functions within the language in terms of their representation by APL arrays. These matters required more fundamental innovations and led to what we have called the system phase.

The most pressing practical need for the application of APL systems to commercial data processing was the provision of file facilities. One of the first commercial systems to provide this was the File Subsystem reported by Sharp [27] in 1970, and defined in a SHARE presentation by L.M. Breed [28], and in a manual published by Scientific Time Sharing Corporation [29]. As its name implies, it was not an integral part of the language but was, like the system commands, a practical ad hoc solution to a pressing problem.

In 1970 R.H. Lathwell proposed what was to become the basis of a general solution to many systems problems of APL\360, a shared variable processor [30] which implemented the shared variable scheme of communication among processors. This work culminated in the APLSV System [31] which became generally available in 1973.

Falkoff's "Some Implications of Shared Variables" [32] presents the essential notion of the shared variable system as follows:

> A user of early APL systems essentially had what appeared to be an "APL machine" at his disposal, but one which lacked access to the rest of the world. In more recent systems, such as APLSV and others, this isolation is overcome and communication with other users and the host system is provided for by shared variables.
>
> Two classes of shared variables are available in these systems. First, there is a general shared variable facility with which a user may establish arbitrary, temporary, interfaces with other users or with auxiliary processors. Through the latter, communication may be had with other elements of the host system, such as its file subsystem, or with other systems altogether. Second, there is a set of system variables which define parts of the permanent interface between an APL program and the underlying processor. These are used for interrogating and controlling the computing environment, such as the origin for array indexing or the action to be taken upon the occurrence of certain exceptional conditions.

4. A DETAILED EXAMPLE

At the risk of placing undue emphasis on one facet of the language, we will now examine in detail the evolution of the treatment of numeric constants, in order to illustrate how substantial changes were commonly arrived at by a sequence of small steps.

Any numeric constant, including a constant vector, can be written as an expression involving APL primitive functions applied to decimal numbers as, for example, in `3.14×10*-5` and `-2.718` and `(3.14×10*-5),(-2.718),5`. At the outset we permitted only non-negative decimal constants of the form `2.718`, and all other values had to be expressed as compound statements.

Use of the monadic negation function in producing negative values in vectors was particularly cumbersome, as in `(-4),3,(-5),-7`. We soon realized that the adoption of a specific "negative" symbol would solve the problem, and familiarity with Beberman's work [33] led us to the adoption of his "high minus" which we had, rather fortuitously, included in our character set. The constant vector used above could now be written as `¯4,3,¯5,¯7`.

Solution of the problem of negative numbers emphasized the remaining awkwardness of factors of the form 10⋆*N*. At a meeting of the principals in Chicago, which included Donald Mitchell and Peter Calingaert of Science Research Associates, it was realized that the introduction of a scaled form of constant in the manner used in FORTRAN would not complicate the syntax, and this was soon adopted.

These refinements left one function in the writing of any vector constant, namely, catenation. The straightforward execution of an expression for a constant vector of *N* elements involved *N*-1 catenations of scalars with vectors of increasing length, the handling of roughly .5×*N*×*N*+1 elements in all. To avoid gross inefficiencies in the input of a constant vector from the keyboard, catenation was therefore given special treatment in the original implementation.

This system had been in use for perhaps six months when it occurred to Falkoff that since commas were not required in the normal representation of a matrix, vector constants might do without them as well. This seemed outrageously simple, and we looked for flaws. Finding none we adopted and implemented the idea immediately, but it took some time to overcome the habit of writing expressions such as (3,3)ρ*X* instead of 3 3ρ*X*.

5. CONCLUSIONS

Nearly all programming languages are rooted in mathematical notation, employing such fundamental notions as functions, variables, and the decimal (or other radix) representation of numbers, and a view of programming languages as part of the longer-range development of mathematical notation can serve to illuminate their development.

Before the advent of the general-purpose computer, mathematical notation had, in a long and painful evolution well-described in Cajori's history of mathematical notations [34], embraced a number of important notions:

1. The notion of assigning an alphabetic name to a variable or unknown quantity (Cajori, Secs. 339-341).

2. The notion of a <u>function</u> which applies to an <u>argument</u> or arguments to produce an explicit result which can itself serve as argument to another function, and the associated adoption of specific symbols (such as + and ×) to denote the more common functions (Cajori, Secs. 200-233).

3. <u>Aggregation</u> or <u>grouping</u> symbols (such as the parentheses) which make possible the use of composite expressions with an unambiguous specification of the order in which the component functions are to be executed (Cajori, Secs. 342-355).

4. Simple, uniform representations for numeric quantities (Cajori, Secs. 276-289).

5. The treatment of quantities without concern for the particular representation used.

6. The notion of treating vectors, matrices, and higher-dimensional arrays as entities, which had by this time become fairly widespread in mathematics, physics, and engineering.

With the first computer languages (machine languages) all of these notions were, for good practical reasons, dropped; variable names were represented by "register numbers", application of a function (as in *A*+*B*) was necessarily broken into a sequence of operations (such as "Load register 801 into the Addend register, Load register 802 into the Augend register, etc."), grouping of operations was therefore non-existent, the various functions provided were represented by numbers rather than by familiar mathematical symbols, results depended sharply on the particular representation used in the machine, and the use of arrays, as such, disappeared.

Some of these limitations were soon removed in early "automatic programming" languages, and languages such as FORTRAN introduced a limited treatment of arrays, but many of the original limitations remain. For example, in FORTRAN and related languages the size of an array is not a language concept, the asterisk is used instead of any of the familiar mathematical symbols for multiplication, the power function is represented by two occurrences of this symbol rather than by a distinct symbol, and concern with representation still survives in declarations.

APL has, in its development, remained much closer to mathematical notation, retaining (or selecting one of) established symbols where possible, and employing mathematical terminology. Principles of simplicity and uniformity have, however, been given precedence, and these have led to certain departures from conventional mathematical notation as, for example, the adoption of a single form (analogous to 3+4) for dyadic functions, a single form (analogous to -4) for monadic functions, and the adoption of a uniform rule for the application of all scalar functions to arrays. This relationship to mathematical notation has been discussed in The Design of APL [1] and in "Algebra as a Language" which occurs as Appendix A in Algebra: an algorithmic treatment [35].

The close ties with mathematical notation are evident in such things as the reduction operator (a generalization of sigma notation), the inner product (a generalization of matrix product), and the outer product (a generalization of the outer product used in tensor analysis). In other aspects the relation to mathematical notation is closer than might appear. For example, the order of execution of the conventional expression *F G H (X)* can be expressed by saying that the right argument of each function is the value of the entire expression to its right; this rule, extended to dyadic as well as monadic functions, is the rule used in APL. Moreover, the term operator is used in the same sense as in "derivative operator" or "convolution operator" in mathematics, and to avoid conflict it is not used as a synonym for function.

As a corollary we may remark that the other major programming languages, although known to the designers of APL, exerted little or no influence, because of their radical departures from the line of development of mathematical notation which APL continued. A concise view of the current use of the language, together with comments on matters such as writing style, may be found in Falkoff's review of the 1975 and 1976 International APL Congresses [36].

Although this is not the place to discuss the future, it should be remarked that the evolution of APL is far from finished. In particular, there remain large areas of mathematics, such as set theory and vector calculus, which can clearly be incorporated in APL through the introduction of further operators.

There are also a number of important features which are already in the abstract language, in the sense that their incorporation requires little or no new definition, but are as yet absent from most implementations. Examples include complex numbers, the possibility of defining functions of ambiguous valence (already incorporated in at least two systems [37, 38]), the use of user defined functions in conjunction with operators, and the use of selection functions other than indexing to the left of the assignment arrow.

We conclude with some general comments, taken from The Design of APL [1], on principles which guided, and circumstances which shaped, the evolution of APL:

> The actual operative principles guiding the design of any complex system must be few and broad. In the present instance we believe these principles to be simplicity and practicality. Simplicity enters in four guises: uniformity (rules are few and simple), generality (a small number of general functions provide as special cases a host of more specialized functions), familiarity (familiar symbols and usages are adopted whenever possible), and brevity (economy of expression is sought). Practicality is manifested in two respects: concern with actual application of the language, and concern with the practical limitations imposed by existing equipment.
>
> We believe that the design of APL was also affected in important respects by a number of procedures and circumstances. Firstly, from its inception APL has been developed by using it in a succession of areas. This emphasis on application clearly favors practicality and simplicity. The treatment of many different areas fostered generalization: for example, the general inner product was developed in attempting to obtain the advantages of ordinary matrix algebra in the treatment of symbolic logic.
>
> Secondly, the lack of any machine realization of the language during the first seven or eight years of its development allowed the designers the freedom to make radical changes, a freedom not normally enjoyed by designers who must observe the needs of a large working population dependent on the language for their daily computing needs. This circumstance was due more to the dearth of interest in the language than to foresight.
>
> Thirdly, at every stage the design of the language was controlled by a small group of not more than five people. In particular, the men who designed (and coded) the implementation were part of the language design group, and all members of the design group were involved in broad decisions affecting the implementation. On the other hand, many ideas were received and accepted from people outside the

design group, particularly from active users of some implementation of APL.

Finally, design decisions were made by Quaker consensus; controversial innovations were deferred until they could be revised or reevaluated so as to obtain unanimous agreement. Unanimity was not achieved without cost in time and effort, and many divergent paths were explored and assessed. For example, many different notations for the circular and hyperbolic functions were entertained over a period of more than a year before the present scheme was proposed, whereupon it was quickly adopted. As the language grows, more effort is needed to explore the ramifications of any major innovation. Moreover, greater care is needed in introducing new facilities, to avoid the possibility of later retraction that would inconvenience thousands of users.

ACKNOWLEDGEMENTS

For critical comments arising from their reading of this paper, we are indebted to a number of our colleagues who were there when it happened, particularly P.S. Abrams of Scientific Time Sharing Corporation, R.H. Lathwell and R.D. Moore of I.P. Sharp Associates, and L.M. Breed and E.E. McDonnell of IBM Corporation.

REFERENCES

1. Falkoff, A.D., and K.E. Iverson, The Design of APL, IBM Journal of Research and Development, Vol.17, No.4, July 1973, pages 324-334.

2. The Story of APL, Computing Report in Science and Engineering, IBM Corp., Vol.6, No.2, April 1970, pages 14-18.

3. Origin of APL, a videotape prepared by John Clark for the Fourth APL Conference , 1974, with the participation of P.S. Abrams, L.M. Breed, A.D. Falkoff, K.E. Iverson, and R.D. Moore. Available from Orange Coast Community College, Costa Mesa, California.

4. Falkoff, A.D., and K.E. Iverson, APL Language, Form No. GC26-3847, IBM Corp., 1975

5. McDonnell, E. E., The Story of ○, APL Quote-Quad, Vol. 8, No. 2, ACM, SIGPLAN Technical Committee on APL (STAPL), December, 1977, pages 48-54.

6. Brooks, F.P., and K.E. Iverson, Automatic Data Processing, John Wiley and Sons, 1973.

7. Falkoff, A.D., Algorithms for Parallel Search Memories, Journal of the ACM, Vol. 9, 1962, pages 488-511.

8. Iverson, K.E., Machine Solutions of Linear Differential Equations: Applications to a Dynamic Economic Model, Harvard University, 1954 (Ph.D. Thesis).

9. Iverson, K.E., The Description of Finite Sequential Processes, Proceedings of the Fourth London Symposium on Information Theory, Colin Cherry, Editor, 1960, pages 447-457.

10. Iverson, K.E., A Programming Language, John Wiley and Sons, 1962.

11. Graduate Program in Automatic Data Processing, Harvard University, 1954, (Brochure).

12. Iverson, K.E., Graduate Research and Instruction, Proceedings of First Conference on Training Personnel for the Computing Machine Field, Wayne State University, Detroit, Michigan, June, 1954, Arvid W. Jacobson, Editor, pages 25-29.

13. Falkoff, A.D., K.E. Iverson, and E.H. Sussenguth, A Formal Description of System/360, IBM Systems Journal, Vol 4, No. 4, October 1964, pages 198-262.

14. Iverson, K.E., Formalism in Programming Languages, Communications of the ACM, Vol.7, No.2, February 1964, pages 80-88.

15. Iverson, K.E., Elementary Functions, Science Research Associates, 1966.

16. Berry, P.C., APL\360 Primer, IBM Corporation (GH20-0689), 1969.

17. Hellerman, H., Experimental Personalized Array Translator System, Communications of the ACM, Vol.7, No.7, July 1964, pages 433-438.

18. Wolontis, V.M., A Complete Floating Point Decimal Interpretive System, Technical Newsletter No. 11, IBM Applied Science Division, 1956.

19. Lathwell, R.H., APL Comparison Tolerance, APL 76 Conference Proceedings, Association for Computing Machinery, 1976, pages 255-258.

20. Breed, L.M., Definitions for Fuzzy Floor and Ceiling, Technical Report No. TR03.024, IBM Corporation, March 1977.

21. Falkoff, A.D., and K.E. Iverson, The APL\360 Terminal System, Symposium on Interactive Systems for Experimental Applied Mathematics, eds. M. Klerer and J. Reinfelds, Academic Press, New York, 1968, pages 22-37.

22. Falkoff, A.D., and K.E. Iverson, APL\360, IBM Corporation, November 1966.

23. Falkoff, A.D., and K.E. Iverson, APL\360 User's Manual, IBM Corporation, August 1968.

24. Abrams, P.S., An Interpreter for Iverson Notation, Technical Report CS47, Computer Science Department, Stanford University, 1966.

25. Breed, L.M., and R.H. Lathwell, The Implementation of APL\360, Symposium on Interactive Systems for Experimental and Applied Mathematics, eds. M. Klerer and J. Reinfelds, Academic Press, New York, 1968, pages 390-399.

26. Jenkins, M.A., The Solution of Linear Systems of Equations and Linear Least Squares Problems in APL, IBM Technical Report No. 320-2989, 1970.

27. Sharp, Ian P., The Future of APL to benefit from a new file system, Canadian Data Systems, March 1970.

28. Breed, L.M., The APL PLUS File System, Proceedings of SHARE XXXV, August, 1970, page 392.

29. APL PLUS File Subsystem Instruction Manual, Scientific Time Sharing Corporation, Washington, D.C., 1970.

30. Lathwell, R.H., System Formulation and APL Shared Variables, IBM Journal of Research and Development, Vol.17, No.4, July 1973, pages 353-359.

31. Falkoff, A.D., and K.E. Iverson, APLSV User's Manual, IBM Corporation, 1973.

32. Falkoff, A.D., Some Implications of Shared Variables, Formal Languages and Programming, R. Aguilar, ed., North Holland Publishing Company, 1976, pages 65-75. Reprinted in APL 76 Conference Proceedings, Association for Computing Machinery, pages 141-148.

33. Beberman, M., and H.E. Vaughn, High School Mathematics Course 1, Heath, 1964.

34. Cajori, F., A History of Mathematical Notations, Vol. I, Notations in Elementary Mathematics, The Open Court Publishing Co., La Salle, Illinois, 1928.

35. Iverson, K.E., Algebra: an algorithmic treatment, Addison Wesley, 1972.

36. Falkoff, A.D., APL75 and APL76: an overview of the Proceedings of the Pisa and Ottawa Congresses, ACM Computing Reviews, Vol. 18, No. 4, April, 1977, Pages 139-141.

37. Weidmann, Clark, APLUM Reference Manual, University of Massachusetts, Amherst, Massachusetts, 1975.

38. Sharp APL Technical Note No. 25, I.P. Sharp Associates, Toronto, Canada.

APPENDIX A

Reprinted from APL\360 User's Manual [23]

ACKNOWLEDGEMENTS

The APL language was first defined by K.E. Iverson in A Programming Language (Wiley, 1962) and has since been developed in collaboration with A.D. Falkoff. The APL\360 Terminal System was designed with the additional collaboration of L.M. Breed, who with R.D. Moore*, also designed the S/360 implementation. The system was programmed for S/360 by Breed, Moore, and R.H. Lathwell, with continuing assistance from L.J. Woodrum⊛, and contributions by C.H. Brenner, H.A. Driscoll**, and S.E. Krueger**. The present implementation also benefitted from experience with an earlier version, designed and programmed for the IBM 7090 by Breed and P.S. Abrams⊛⊛.

The development of the system has also profited from ideas contributed by many other users and colleagues, notably E.E. McDonnell, who suggested the notation for the signum and the circular functions.

In the preparation of the present manual, the authors are indebted to L.M. Breed for many discussions and

---

*I.P. Sharp Associates, Toronto, Canada.

⊛General Systems Architecture, IBM Corporation, Poughkeepsie, N.Y.

**Science Research Associates, Chicago, Illinois.

⊛⊛Computer Science Department, Stanford University, Stanford, California.

suggestions; to R.H. Lathwell, E.E. McDonnell, and J.G. Arnold*® for critical reading of successive drafts; and to Mrs. G.K. Sedlmayer and Miss Valerie Gilbert for superior clerical assistance.

A special acknowledgement is due to John L. Lawrence, who provided important support and encouragement during the early development of APL implementation, and who pioneered the application of APL in computer-related instruction.

*®Industry Development, IBM Corporation, White Plains, N.Y.

APL LANGUAGE SUMMARY

APL is a general-purpose programming language with the following characteristics (reprinted from APL Language [4]):

> The primitive objects of the language are arrays (lists, tables, lists of tables, etc.). For example, *A+B* is meaningful for any arrays *A* and *B*, the size of an array (⍴*A*) is a primitive function, and arrays may be indexed by arrays as in *A*[3 1 4 2].
>
> The syntax is simple: there are only three statement types (name assignment, branch, or neither), there is no function precedence hierarchy, functions have either one, two, or no arguments, and primitive functions and defined functions (programs) are treated alike.
>
> The semantic rules are few: the definitions of primitve functions are independent of the representations of data to which they apply, all scalar functions are extended to other arrays in the same way (that is, item-by-item), and primitive functions have no hidden effects (so-called side-effects).
>
> The sequence control is simple: one statement type embraces all types of branches (conditional, unconditional, computed, etc.), and the termination of the execution of any function always returns control to the point of use.
>
> External communication is established by means of variables which are shared between APL and other systems or subsystems. These shared variables are treated both syntactically and semantically like other variables. A subclass of shared variables, system variables, provides convenient communication between APL programs and their environment.
>
> The utility of the primitive functions is vastly enhanced by operators which modify their behavior in a systematic manner. For example, reduction (denoted by /) modifies a function to apply over all elements of a list, as in *+/L* for summation of the items of *L*. The remaining operators are scan (running totals, running maxima, etc.), the axis operator which, for example, allows reduction and scan to be applied over a specified axis (rows or columns) of a table, the outer product, which produces tables of values as in *RATE∘.⋆YEARS* for an interest table, and the inner product, a simple generalization of matrix product which is exceedingly useful in data processing and other non-mathematical applications.
>
> The number of primitive functions is small enough that each is represented by a single easily-read and easily-written symbol, yet the set of primitives embraces operations from simple addition to grading (sorting) and formatting. The complete set can be classified as follows:
>
> Arithmetic: + - × ÷ ⋆ ⍟ ○ | ⌊ ⌈ ! ⌹
> Boolean and Relational: ∨ ∧ ⍱ ⍲ ~ < ≤ = ≥ > ≠
> Selection and Structural: / \ ⌿ ⍀ [;] ↑ ↓ ⍴ , ⌽ ⍉ ⊖
> General: ∊ ⍳ ? ⊥ ⊤ ⍋ ⍒ ⍎ ⍕

6 *Programming Style in APL*

PROGRAMMING STYLE IN APL

Kenneth E. Iverson
IBM Thomas J. Watson Research Center
Yorktown Heights, New York

When all the techniques of program management and programming practice have been applied, there remain vast differences in quality of code produced by different programmers. These differences turn not so much upon the use of specific tricks or techniques as upon a general manner of expression, which, by analogy with natural language, we will refer to as **style**. This paper addresses the question of developing good programming style in APL.

Because it does not rest upon specific techniques, good style cannot be taught in a direct manner, but it can be fostered by the acquisition of certain habits of thought. The following sections should therefore be read more as examples of general habits to be identified and fostered, than as specific prescriptions of good technique.

In programming, as in the use of natural languages, questions of style depend upon the purpose of the writing. In the present paper, emphasis is placed upon clarity of expression rather than upon efficiency in space and time in execution. However, clarity is often a major contributor to efficiency, either directly, in providing a fuller understanding of the problem and leading to the choice of a better, more flexible, and more easily documented solution, or indirectly, by providing a clear and complete model which may then be adapted (perhaps by programmers other than the original designer) to the characteristics of any particular implementation of APL.

All examples are expressed in 0-origin. Examples chosen from fields unfamiliar to any reader should perhaps be skimmed lightly on first reading.

1. Assimilation of Primitives and Phrases

Knowledge of the bare definition of a primitive can permit its use in situations where its applicability is clearly recognizable. Effective use, however, must rest upon a more intimate knowledge, a feeling of familiarity, an ability to view it from different vantage points, and an ability to recognize similar uses in seemingly dissimilar applications.

One technique for developing intimate knowledge of a primitive or a phrase is to create at least one clear and general example of its use, an example which can be retained as a graphic picture of its behavior when attempting to apply it in complex situations. We will now give examples of creating such pictures for three important cases, the outer product, the inner product, and the dyadic transpose.

Outer product. The formal definition of the result of the expression R←A∘.fB for a specified primitive f and arrays A and B of ranks 3 and 4 respectively, may be expressed as:

```
R[H;I;J;K;L;M;N]↔A[H;I;J] f B[K;L;M;N]
```

Although this definition is essentially complete, it may not be very helpful to the beginner in forming a manageable picture of the outer product.

To this end it might be better to begin with the examples:

```
      N∘.+N←1 2 3 4                      N∘.×N
 2 3 4 5                           1  2  3  4
 3 4 5 6                           2  4  6  8
 4 5 6 7                           3  6  9 12
 5 6 7 8                           4  8 12 16
```

and emphasize the fact that these outer products are the familiar addition and multiplication tables, and that, more generally, *A*∘.f*B* yields a **function table** for the function f applied to the sets of arguments *A* and *B*.

One might reinforce the idea by examples in which the outer product illuminates the definition, properties, or applicability of the functions involved. For example, the expressions *S*∘.×*S*←¯3 ¯2 ¯1 0 1 2 3, and ×*S*∘.×*S* yield an interesting picture of the rule of signs in multiplication, and the expressions *R*∘.=*V* and *R*∘.≤*V* and ' ⋆'[*R*∘.=*V*] (with *V*←(*X*-3)×(*X*←1+⍳7)-5 and with *R* specified as the range of *V*, that is, *R*←8 7 6 5 4 3 2 1 0 ¯1) illustrate the applicability of outer products in defining and producing graphs and bar charts. These and other uses of outer products as function tables are treated in Iverson [1].

Useful pictures of outer products of higher rank may also be formed. For example, *D*∘.∨*D*∘.∨*D*←0 1 gives a rank three function table for the **or** function with three arguments, and if *A* is a matrix of altitudes of points in a rectangular area of land and *C* is a vector of contour levels to be indicated on a map of the area, then the expression *C*∘.≤*A* relates the points to the contour levels and +⌿*C*∘.≤*A* gives the index of the contour level appropriate to each point.

Inner Product. Although the inner product is perhaps most used with at least one argument of rank two or more, a picture of its behavior and wide applicability is perhaps best obtained (in the manner employed in Chapter 13 of Reference 1) by first exploring its significance when applied to vector arguments. For example:

```
      P←2  3  5  7 11
      Q←2  0  2  1  0

      +/P×Q              Total cost in terms of price and quantity.
21

      ⌊/P+Q              Minimum trip of two legs with distances to and from
3                        connecting point given by P and Q.

      ×/P⋆Q              The number whose prime factorization is specified by
700                      the exponents Q.

      +/P×Q              Torque due to weights Q placed at positions P
21                       relative to the axis.
```

The first and last examples above illustrate the fact that the same expression may be given different interpretations in different fields of application.

The inner product is defined in terms of expressions of the form used above. Thus, *P*+.×*Q* ↔ +/*P*×*Q* and, more generally for any pair of scalar functions f and g, *P*f.g*Q* ↔ f/*P*g*Q*. The extension to arrays of higher rank is made in terms of the definition for vectors; each element of the result is the inner product of a pair of vectors from the two arguments. For the case of matrix arguments, this can be represented by the following picture:

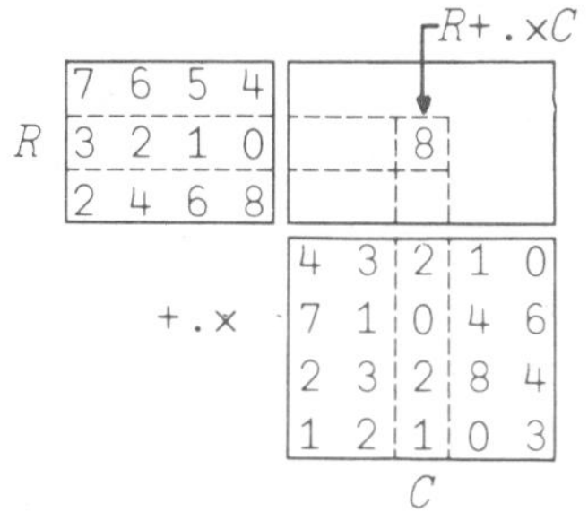

The +.× inner product applied to two vectors *V* and *W* (as in *V*+.×*W*) can be construed as a **weighted sum** of the vector *V*, whose elements are each "weighted" by multiplication by the corresponding elements of *W*, and then summed. This notion can be extended to give a useful interpretation of the expression *M*+.×*W*, for a matrix *M*, as a weighted sum of the column vectors of *M*. Thus:

```
      W←3 1 4
      ⎕←M←1+3 3⍴⍳9
 1 2 3
 4 5 6
 7 8 9
      M+.×W
17 41 65
```

This result can be seen to be equivalent to writing the elements of *W* below the columns of *M*, multiplying each column vector of *M* by the element below it, and adding.

If *W* is replaced by a boolean vector *B* (whose elements are zeros or ones), then *M*+.×*B* can still be construed as a weighted sum, but can also be construed as **sums over subsets** of the rows of *M*, the subsets being chosen by the 1's in the boolean vector. For example:

```
      B←1 0 1
      M+.×B
4 10 16
      B/M
 1 3
 4 6
 7 9
      +/B/M
4 10 16
```

Finally, by using an expression of the form *M*×.⋆*B* instead of *M*+.×*B*, a boolean vector can be used to apply multiplication over a specified subset of each of the rows of *M*. Thus:

```
      M×.⋆B
3 24 63
      ×/B/M
3 24 63
```

This use of boolean vectors to apply functions over specified subsets of arrays will be pursued further in the section on generalization, using boolean matrices as well as vectors.

Dyadic transpose. Although the transposition of a matrix is easy to picture (as an interchange of rows and columns), the dyadic transpose of an array of higher rank is not, as may be seen by trying to compare the following arrays:

```
      A                          2 1 3⍉A                 3 2 1⍉A
ABCD                     ABCD                    AM
EFGH                     MNOP                    EQ
IJKL                                             IU
                         EFGH
MNOP                     QRST                    BN
QRST                                             FR
UVWX                     IJKL                    JV
                         UVWX
                                                 CO
                                                 GS
                                                 KW

                                                 DP
                                                 HT
                                                 LX
```

The difficulty increases when we permit left arguments with repeated elements which produce "diagonal sections" of the original array. This general transpose is, however, a very useful function and worth considerable effort to assimilate. The following example of its use may help.

The associativity of a function f is normally expressed by the identity:

```
      Xf(YfZ)↔(XfY)f
Z
```

and a **test** of the associativity of the function on some specified domain D←1 2 3 can be made by comparing the two function tables D∘.f(D∘.fD) and (D∘.f
D)∘.fD corresponding to the left and right sides of the identity. For example:

```
      D←1 2 3
      ⎕←L←D∘.-(D∘.-D)            ⎕←R←(D∘.-D)∘.-D          L=R
 1  2  3                   ¯1 ¯2 ¯3                  0 0 0
 0  1  2                   ¯2 ¯3 ¯4                  0 0 0
¯1  0  1                   ¯3 ¯4 ¯5                  0 0 0

 2  3  4                    0 ¯1 ¯2                  0 0 0
 1  2  3                   ¯1 ¯2 ¯3                  0 0 0
 0  1  2                   ¯2 ¯3 ¯4                  0 0 0

 3  4  5                    1  0 ¯1                  0 0 0
 2  3  4                    0 ¯1 ¯2                  0 0 0
 1  2  3                   ¯1 ¯2 ¯3                  0 0 0
```

```
      ∧/,L=R
0
      ⎕←L←D∘.+(D∘.+D)          ⎕←R←(D∘.+D)∘.+D        L=R
 3 4 5                       3 4 5                    1 1 1
 4 5 6                       4 5 6                    1 1 1
 5 6 7                       5 6 7                    1 1 1

 4 5 6                       4 5 6                    1 1 1
 5 6 7                       5 6 7                    1 1 1
 6 7 8                       6 7 8                    1 1 1

 5 6 7                       5 6 7                    1 1 1
 6 7 8                       6 7 8                    1 1 1
 7 8 9                       7 8 9                    1 1 1
```

For the case of logical functions, the test made by comparing the function tables can be made complete, since the functions are defined on a finite domain `D←0 1`. For example:

```
      D←0 1
      ∧/,(D∘.∨(D∘.∨D))=((D∘.∨D)∘.∨D)
1
      ∧/,(D∘.≠(D∘.≠D))=((D∘.≠D)∘.≠D)
1
      ∧/,(D∘.⍲(D∘.⍲D))=((D∘.⍲D)∘.⍲D)
0
```

Turning to the identity for the distribution of one function over another we have expressions such as:

```
      X×(Y+Z)←→(X×Y)+(X×Z)
```

and

```
      X∧(Y∨Z)←→(X∧Y)∨(X∧Z)
```

Attempting to write the function table comparison for the latter case as:

```
      L←D∘.∧(D∘.∨D)
      R←(D∘.∧D)∘.∨(D∘.∧D)
```

we encounter a difficulty since the two sides *L* and *R* do not even agree in rank, being of ranks 3 and 4.

The difficulty clearly arises from the fact that the axes of the left and right function tables must agree according to the names in the original identity; in particular, the *X* in position 0 on the left and in positions 0 and 2 on the right implies that axes 0 and 2 on the right must be "run together" to form a single axis in position 0. The complete disposition of the four axes on the right can be seen to be described by the vector `0 1 0 2`, showing where in the result each of the original axes is to appear. This is a paraphrase of the definition of the dyadic transpose, and we can therefore compare *L* with `0 1 0 2⍉R`. Thus:

```
      ∧/,(D∘.∧(D∘.∨D))=0 1 0 2⍉((D∘.∧D)∘.∨(D∘.∧D))
1
```

The idea of thorough assimilation discussed thus far in terms of primitive expressions can be applied equally to commonly used phrases and defined functions. For example:

`ιρV`	The indices of vector *V*
`ιρρA`	The axes of *A*
`×/ρA`	The number of elements in *A*
`V[⍋V]`	Sorting the vector *V*
`M[⍋+⌿R<.-⍉R←M,0;]`	Sorting the rows of *M* into lexical order
`⍉F⍉M`	Applying to columns a function *F* defined on rows

Collections of commonly used phrases and functions may be found in Perlis and Rugaber [2] and in Macklin [3].

2. Function Definition

A complex system should best be designed not as a single monolithic function, but as a structure built from component functions which are meaningful in themselves and which may in turn be realized from simpler components. In order to interact with other elements of a system, and therefore serve as a "building block", a component must possess inputs and outputs. A defined function with an explicit argument, or arguments, and an explicit result provides such a component.

If a component function produces **side effects** by setting global variables used by other components, the interaction between components becomes much more difficult to analyze and comprehend than if communication between components is limited to their explicit arguments and explicit results. Ideally, systems should be designed with communication so constrained and, in practice, the number of global variables employed should be severely limited.

Because the fundamental definition form in APL (produced by the use of ∇ or by ⎕*FX*, and commonly called the **del** form) is necessarily general, it permits the definition of functions which produce side effects, which have no explicit arguments, and which have no explicit results. The **direct** form which uses the symbols α and ω (as defined in Iverson [4]) exercises a discipline more appropriate to good design, allowing only the definition of functions with explicit results, and localizing all names which are specified within the function, thereby eliminating side effects outside of it.

The direct form of definition may be either simple or conditional. The latter form will be discussed in section 6. The simple form may be illustrated as follows. The expression

```
      F:ω+4÷α
```

may be read as "*F* is defined by the expression `ω+4÷α`, where α represents the first argument of *F* and ω represents the second". Thus `8 F 3` yields `3.5`.

If a direct definition is to produce a machine executable function, the definition must be translated by a suitable function. For example, if this translation is called *DEF*, then:

```
      DEF
F:α+÷ω
F
      3 F 4
3.25

      DEF
P:+/α×ω*ιρα
P
      1 3 3 1 P 4
125
```

```
      DEF
SORT:ω[⍋ω]
SORT
      SORT 3 1 4 3 6 2 7 6
1 2 3 3 4 6 6 7

      DEF
POL:(ω∘.*ιρα)+.×α
POL
      1 3 3 1 POL 0 1 2 3 4
1 8 27 64 125
```

The direct form of definition will be used in the examples which follow. The question of the translation function *DEF* is discussed in Appendix A.

3. Generality

It is often possible to take a function defined for a specific purpose and modify it so that it applies to a wider class of problems. For example, the function `AV:(+/⍵)÷⍴⍵` may be applied to a numeric vector to produce its average. However, it fails to apply to average all rows in a matrix; the simple modification `AV2:(+/⍵)÷¯1↑⍴⍵` not only permits this, but applies to average the vectors along the last axis of any array, including the case of a vector.

The problem might also be generalized to a weighted average, in which a vector left argument specifies the weights to be applied in summation, the result being normalized by division by the total weight. Again this function could be defined to apply to a vector right argument in the form `WAV:(+/⍺×⍵)÷+/⍺`, but, applying the inner product in the manner discussed in the preceding section, we may define a function which applies to matrices:

```
      WAV2:(⍵+.×⍺)÷+/⍺
```

Thus:

```
      ⎕←M←3 4⍴⍳12
 0  1  2  3
 4  5  6  7
 8  9 10 11
      W←2 1 3 4
      W WAV2 M
1.9 5.9 9.9
```

The same function may be interpreted in different ways in different disciplines. For example, if column `I` of `M` gives the coordinates of a mass of weight `W[I]`, then `W WAV2 M` is the center of gravity of the set of masses. Moreover, if the elements of `W` are required to be non-negative, then the result `W WAV2 M` is always a point in the convex space defined by the points of *M*, that is a point within the body whose vertices are given by *M*. This can be more easily seen in the following equivalent function:

```
      WAV3:⍵+.×(⍵÷+/⍺)
```

in which the weights are normalized to sum to `1`.

Striving to write functions in a general way not only leads to functions with wider applicability, but often provides greater insight into the problem. We will attempt to illustrate this in three areas, functions on subsets, indexing, and polynomials.

Functions on subsets. It is often necessary to apply some function (such as addition or maximum) over all elements in some subset of a given list. For example, to sum all non-negative elements in the list `X←3 ¯4 2 0 ¯3 7`, we might first define the boolean vector which identifies the desired subset, then select the set, and then sum it:

```
      X
3 ¯4 2 0 ¯3 7
      X≥0                    (X≥0)/X            +/(X≥0)/X
1 0 1 1 0 1             3 2 0 7            12
```

In general, if B is a boolean vector which defines a subset, we may write +/B/X. However, as seen in the discussion of inner product, this may also be written in the form X+.×B, and in this form it applies more generally to a boolean matrix (or higher rank array) in which the columns (or vectors along the leading axis) determine the different subsets. For example, if

```
      ⎕←B←(4⍴2)⊤⍳2*4
0 0 0 0 0 0 0 0 1 1 1 1 1 1 1 1
0 0 0 0 1 1 1 1 0 0 0 0 1 1 1 1
0 0 1 1 0 0 1 1 0 0 1 1 0 0 1 1
0 1 0 1 0 1 0 1 0 1 0 1 0 1 0 1
```

then the columns of B represent all possible subsets of a vector of four elements, and if X←2 3 5 7 then:

```
      X+.×B
0 7 5 12 3 10 8 15 2 9 7 14 5 12 10 17
```

yields the sums over all subsets of X, including the empty set (0 0 0 0), and the complete set (1 1 1 1).

It is also easy to establish that

```
      X×.*B
1 7 5 35 3 21 15 105 2 14 10 70 6 42 30 210
```

yields the products over all subsets, and that (for non-negative vectors X) the expression

```
      X⌈.×B
0 7 5 7 3 7 5 7 2 7 5 7 3 7 5 7
```

yields the maxima over all subsets of X. This last expression holds only for non-negative values of X, but could be replaced by the more general expression M+(X-M←⌊/X)⌈.×B. A more general approach to this problem (in terms of a new operator) is discussed in Section 2 of Iverson [5].

If we have a list A with repeated elements, and if we need to evaluate some costly function F on each element of A, then it may be efficient to evaluate F only on the **nub** of A (consisting of the distinct elements of A) and then distribute the results to the appropriate positions to yield FA. Thus:

Function	Definition	Example
		`A←3 2 3 5 2 3`
Nub	`NUB:((⍳⍴⍵)=⍵⍳⍵)/⍵`	`NUB A` `3 2 5`

Distribution	`DIS:(NUB)∘.=⍵`	`DIS A`
		`1 0 1 0 0 1`
		`0 1 0 0 1 0`
		`0 0 0 1 0 0`

Example	`F:⍵*2`	`F A`
		`9 4 9 25 4 9`
		`F NUB A`
		`9 4 25`
		`(F NUB A)+.×DIS A`
		`9 4 9 25 4 9`

From the foregoing it may be seen that an inner product post-multiplication by the distribution matrix `DIS A` distributes the results `F NUB A` appropriately. The distribution function may also be used to perform aggregation or summarization. For example, if `C` is a vector of costs associated with the account numbers recorded in `A`, then summarization of the costs for each account may be obtained by pre-multiplication by `DIS A`. Thus:

```
      C←1 2 3 4 5 6
      (DIS A)+.×C
10 7 4
```

Indexing. If `M` is a matrix of `N←¯1↑ρM` columns, and if `I` and `J` are scalars, then element `M[I;J]` can be selected from the ravel `R←,M` by the expression `R[(N×I)+J]`. More generally, if `K` is a two-rowed matrix whose columns are indices to elements of `M`, then these elements may be selected much more easily from `R` (by the expression `R[(N×K[0;])+K[1;]]`) than from `M` itself. Moreover, the indexing expression can be simplified to `R[(N,1)+.×K]`, or to `R[(ρM)⊥K]`.

The last form is interesting in that it applies to an array `M` of any rank `P`, provided that `K` has `P` rows. More generally, it applies to an index array `K` of any rank (provided that `(ρρM)=1↑ρK`) to produce a result of shape `1↓ρK`. To summarize, we may define a general indexing function:

```
      SUB:(,α)[(ρα)⊥ω]
```

and use it as in the following examples:

```
      ⎕←M←3 3ρι9
 0 1 2
 3 4 5
 6 7 8
      M SUB K
2 3 7 2 3
      M SUB 3|2 3 5ρι30
 0 4 8 0 4
 8 0 4 8 0
 4 8 0 4 8
      (4 4 4ρι4*3) SUB 4|3 2 6ρ2×ι36
  0 42  0 42  0 42
  0 42  0 42  0 42
```

```
      ⎕←K←3|2 5ρι10
0 1 2 0 1
2 0 1 2 0
```

This use of the base value function in the expression `(ρα)⊥ω` correctly suggests the possible use of the inverse expression `(ρα)⊤ω` to obtain the indices to an array `α` in terms of the index to its ravel (that is, `ω`).

Polynomials. If `F:+/α×ω*ιρα`, then the expression `C F X` evaluates the polynomial with coefficients `C` for the scalar argument `X`. The more general function:

```
      P:(ω∘.*ιρα)+.×α
```

applies to a vector right argument and (since `ω∘.*ιρα` is then a matrix `M`, and since `M+.×α` is a linear function of `α`) emphasizes the fact that the polynomial is a linear function of its coefficients. If `(ρω)=ρα`, then `M` is square, and if the elements of `ω` are all distinct (that is, `(ρω)=ρNUB)`), then `MIN` is non-singular, and the function:

```
      FIT:(⌹ω∘.*ιρα)+.×α
```

is inverse to *P* in the sense that:

C ↔ (*C P X*) *FIT X* and *Y* ↔ (*Y FIT X*)*P X*

In other words, if *Y*←*F X* for some scalar function *F*, then *Y FIT X* yields the coefficients of the polynomial which fits the function *F* at the points (arguments) *X*. For example:

```
      3⍕Y←*X←0 .5 1 1.5
1.000 1.649 2.718 4.482
      3⍕C←Y FIT X
1.000 1.059  .296  .364
      3⍕C P X
1.000 1.649 2.718 4.482
```

The function *F* can be defined in a neater equivalent form, using the dyadic form of ⌹, as *FIT*:α⌹ω∘.*⍳⍴α. Moreover, the more general function:

```
      LSF:α⌹ω∘.*⍳N
```

(which depends upon the global variable *N*) yields the *N* coefficients of the polynomial of order *N*-1 which best fits the function α←*F*ω in the least squares sense. Thus:

```
      N←4
      3⍕Y LSF X
1.000 1.059  .296  .364
      N←3
      3⍕C←Y LSF X
1.014  .631 1.115
      3⍕C P X
1.014 1.608 2.759 4.468
```

```
      N←2
      3⍕C←YLSF X
.735 2.303
      3⍕C P X
.735 1.886 3.038 4.189
```

The case *N*←2 yields the best straight line fit. It can be used, for example, in estimating the "compound interest" or "growth rate" of a function that is assumed to be approximately exponential. This is done by fitting the logarithm of the values and then taking the exponential of the result. For example:

```
      X←0 1 2 3 4 5
      3⍕Y←300×1.09*X
 300.000 327.000 356.430 388.509 423.474 461.587
      N←2
      3⍕E←(⍟Y) LSF X
 5.704  .086
      *E
300 1.09
      3⍕(*E[0])×(*E[1])*X
 300.000 327.000 356.430 388.509 423.474 461.587
      3⍕Y←Y+?6⍴⎕RL←50
 300.000 355.000 395.430 434.509 454.474 508.587
      3⍕E←(⍟Y) LSF X
 5.749  .099
      *E
313.7594974 1.104368699
      3⍕(*E[0])×(*E[1])*X
 313.759 346.506 382.671 422.609 466.717 515.427
```

The growth rate is ⋆E[1], and the estimated compound interest rate is therefore given by the function

```
      ECI:100×¯1+⋆1↓(⍟α) LSF ω
```

For example:

```
      1⍕I←Y ECI X
10.4
      3⍕(⋆E[0])×(1+.01×I)⋆X
313.759 346.506 382.671 422.609 466.717 515.427
```

General considerations can often lead to simple solutions of specific problems. Consider, for example, the definition of a "times" function T for the multiplication of polynomials, that is:

```
      (C P X)×(D P X) ↔ (C T D) P X
```

The function T is easily shown to be linear in both its left and right arguments, and can therefore be expressed in the form C+.×B+.×D. The array B is a boolean array whose unit elements serve to multiply together appropriate elements of C and D, and whose zeros suppress contributions from other pairs of elements. The elements of B are determined by the exponents associated with C, with D, and with the result vector, that is, ⍳⍴C and ⍳⍴D and ⍳⍴1↓C,D. For each element of the result, the "deficiency" of each element of the exponents associated with D is given by the table S←(⍳⍴1↓C,D)∘.-⍳⍴D, and the array B is obtained by comparing this deficiency with the contributions from the exponents associated with C, that is, (⍳⍴C)∘.=S. To summarize, the times function may be defined as follows:

```
      T:α+.×(αBω)+.×ω
      B:(⍳⍴α)∘.=(⍳⍴1↓α,ω)∘.-⍳⍴ω
```

For example:

```
      ⎕←E←(C←1 2 1) T (D←1 3 3 1)
1 5 10 10 5 1
```

Since the expression α+.×(αBω) yields a matrix, it appears that the inverse problem of defining a function DB (divided by) for polynomial division might be solved by inverting this matrix. To this end we define a related function BQ expressed in terms of E and C, rather than in terms of C and D:

```
      BQ:(⍳⍴α)∘.=(⍳⍴ω)∘.-⍳1+(⍴ω)-⍴α
```

and consider the matrix M←C+.×C BQ E.

The expression (⌹M)+.×E fails to work properly because M is not square, and we recognize two cases, the first being given by inverting the top part of M (that is, ⌹(2⍴⌊/⍴M)↑M) and yielding a quotient with high-order remainder, and the second by inverting the bottom part and yielding a quotient with low order remainder. Thus:

```
      DBHO:(D↑α)⌹(2⍴D← ⌊/⍴M)↑M←ω+.×ωBQα
      DBLO:(D↑α)⌹(2⍴D←-⌊/⍴M)↑M←ω+.×ωBQα
```

For example:

```
      E←1 5 10 10 7 4
      C←1 2 1
      ⎕←Q←E DBHO C
1 3 3 1
      0⍕R←E-C T Q
  0  0  0  0  2  3
```

```
      E←47101051
      C←1 2 1
      ⎕←Q←E DBLO C
1 3 3 1
      0⍕R←E-C T Q
 3 2 0 0 0 0
```

The treatment of polynomials is a prolific source of examples of the insights provided by precise general functions for various processes, insights which often lead to better ways of carrying out commonly-needed hand calculations. For example, a function *E* for the expansion of a polynomial *C* (defined more precisely by the relation `(E C)P X ↔ C P X+1`) can be defined as:

```
      E:(BC ⍴⍵)+.×⍵                    BC:(⍳⍵)∘.!⍳⍵
```

Working out an example shows that manual expansion of *C* can be carried out be jotting down the table of binomial coefficients of order `⍴C` (that is, `BC ⍴⍵`) and then taking a weighted sum of its columns, the weights being the elements of *C*.

4. Identities

An identity is an equivalence between two different expressions. Although identities are commonly thought of only as tools of mathematical analysis, they can be an important practical tool for simplfying and otherwise modifying expressions used in defining functions.

Consider, for example, a function *F* which applied to a boolean vector suppresses all 1's after the first. It could be used, for example, in the expression `(~F X='D')/X` to suppress the first *D* in a character string *X*. The function could be defined as `F:(⍵⍳1)=⍳⍴⍵`. However, the following identity holds:

```
      (⍵⍳1)=⍳⍴⍵↔<\⍵
```

and we may therefore use one or other of the equivalent functions:

```
      F:(⍵⍳1)=⍳⍴⍵                      G:<\⍵
```

One may react to a putative identity in several ways: accept it on faith and use it as a practical tool, work some examples to gain confidence and a feeling for why it works, or prove its validity in a general way. The last two take more time, but often lead to further insights and further identities. Thus the application of the functions *F* and *G* to a few examples might lead one to see that *G* applies in a straightforward way to the rows of a matrix, but *F* does not, that both can be applied to locate the first **zero** by the expressions `~F~B` and `~G~B`, and (perhaps) that the latter case (that is, `~<\~B`) can be replaced by the simpler expression `≤\B`.

As a second example, consider the expression `Y←((~B)/X),B/X` with `B←X≤2`. The result is to **classify** the elements of *X* by placing all those in a specified class (those less than or equal to 2) at the tail end of *Y*. More generally, we may define a **classification** function *C* which classifies the elements of its right argument according to its boolean left argument:

```
      C:((~⍺)/⍵),⍺/⍵
```

For example:

```
      X←3 1 4 7 2
      ⎕←B←X≤2
0 1 0 0 1
      B C X
3 4 7 1 2
```

Since the result of *C* is a permutation of its right argument, it should be possible to define an equivalent function in the form ⍵[*V*], where *V* is some permutation vector. It can be shown that the appropriate permutation vector is simply ⍋⍺. For example:

```
      ⍋B                              X[⍋B]
 0 2 3 1 4                       3 4 7 1 2
```

Thus:

```
      P:⍵[⍋⍺]     and      C:((~⍺)/⍵),⍺/⍵
```

are equivalent functions.

For any given function there are often related functions (such as an inverse) of practical interest. For example, if *V*←*B C X*, then there is some inverse function *CI* such that *B CI V* yields *X*. Moreover, the definition of a related function may be much easier to derive from one of several different equivalent definitions of the original function than from the others. Thus the definition of the inverse *CI* may not be immediately evident from the definition *C*, but from the definition *P* it is clear that what is needed is the inverse permutation. Thus:

```
      CI:⍵[⍋⍋⍺]

      ⎕←V←B C X                        B CI V
3 4 7 1 2                        3 1 4 7 2
```

Finally, a given formulation of a function may suggest a simple formulation for a similar function. For example, the application of the function *P* with a left argument containing a single 1 can be seen to effect a rotation of that suffix of the right argument marked off by the location of the 1. This suggests the following formulation for a function which rotates each of the segments marked off by the 1's in the left argument:

```
      RS:⍵[⍋⍺++\⍺]

      1 0 0 1 0 0 0 1 0 RS 'ABCDEFGHI'
BCAEFGDIH
```

Dualities. We will now consider one class of very useful identities in some detail. The most familiar example of the class is known as deMorgan's law and is expressed as follows:

```
      X∧Y ↔ ~(~X)∨(~Y)
```

Useful related forms of deMorgan's law are:

```
      ∧/V ↔ ~∨/~V
      ∧\V ↔ ~∨\~V
      M∨.∧N ↔ (~M)∧.∨(~N)
```

DeMorgan's law concerns a relation between the functions **and, or,** and **not** (∧ ∨ ~), and we say that ∧ is the **dual of** ∨ **with respect to** ~. Each of the boolean functions of two arguments possess a dual with respect to ~. For example, *X*≤*Y* ↔ ~(~*X*)<(~*Y*), and from this the three related identities ≤/*V* ↔ ~</~*V*, etc.) follow in the manner shown above. The five dual pairs of boolean functions are:

```
∨ ⍱ < = >
∧ ⍲ ≤ ≠ ≥
```

These dualities are frequently useful in simplifying expressions used in logical selections. For example, we have already seen the use of the duality between ≤ and < to replace the expression ~<\~⍵ by ≤\⍵.

Useful dualities are not limited to boolean functions. For example, **maximum** and **minimum** (⌈ and ⌊) are dual with respect to **arithmetic** negation (-) as follows:

```
X⌈Y ↔ -(-X)⌊(-Y)
```

Again the related forms of duality follow.

More generally, duality is defined in terms of any monadic function *M* and its inverse *MI* as follows: a function *F* is said to be the dual of a function *G* with respect to *M* if:

```
X F Y ↔ MI (M X)G(M Y)
```

In the preceding examples of duality, each of the monadic functions used (~ and -) happened to be self-inverse and *MI* was therefore indistinguishable from *M*.

The general form includes the duality with respect to the natural logarithm function ⍟ which lies at the root of the use of logarithm tables and addition to perform multiplication, namely:

```
×/X ↔ *+/⍟X
```

The use of base ten logarithms rests similarly on duality with respect to the monadic function 10⍟⍵ and its inverse 10*⍵:

```
×/X ↔ 10*+/10⍟X
```

5. Proofs

A proof is a demonstration of the validity of an identity based upon other identities or facts already proven or accepted. For example, deMorgan's law may be proved by simply evaluating the two supposedly equivalent expressions (*X*∧*Y* and ~(~*X*)∨(~*Y*)) for all possible combinations of boolean values of *X* and *Y*:

X	Y	X∧Y	~X	~Y	(~X)∨(~Y)	~(~X)∨(~Y)
0	0	0	1	1	1	0
0	1	0	1	0	1	0
1	0	0	0	1	1	0
1	1	1	0	0	0	1

An identity which is useful and important enough to be used in the proofs of other identities is commonly called a theorem. Thus:

Theorem 1 `(A×B)∘.×(P×Q) ↔ (A∘.×P)×(B∘.×Q)`

We will prove theorem 1 itself for vectors `A,B,P,` and `Q` by calling the results of the left and right expressions `L` and `R` and showing that for any indices `I` and `J`, the values of `L[I;J]` and `R[I;J]` agree. We do this by writing a sequence of equivalent expressions, citing at the right of each expression the basis for believing it to be equivalent to the preceding one. Thus:

```
L[I;J]
((A×B)∘.×(P×Q))[I;J]              Def of L
(A×B)[I]×(P×Q)[J]                 Def of ∘.×
(A[I]×B[I])×(P[J]×Q[J])           Def of vector ×

R[I;J]
((A∘.×P)×(B∘.×Q))[I;J]            Def of R
(A∘.×P)[I;J]×(B∘.×Q)[I;J]         Def of matrix ×
(A[I]×P[J])×(B[I]×Q[J])           Def of ∘.×
(A[I]×B[I])×(P[J]×Q[J])           × associates and commutes
```

Comparison of the expressions ending the two sequences completes the proof.

We will now state a second theorem (whose proof for vector variables is given in Iverson [6]), and use it in a proof that the product of two polynomials `C P X` and `D P X` is equivalent to the expression `+/,(C∘.×D)×X*(⍳⍴C)∘.+⍳⍴D`:

Theorem 2 `+/,V∘.×W ↔ (+/V)×(+/W)`

Thus:

Theorem 3

```
(C P X)×(D P X)
(+/C×X*E←⍳⍴C)×(+/D×X*F←⍳⍴D)       Def of P
+/,(C×X*E)∘.×(D×X*F)               Theorem 2
+/,(C∘.×D)×((X*E)∘.×(X*F))         Theorem 1
+/,(C∘.×D)×X*E∘.+F
```

The final step is based on the fact that `(X*A)×(X*B) ↔ X*A+B`.

A proof in which every step is fully justified is called a **formal** proof; a step which is justified less formally by the observation of some general pattern is called an **informal** proof. We will now illustrate an informal proof by assigning values to the arguments `C` and `D` and displaying the tables `C∘.×D` and `E∘.+F` occurring in the last line of theorem 3:

```
      C←3 1 4                        E←⍳⍴C
      D←2 0 3 1                      F←⍳⍴D
      C∘.×D                          E∘.+F
6  0  9  3                       0 1 2 3
2  0  3  1                       1 2 3 4
8  0 12  4                       2 3 4 5
```

Since the elements of `E∘.+F` are exponents of `X`, and since the `I`th diagonal of `E∘.+F` (beginning with the zeroth) has the values `I`, each element of the `I`th diagonal of `C∘.×D` is multiplied by `X*I`. We may therefore conclude (informally) that the expression is equivalent to a polynomial whose coefficient vector is formed by summing the diagonals of `C∘.×D`. Using theorem 3 as well, we therefore conclude that this polynomial is equivalent to the product of the polynomials `C P ⍵` and `D P ⍵`.

Many useful identities concern what are called (in **APL Language** [7]) **structural** and **selection** functions, such as reshape, transpose, indexing, and compression. For example, a succession of dyadic transpositions can be reduced to a single equivalent transposition by the following identity:

```
I⍉J⍉A ↔ I[J]⍉A
```

The proof is given in Iverson [5]. Further examples of proofs in APL may be found in Orth [8] and in Iverson [1,4].

6. Recursive Definition

A function can sometimes be defined very neatly by using it in its own definition. For example, the factorial function `F:×/1+⍳ω` could be defined alternatively by saying that `F ω ↔ ω×F ω-1` and giving the auxiliary information that in the case `ω=0` the value of the function is `1`. Such a definition which utilizes the function being defined is called a **recursive** definition.

The direct definition form as defined in Iverson [4] permits a "conditional" definition such as:

```
G:ω:ω<0:-ω
```

Such a definition includes three expressions separated by colons and is interpreted by executing the middle one, then executing the first or the last, according to whether the value of the (first element of the) middle one is zero or not. Thus `G ω` is (for scalar arguments) equivalent to `|ω`.

This conditional form is convenient for making recursive definitions. For example, the factorial function discussed above could be defined as `F:ω×Fω-1:ω=0:1`, and a function to generate the binomial coefficients of a given order could be defined recursively as:

```
BC:(Z,0)+0,Z←BCω-1:ω=0:1
```

For example

```
      BC 2              BC 3                      BC 4
1 2 1             1 3 3 1                  1 4 6 4 1
```

Recursive definition can be an extremely useful tool, but one that may require considerable effort to assimilate. The study of existing recursive definitions (as in Chapters 7 and 8 of Orth [8] and Chapter 10 of Iverson [4]) may prove helpful. Perhaps the best way to grasp a particular definition is to execute it in detail for a few simple cases, either manually or on the computer. The details of computer execution can usually be suitably exhibited by inserting `⎕←` at one or more points in the definition. We might, for example, modify and execute the binomial coefficient function `BC` as follows:

```
      BC:(Z,0)+0,Z←⎕←BCω-1:ω=0:1

      Q←BC 3
1
1 1
1 2 1
      Q
1 3 3 1
```

We will now give two less trivial recursive definitions for study. The first generates all permutations of a specified order as follows:

```
      PER:(-⌊(⍳!⍵)÷!X)⌽X,((!⍵),X)⍴PER X←⍵-1:⍵=1:1 1⍴0

      PER 3                                         ⍉'ABCD'[PER 4]
 2 1 0                                        DDDDDDABBACCBACCABCCABBA
 2 0 1                                        CCABBADDDDDDABBACCBACCAB
 0 2 1                                        BACCABCCABBADDDDDDABBACC
 1 2 0                                        ABBACCBACCABCCABBADDDDDD
 1 0 2
 0 1 2
```

The second is a solution of the "topological sort" problem discussed on pages 258-268 of Knuth [9]. Briefly stated, an *N* by *N* boolean matrix can specify "precedences" required in the ordering of *N* items (which may represent the steps to be carried out in some production process). If the positions of the 1's in row *I* indicate which items must precede item *I*, then the function:

```
      PR:⍺[⍋(-⍴⍺)↑S] PR S≠S/⍵:∧/S←∨/⍵:(-1↑⍴⍵)↓⍺
```

provides a solution in the sense that it permutes its vector left argument to satisfy the constraints imposed by the matrix right argument. For example:

```
      C←'ATSFX'
      M              C PR M           PROC           PROC[(⍳5)PR M;]
 0 1 0 1 1     TFXAS              ADDRESS       TEXT
 0 0 0 0 0                        TEXT          FIGURES
 0 1 0 1 1                        STAMP         XEROX
 0 0 0 0 0                        FIGURES       ADDRESS
 0 1 0 1 0                        XEROX         STAMP
```

If the required orderings among certain items are inconsistent and cannot be satisfied, they are suppressed from the result.

7. Properties of Defined Functions

Defined functions used as building blocks in the development of a complex system play much the same role as primitives, and the comments made on the assimilation of primitives apply equally to such defined functions. Moreover, a clear understanding of the properties of functions under design may contribute to their design.

Many of the general properties of primitives (such as their systematic extension to arrays and the existence of primitive inverse functions) are also useful in defined functions and should be preserved as much as possible. The section on generality addressed certain aspects of this, and we now briefly address some others, including choice of names, application of operators, and the provision of inverse functions.

The names of primitive functions are graphic symbols, and the ease of distinguishing them from the names of arguments contributes to the readability of expressions. It is also possible to adopt naming schemes which distinguish defined functions from arguments, or which even distinguish several sub-classes of defined functions. The choice of mnemonic names for functions can also contribute to clarity; the use of the direct form of definition properly focusses attention on the choice of function names rather than on the choice of argument names.

Present APL implementations limit the application of operators (such as reduction and inner product) to primitive functions, and do not allow the use of defined functions in expressions such as *F/* and

∘.*F*. For any defined function *F* it is sometimes useful (although questions of efficiency may limit the usefulness to experimentation rather than general use) to define a corresponding outer product function *OPF*, and a corresponding reduction function *RF*. For example:

```
      F:α+÷ω
    OPF:(α∘.+0×ω) F (α×0)∘.+ω
     RF:(1↑ω) F RF 1↓ω:1=ρω:ω[0]

      A←3 7 11
      B←2 5 10

      A F B                    A OPF B                 RF B
3.5 7.2 11.1              3.5  3.2  3.1           2.196078431
                          7.5  7.2  7.1
                         11.5 11.2 11.1
```

The importance of inverse functions in mathematics is indicated in part by the number of inverse pairs of functions provided, such as the pair *K*○ω and (-*K*)○ω, the pair *B*⍟ω and *B*⋆ω, and the pair ω⋆*N* and ω⋆÷*N*. Their importance in non-numeric applications is not so commonly recognized, and it is well to keep the matter in mind in designing functions. For example, in designing functions *GET* and *PUT* for accessing files, it is advantageous to design them as inverses in the sense that the expression *K PUT K GET* '*FILENAME*' will produce no change in the file.

Other examples of useful inverse pairs include the permutations ω[*P*] and ω[⍋*P*] defined by a given permutation vector *P*, the classification function *C*:ω[⍋α] and its inverse (discussed in Section 4) *CI*:ω[⍋⍋α], and the "cumulative sum" or "integration" function *CS* and its inverse, the "difference function" *DF* defined as follows:

```
      CS:+\ω
      DF:ω-0,¯1↓ω

      A←3 5 7 11 13 17
      CS A                           DF A
3 8 15 26 39 56                3 2 2 4 2 4
      DF CS A                      CS DF A
3 5 7 11 13 17                 3 5 7 11 13 17
```

8. Efficiency

Emphasis on clarity of expression in designing a system may contribute greatly to its efficiency by leading to the choice of a superior overall approach, but it may also lead to solutions which violate the space constraints of a particular implementation or make ineffective use of the facilities which it provides. It is therefore necessary at some point to consider the characteristics of the particular implementation to be used. The speed and space characteristics of the various implementations of APL are too varied to be considered here. There are, however, a number of identities which are of rather general use.

Expressions involving inner and outer products often lead to space requirements which can be alleviated by partitioning the arguments. For example, if *A* and *B* are vectors and *R*←*A*∘.f *B*, then the *M* by *N* segment of the result represented by (*M*,*N*)↑*R* can be computed as (*M*↑*A*)∘.f (*N*↑*B*), and *M* and *N* can be chosen to make the best use of available space. The resulting segments may be stored in files or, if the subsequent expressions to be applied to the result permit it, they may be applied to the segments. For example, if the complete expression is +/*A*∘.f*B*, then each of the segments may be summed as they are produced. Expressions of the form (M,N)↑R can also be generalized to apply to higher rank arrays and to select any desired rectangular segment.

If X is a vector, the reduction +/X can be partitioned by use of the identity:

```
+/X ↔ (+/K↑X)+(+/K↓X)
```

and this identity applies more generally for reduction by any associative function F. Moreover, this identity provides the basis for the partitioning of inner products, a generalization of the partitioning used in matrix algebra which is discussed more fully in Iverson [6].

The direct use of the distribution function DIS of Section 3 for summarization (in the form (DIS A)+.×C) may lead to excessive use of both time and space. Such problems can often be alleviated in a general way by the use of sorting. For example, the expression R←A[P←⍋A] produces an ordered list of the account numbers in which all repetitions of any one account number are adjacent. The points of change in account numbers are therefore given by the boolean vector B←R≠¯1⌽R and if the costs C are ordered similarly by S←C[P], then the summarization may be performed by summing over the intervals of S marked off by B.

The sorting process discussed above may itself be partitioned, and the subsequent summarization steps may, for reasons of efficiency, be incorporated directly in the sorting process. Many of the uses of sorting in data processing are in fact obvious or disguised realizations of some classification problem, and a simpler statement of the essential process may lead simply to different efficient realizations appropriate to different implementations of APL.

Like the inner and outer product, recursive definitions often make excessive demands on space. In some cases, as in the function PER discussed in Section 6, the size of the arguments to which the function is successively applied decreases so rapidly that the recursive definition does not greatly increase the space requirements. In others, as in the function PR of Section 6, the space requirements may be excessive, and the recursive definition can be translated (usually in a straightforward manner) into a more space-efficient iterative program. For example, the following non-recursive definition is such a translation of the function PR:

```
X←A PRN W
L1:→(∧/S←∨/W)/L2
A←A[⍋(-ρA)↑S]
W←S⌿S/W
→L1
L2:Z←(-1↑ρW)↓A
```

9. Reading

Perhaps the most important habit in the development of good style in a language remains to be mentioned, the habit of critical reading. Such reading should not be limited to collections of well-turned and useful phrases, such as Bartlett's Quotations or the collections of References 2 and 3, nor should it be limited to topics in a reader's particular speciality.

Manuals and other books **about** a language are, like grammars and dictionaries in natural language, essential, but reading should not be confined to them. Emphasis should be placed rather on the reading of books which use the language in the treatment of other topics, as in the references already cited, in Berry et al [10,11], in Blaauw [12], and in Spence [13].

The APL neophyte should not be dissuaded from reading by the occurrence of long expressions whose meanings are not immediately clear; because the sequence of execution is clear and unambiguous, the reader can always work through sample executions accurately, either with pencil and paper, with a computer, or both. An example of this is discussed at length in Section 1.1 of Iverson [4].

Moreover, the neophyte need not be dissuaded from reading by the occurrence of some unfamiliar primitives, since all primitives can be summarized (together with examples) in two brief tables (pages 32 and 44 of APL Language [7]), and since these tables are usable after the reading of two short sections: Fundamentals (pages 21-28) and Operators (pages 39-43).

Finally, one may benefit from the critical reading of mediocre writing as well as good; good writing may present new turns of phrase, but mediocre writing may spur the reader to improve upon it.

10. Conclusions

This paper has addressed the question of **style**, the **manner** in which something is said as distinct from the substance. The techniques suggested for fostering good style are analogous to techniques appropriate to natural language: intimate knowledge of vocabulary (primitives) and commonly used phrases (certain defined functions), facility in abstract expression (generality), mastery of a variety of equivalent ways of expressing a matter (identities), a knowledge of techniques for examining and establishing such equivalences (proofs), a precise general method for using an expression in its own definition (recursion), and an emphasis on wide critical reading **in** rather than **about** the language.

If one accepts the importance of good style in APL, then one should consider the implications of these techniques for the teaching of APL. Current courses and textbooks typically follow the inappropriate model set by the teaching of earlier programming languages, which are not so simply structured and not so easy to introduce (as one introduces mathematical notation) in the context of some reasonably elaborate **use** of the language. Moreover, they place little or no emphasis on reading in APL and little on the structure of the language, often confusing, for example, the crucial distinction between operators and functions by using the same term for both. **APL Language** [7] does present this structure, but, being designed for reference, is not itself a sufficient basis for a course.

Appendix A

Translation from Direct to Del Form

The problem of translation from the direct to the del form of function definition is fully discussed in Section 10.4 of Iverson [4], the discussion culminating in a set of translation functions usable (or easily adapted for use) on most implementations of APL. Because it is aimed primarily at an exposition of the translation problem, the functions developed in this presentation leave many secondary problems (such as the avoidance of name conflicts) to the user, and the following translation functions and associated variables may be found more convenient for experimentation with the use of direct definition:

```
D←F9 E;F;I;J;K;Q;⎕IO
→((2|+/E='''')∨∧/ 1 3 ≠+/':' I9 E)/ρD←(2ρ⎕IO←0)ρ''
F←'α X9 ' R9 'ω Y9 ' R9 E←, 1 1 ↓⎕CR ⎕FX 'Q',' ',[¯0.5],E
F←1↓ρD←(0,-6-+/I)↓(-(3×I)++\I←':' I9 F)⌽⍉(7,ρF)ρ(7×ρF)↑F
D←3⌽(C9[((2⌊2⊥∨/'αω' I9 E),1+I),5;]),⍉D[;0,(I←2+⍳F-2),1]
J←((¯1⌽I)∧J←>≠ 0 ¯1 ⌽'←⎕' I9 E)/K←+\I<0,¯1↓I←E∊A9
K←∨/((-K)⌽I∘.>⍳1+⌈/K)[;J-1]
D←D,(F,ρE)↑⍉ 0 ¯2 ↓(K+2×K<1⌽K)⌽' ',E,[0.5] ';'

Z←X R9 Y;N
Z←(,((1↑X) I9 Y)∘.≠N↑1)/,Y,((ρY),¯1+N←ρX)ρ1↓X

Z←A I9 B
Z←(A∘.=B)∧((ρA),ρB)ρ~2|+\B=''''

Z9←DEF
Z9←⎕FX F9 ⍞


        C9
    Z9←
  Y9Z9←
  Y9Z9←X9
)/3→(0=1↑,
    →0,0ρZ9←
    Z9←


        A9
0123456789ABCDEFGHIJKLMNOPQRSTUVWXYZABCDEFGHIJKLMNOPQRSTUVWXYZ⎕
```

The foregoing functions were designed more for brevity than clarity; nevertheless the reader who wishes to study the translation process in detail may find it useful to compare them with those of Reference 4.

For serious use of direct definition, one should augment the foregoing with functions which record the definitions presented, display them on demand, and provide for convenient editing. For example, execution of:

```
      DEF
DEFR:0ρ⍎'R',Y,'←X',0ρY←⎕FX F9 X←⍞
DEFR
```

produces a function *DEFR* which, like *DEF*, fixes the definition of any function *F* presented to it in direct form, but which also records the original definition (for later display or editing) in the associated variable *R̲F*. The display of a desired function could then be produced by the following definition:

```
      DEFR
DISPLAY:⍎,(N∧.=(¯1↑ρN)↑'R̲',⍞)⌿N←⎕NL 2
```

For example:

```
      DEFR
PLUS:α+ω
      DISPLAY
PLUS
PLUS:α+ω
```

References

1. Iverson, K.E., **Algebra, an Algorithmic Treatment**, APL Press, 1976.

2. Perlis, A.J., and S. Rugaber, **The APL Idiom List**, Research Report 87, Computer Sciences Department, Yale University, 1977.

3. Macklin, D., **The APL Handbook of Techniques**, Form Number S320-5996, IBM Corporation, 1977.

4. Iverson, K.E., **Elementary Analysis**, APL Press, 1976.

5. Iverson, K.E., **Operators and Functions**, Research Report 7091, IBM Corporation, 1978.

6. Iverson, K.E., **An Introduction to APL for Scientists and Engineers**, APL Press, 1976.

7. **APL Language**, Form Number GC26-3847, IBM Corporation.

8. Orth, D.L., **Calculus in a New Key**, APL Press, 1976.

9. Knuth, D.E., **The Art of Computer Programming**, Addison Wesley, 1968.

10. Berry, P.C., J. Bartoli, C. Dell'Aquila, V. Spadavecchia, **APL and Insight**, APL Press, 1978.

11. Berry, P.C., and J. Thorstensen, **Starmap**, APL Press, 1978.

12. Blaauw, G.A., **Digital System Implementation**, Prentice-Hall, 1977.

13. Spence, R.L., **Resistive Circuit Theory**, APL Press, 1974.

7 *Notation as a Tool of Thought*

Notation as a Tool of Thought

Kenneth E. Iverson
IBM Thomas J. Watson Research Center

The importance of nomenclature, notation, and language as tools of thought has long been recognized. In chemistry and in botany, for example, the establishment of systems of nomenclature by Lavoisier and Linnaeus did much to stimulate and to channel later investigation. Concerning language, George Boole in his *Laws of Thought* [1, p.24] asserted "That language is an instrument of human reason, and not merely a medium for the expression of thought, is a truth generally admitted."

Mathematical notation provides perhaps the best-known and best-developed example of language used consciously as a tool of thought. Recognition of the important role of notation in mathematics is clear from the quotations from mathematicians given in Cajori's *A History of Mathematical Notations* [2, pp.332,331]. They are well worth reading in full, but the following excerpts suggest the tone:

> By relieving the brain of all unnecessary work, a good notation sets it free to concentrate on more advanced problems, and in effect increases the mental power of the race.
>
> A.N. Whitehead

> The quantity of meaning compressed into small space by algebraic signs, is another circumstance that facilitates the reasonings we are accustomed to carry on by their aid.
>
> Charles Babbage

Nevertheless, mathematical notation has serious deficiencies. In particular, it lacks universality, and must be interpreted differently according to the topic, according to the author, and even according to the immediate context. Programming languages, because they were designed for the purpose of directing computers, offer important advantages as tools of thought. Not only are they universal (general-purpose), but they are also executable and unambiguous. Executability makes it possible to use computers to perform extensive experiments on ideas expressed in a programming language and the lack of ambiguity makes possible precise thought experiments. In other respects, however, most programming languages are decidedly inferior to mathematical notation and are little used as tools of thought in ways that would be considered significant by, say, an applied mathematician.

The thesis of the present paper is that the advantages of executability and universality found in programming languages can be effectively combined, in a single coherent language, with the advantages offered by mathematical notation. It is developed in four stages:

(a) Section 1 identifies salient characteristics of mathematical notation and uses simple problems to illustrate how these characteristics may be provided in an executable notation.

(b) Sections 2 and 3 continue this illustration by deeper treatment of a set of topics chosen for their general interest and utility. Section 2 concerns polynomials, and Section 3 concerns transformations between representations of functions relevant to a number of topics, including permutations and directed graphs. Although these topics might be characterized as mathematical, they are directly relevant to computer programming, and their relevance will increase as programming continues to develop into a legitimate mathematical discipline.

(c) Section 4 provides examples of identities and formal proofs. Many of these formal proofs concern identities established informally and used in preceeding sections.

(d) The concluding section provides some general comparisons with mathematical notation, references to treatments of other topics, and discussion of the problem of introducing notation in context.

The executable language to be used is APL, a general purpose language which originated in an attempt to provide clear and precise expression in writing and teaching, and which was implemented as a programming language only after several years of use and development [3].

Although many readers will be unfamiliar with APL, I have chosen not to provide a separate introduction to it, but rather to introduce it in context as needed. Mathematical notation is always introduced in this way rather than being taught, as programming languages commonly are, in a separate course. Notation suited as a tool of thought in any topic should permit easy introduction in the context of that topic; one advantage of introducing APL in context here is that the reader may assess the relative difficulty of such introduction.

However, introduction in context is incompatible with complete discussion of all nuances of each bit of notation, and the reader must be prepared to either extend the definitions in obvious and systematic ways as required in later uses, or to consult a reference work. All of the notation used here is summarized in Appendix A, and is covered fully in pages 24-60 of *APL Language* [4].

Readers having access to some machine embodiment of APL may wish to translate the function definitions given here in *direct definition* form [5, p.10] (using ⍺ and ⍵ to represent the left and right arguments) to the *canonical* form required for execution. A function for performing this translation automatically is given in Appendix B.

1. Important Characteristics of Notation

In addition to the executability and universality emphasized in the introduction, a good notation should embody characteristics familiar to any user of mathematical notation:

- Ease of expressing constructs arising in problems.
- Suggestivity.
- Ability to subordinate detail.
- Economy.
- Amenability to formal proofs.

The foregoing is not intended as an exhaustive list, but will be used to shape the subsequent discussion.

Unambiguous executability of the notation introduced remains important, and will be emphasized by displaying below an expression the explicit result produced by it. To maintain the distinction between expressions and results, the expressions will be indented as they automatically are on APL computers. For example, the *integer* function denoted by ⍳ produces a vector of the first N integers when applied to the argument N, and the *sum reduction* denoted by +/ produces the sum of the elements of its vector argument, and will be shown as follows:

```
      ⍳5
1 2 3 4 5
      +/⍳5
15
```

We will use one non-executable bit of notation: the symbol ←→ appearing between two expressions asserts their equivalance.

1.1 Ease of Expressing Constructs Arising in Problems

If it is to be effective as a tool of thought, a notation must allow convenient expression not only of notions arising directly from a problem, but also of those arising in subsequent analysis, generalization, and specialization.

Consider, for example, the crystal structure illustrated by Figure 1, in which successive layers of atoms lie not directly on top of one another, but lie "close-packed" between those below them. The numbers of atoms in successive rows from the top in Figure 1 are therefore given by ⍳5, and the total number is given by +/⍳5.

The three-dimensional structure of such a crystal is also close-packed; the atoms in the plane lying above Figure 1 would lie between the atoms in the plane below it, and would have a base row of four atoms. The complete three-dimensional structure corresponding to Figure 1 is therefore a tetrahedron whose planes have bases of lengths 1, 2, 3, 4, and 5. The numbers in successive planes are therefore the *partial* sums of the vector ⍳5, that is, the sum of the first element, the sum of the first two elements, etc. Such partial sums of a vector V are denoted by +\V, the function +\ being called *sum scan*. Thus:

```
      +\⍳5
1 3 6 10 15
      +/+\⍳5
35
```

The final expression gives the total number of atoms in the tetrahedron.

The sum +/⍳5 can be represented graphically in other ways, such as shown on the left of Figure 2. Combined with the inverted pattern on the right, this representation suggests that the sum may be simply related to the number of units in a rectangle, that is, to a product.

The lengths of the rows of the figure formed by pushing together the two parts of Figure 2 are given by adding the vector ⍳5 to the same vector reversed. Thus:

```
      ⍳5
1 2 3 4 5
      ⌽⍳5
5 4 3 2 1
      (⍳5)+(⌽⍳5)
6 6 6 6 6
```

Fig. 1.

```
    ○
   ○ ○
  ○ ○ ○
 ○ ○ ○ ○
○ ○ ○ ○ ○
```

Fig. 2.

```
□      □□□□□
□□      □□□□
□□□      □□□
□□□□      □□
□□□□□      □
```

This pattern of 5 repetitions of 6 may be expressed as 5⍴6, and we have:

```
      5⍴6
6 6 6 6 6
      +/5⍴6
30
      6×5
30
```

The fact that +/5⍴6 ←→ 6×5 follows from the definition of multiplication as repeated addition.

The foregoing suggests that +/⍳5 ←→ (6×5)÷2, and, more generally, that:

```
      +/⍳N ←→ ((N+1)×N)÷2                    A.1
```

1.2 Suggestivity

A notation will be said to be *suggestive* if the forms of the expressions arising in one set of problems suggest related expressions which find application in other problems. We will now consider related uses of the functions introduced thus far, namely:

```
      ⍳    ⌽    ⍴    +/    +\
```

The example:

```
      5⍴2
2 2 2 2 2
      ×/5⍴2
32
```

suggests that ×/M⍴N ←→ N*M, where * represents the power function. The similiarity between the definitions of power in terms of times, and of times in terms of plus may therefore be exhibited as follows:

```
      ×/M⍴N ←→ N*M
      +/M⍴N ←→ N×M
```

Similar expressions for partial sums and partial products may be developed as follows:

```
      ×\5⍴2
2 4 8 16 32
      2*⍳5
2 4 8 16 32

      ×\M⍴N ←→ N*⍳M
      +\M⍴N ←→ N×⍳M
```

Because they can be represented by a triangle as in Figure 1, the sums +\⍳5 are called *triangular* numbers. They are a special case of the *figurate* numbers obtained by repeated applications of sum scan, beginning either with +\⍳N, or with +\N⍴1. Thus:

```
      5⍴1                     +\+\5⍴1
1 1 1 1 1               1 3 6 10 15

      +\5⍴1                   +\+\+\5⍴1
1 2 3 4 5               1 4 10 20 35
```

Replacing sums over the successive integers by products yields the factorials as follows:

```
      ⍳5
1 2 3 4 5
      ×/⍳5                    ×\⍳5
120                     1 2 6 24 120
      !5                      !⍳5
120                     1 2 6 24 120
```

Part of the suggestive power of a language resides in the ability to represent identities in brief, general, and easily remembered forms. We will illustrate this by expressing *dualities* between functions in a form which embraces DeMorgan's laws, multiplication by the use of logarithms, and other less familiar identities.

If V is a vector of positive numbers, then the product ×/V may be obtained by taking the natural logarithms of each element of V (denoted by ⍟V), summing them (+/⍟V), and applying the exponential function (*+/⍟V). Thus:

```
      ×/V ←→ *+/⍟V
```

Since the exponential function * is the inverse of the natural logarithm ⍟, the general form suggested by the right side of the identity is:

```
      IG F/G V
```

where IG is the function inverse to G.

Using ∧ and ∨ to denote the functions *and* and *or*, and ~ to denote the self-inverse function of logical negation, we may express DeMorgan's laws for an arbitrary number of elements by:

```
∧/B ↔ ~∨/~B
∨/B ↔ ~∧/~B
```

The elements of B are, of course, restricted to the boolean values 0 and 1. Using the relation symbols to denote *functions* (for example, X<Y yields 1 if X is less than Y and 0 otherwise) we can express further dualities, such as:

```
≠/B ↔ ~=/~B
=/B ↔ ~≠/~B
```

Finally, using ⌈ and ⌊ to denote the *maximum* and *minimum* functions, we can express dualities which involve arithmetic negation:

```
⌈/V ↔ -⌊/-V
⌊/V ↔ -⌈/-V
```

It may also be noted that scan (F\) may replace reduction (F/) in any of the foregoing dualities.

1.3 Subordination of Detail

As Babbage remarked in the passage cited by Cajori, brevity facilitates reasoning. Brevity is achieved by subordinating detail, and we will here consider three important ways of doing this: the use of arrays, the assignment of names to functions and variables, and the use of operators.

We have already seen examples of the brevity provided by one-dimensional arrays (vectors) in the treatment of duality, and further subordination is provided by matrices and other arrays of higher rank, since functions defined on vectors are extended systematically to arrays of higher rank.

In particular, one may specify the axis to which a function applies. For example, ⌽[1]M acts along the first axis of a matrix M to reverse each of the columns, and ⌽[2]M reverses each row; M,[1]N catenates columns (placing M above N), and M,[2]N catenates rows; and +/[1]M sums columns and +/[2]M sums rows. If no axis is specified, the function applies along the last axis. Thus +/M sums rows. Finally, reduction and scan along the *first* axis may be denoted by the symbols ⌿ and ⍀.

Two uses of names may be distinguished: *constant* names which have fixed referents are used for entities of very general utility, and ad hoc names are assigned (by means of the symbol ←) to quantities of interest in a narrower context. For example, the constant (name) 144 has a fixed referent, but the names CRATE, LAYER, and ROW assigned by the expressions

```
CRATE ← 144
LAYER ← CRATE÷8
ROW ← LAYER÷3
```

are ad hoc, or *variable* names. Constant names for vectors are also provided, as in 2 3 5 7 11 for a numeric vector of five elements, and in 'ABCDE' for a character vector of five elements.

Analogous distinctions are made in the names of functions. Constant names such as +, ×, and * are assigned to so-called *primitive* functions of general utility. The detailed definitions, such as +/MρN for N×M and ×/MρN for N*M, are subordinated by the constant names × and *.

Less familiar examples of constant function names are provided by the comma which *catenates* its arguments as illustrated by:

```
(⍳5),(⌽5) ↔ 1 2 3 4 5 5 4 3 2 1
```

and by the *base-representation* function ⊤, which produces a representation of its right argument in the radix specified by its left argument. For example:

```
      2 2 2 ⊤ 3 ↔ 0 1 1

      2 2 2 ⊤ 4 ↔ 1 0 0

      BN←2 2 2 ⊤ 0 1 2 3 4 5 6 7
      BN
0 0 0 0 1 1 1 1
0 0 1 1 0 0 1 1
0 1 0 1 0 1 0 1

      BN,⌽BN
0 0 0 0 1 1 1 1 1 1 1 1 0 0 0 0
0 0 1 1 0 0 1 1 1 1 0 0 1 1 0 0
0 1 0 1 0 1 0 1 1 0 1 0 1 0 1 0
```

The matrix BN is an important one, since it can be viewed in several ways. In addition to representing the binary numbers, the columns represent all subsets of a set of three elements, as well as the entries in a truth table for three boolean arguments. The general expression for N elements is easily seen to be (Nρ2)⊤(⍳2*N)-1, and we may wish to assign an ad hoc name to this function. Using the direct definition form (Appendix B), the name T is assigned to this function as follows:

```
T:(ωρ2)⊤(⍳2*ω)-1                                   A.2
```

The symbol ω represents the argument of the function; in the case of two arguments the left is represented by α. Following such a definition of the function T, the expression T 3 yields the boolean matrix BN shown above.

Three expressions, separated by colons, are also used to define a function as follows: the middle expression is executed first; if its value is zero the first expression is executed, if not, the last expression is executed. This form is convenient for recursive definitions, in which the function is used in its own definition. For example, a function which produces binomial coefficients of an order specified by its argument may be defined recursively as follows:

```
      BC:(X,0)+(0,X←BC ⍵-1):⍵=0:1                    A.3
```

Thus `BC 0 ↔ 1` and `BC 1 ↔ 1 1` and `BC 4 ↔ 1 4 6 4 1`.

The term *operator*, used in the strict sense defined in mathematics rather than loosely as a synonym for *function*, refers to an entity which applies to functions to produce functions; an example is the derivative operator.

We have already met two operators, *reduction*, and *scan*, denoted by `/` and `\`, and seen how they contribute to brevity by applying to different functions to produce families of related functions such as `+/` and `×/` and `∧/`. We will now illustrate the notion further by introducing the *inner product* operator denoted by a period. A function (such as `+/`) produced by an operator will be called a *derived* function.

If `P` and `Q` are two vectors, then the inner product `+.×` is defined by:

```
      P+.×Q ↔ +/P×Q
```

and analogous definitions hold for function pairs other than `+` and `×`. For example:

```
      P←2 3 5
      Q←2 1 2
      P+.×Q
17
      P×.*Q
300
      P⌊.+Q
4
```

Each of the foregoing expressions has at least one useful interpretation: `P+.×Q` is the total cost of order quantities `Q` for items whose prices are given by `P`; because `P` is a vector of primes, `P×.*Q` is the number whose prime decomposition is given by the exponents `Q`; and if `P` gives distances from a source to transhipment points and `Q` gives distances from the transhipment points to the destination, then `P⌊.+Q` gives the minimum distance possible.

The function `+.×` is equivalent to the inner product or dot product of mathematics, and is extended to matrices as in mathematics. Other cases such as `×.*` are extended analogously. For example, if `T` is the function defined by A.2, then:

```
      T 3
0 0 0 0 1 1 1 1
0 0 1 1 0 0 1 1
0 1 0 1 0 1 0 1
      P+.×T 3                        P×.*T 3
0 5 3 8 2 7 5 10             1 5 3 15 2 10 6 30
```

These examples bring out an important point: if `B` is boolean, then `P+.×B` produces sums over subsets of `P` specified by `1`'s in `B`, and `P×.*B` produces products over subsets.

The phrase `∘.×` is a special use of the inner product operator to produce a derived function which yields products of each element of its left argument with each element of its right. For example:

```
      2 3 5∘.×⍳5
2  4  6  8 10
3  6  9 12 15
5 10 15 20 25
```

The function `∘.×` is called *outer product*, as it is in tensor analysis, and functions such as `∘.+` and `∘.*` and `∘.<` are defined analogously, producing "function tables" for the particular functions. For example:

```
      D←0 1 2 3
      D∘.⌈D                 D∘.≥D                D∘.!D
0 1 2 3               1 0 0 0               1 1 1 1
1 1 2 3               1 1 0 0               0 1 2 3
2 2 2 3               1 1 1 0               0 0 1 3
3 3 3 3               1 1 1 1               0 0 0 1
```

The symbol `!` denotes the binomial coefficient function, and the table `D∘.!D` is seen to contain Pascal's triangle with its apex at the left; if extended to negative arguments (as with `D←¯3 ¯2 ¯1 0 1 2 3`) it will be seen to contain the triangular and higher-order figurate numbers as well. This extension to negative arguments is interesting for other functions as well. For example, the table `D∘.×D` consists of four quadrants separated by a row and a column of zeros, the quadrants showing clearly the rule of signs for multiplication.

Patterns in these function tables exhibit other properties of the functions, allowing brief statements of proofs by exhaustion. For example, commutativity appears as a symmetry about the diagonal. More precisely, if the result of the transpose function `⍉` (which reverses the order of the axes of its argument) applied to a table `T←D∘.fD` agrees with `T`, then the function `f` is commutative on the domain. For example, `T=⍉T←D∘.⌈D` produces a table of `1`'s because `⌈` is commutative.

Corresponding tests of associativity require rank `3` tables of the form `D∘.f(D∘.fD)` and `(D∘.fD)∘.fD`. For example:

```
      D←0 1
D∘.∧(D∘.∧D)    (D∘.∧D)∘.∧D    D∘.≤(D∘.≤D)    (D∘.≤D)∘.≤D

    0 0            0 0            1 1            0 1
    0 0            0 0            1 1            0 1

    0 0            0 0            1 1            1 1
    0 1            0 1            0 1            0 1
```

1.4 Economy

The utility of a language as a tool of thought increases with the range of topics it can treat, but decreases with the amount of vocabulary and the complexity of grammatical rules which the user must keep in mind. Economy of notation is therefore important.

Economy requires that a large number of ideas be expressible in terms of a relatively small vocabulary. A fundamental scheme for achieving this is the introduction of grammatical rules by which meaningful phrases and sentences can be constructed by combining elements of the vocabulary.

This scheme may be illustrated by the first example treated -- the relatively simple and widely useful notion of the sum of the first N integers was not introduced as a primitive, but as a phrase constructed from two more generally useful notions, the function ⍳ for the production of a vector of integers, and the function +/ for the summation of the elements of a vector. Moreover, the derived function +/ is itself a phrase, summation being a derived function constructed from the more general notion of the reduction operator applied to a particular function.

Economy is also achieved by generality in the functions introduced. For example, the definition of the factorial function denoted by ! is not restricted to integers, and the gamma function of X may therefore be written as !X-1. Similiarly, the *relations* defined on all real arguments provide several important logical functions when applied to boolean arguments: exclusive-or (≠), material implication (≤), and equivalence (=).

The economy achieved for the matters treated thus far can be assessed by recalling the vocabulary introduced:

```
⍳   ⍴   ⌽   ⊤   ,
/   \   .

+-×÷*⍟!⌈⌊⍉
∨∧~<≤=≥>≠
```

The five functions and three operators listed in the first two rows are of primary interest, the remaining familiar functions having been introduced to illustrate the versatility of the operators.

A significant economy of symbols, as opposed to economy of functions, is attained by allowing any symbol to represent both a *monadic* function (i.e. a function of one argument) and a *dyadic* function, in the same manner that the minus sign is commonly used for both subtraction and negation. Because the two functions represented may, as in the case of the minus sign, be related, the burden of remembering symbols is eased.

For example, X*Y and *Y represent power and exponential, X⍟Y and ⍟Y represent base X logarithm and natural logarithm, X÷Y and ÷Y represent division and reciprocal, and X!Y and !Y represent the binomial coefficient function and the factorial (that is, X!Y←→(!Y)÷(!X)×(!Y-X)). The symbol ⍴ used for the dyadic function of replication also represents a monadic function which gives the shape of the argument (that is, X←→⍴X⍴Y), the symbol ⌽ used for the monadic reversal function also represents the dyadic *rotate* function exemplified by 2⌽⍳5←→3 4 5 1 2, and by ¯2⌽⍳5←→4 5 1 2 3, and finally, the comma represents not only catenation, but also the monadic *ravel*, which produces a vector of the elements of its argument in "row-major" order. For example:

```
    T̲ 2                    ,T̲ 2
0 0 1 1             0 0 1 1 0 1 0 1
0 1 0 1
```

Simplicity of the grammatical rules of a notation is also important. Because the rules used thus far have been those familiar in mathematical notation, they have not been made explicit, but two simplifications in the order of execution should be remarked:

(1)All functions are treated alike, and there are no rules of precedence such as × being executed before +.

(2)The rule that the right argument of a monadic function is the value of the entire expression to its right, implicit in the order of execution of an expression such as SIN LOG !N, is extended to dyadic functions.

The second rule has certain useful consequences in reduction and scan. Since F/V is equivalent to placing the function F between the elements of V, the expression -/V gives the alternating sum of the elements of V, and ÷/V gives the alternating product. Moreover, if B is a boolean vector, then <\B "isolates" the first 1 in B, since all elements following it become 0. For example:

```
<\0 0 1 1 0 1 1 ←→ 0 0 1 0 0 0 0
```

Syntactic rules are further simplified by adopting a single form for all dyadic functions, which appear between their arguments, and for all monadic functions, which appear before their arguments. This contrasts with the variety of rules in mathematics. For example, the symbols for the monadic functions of negation, factorial, and magnitude precede, follow, and surround their arguments, respectively. Dyadic functions show even more variety.

1.5 Amenability to Formal Proofs

The importance of formal proofs and derivations is clear from their role in mathematics. Section 4 is largely devoted to formal proofs, and we will limit the discussion here to the introduction of the forms used.

Proof by exhaustion consists of exhaustively examining all of a finite number of special cases. Such exhaustion can often be simply expressed by applying some outer product to arguments which include all elements of the relevant domain. For example, if `D←0 1`, then `D∘.∧D` gives all cases of application of the *and* function. Moreover, DeMorgan's law can be proved exhaustively by comparing each element of the matrix `D∘.∧D` with each element of `~(~D)∘.∨(~D)` as follows:

```
      D∘.∧D                        ~(~D)∘.∨(~D)
 0 0                          0 0
 0 1                          0 1
      (D∘.∧D)=(~(~D)∘.∨(~D))
 1 1
 1 1
      ∧/,(D∘.∧D)=(~(~D)∘.∨(~D))
1
```

Questions of associativity can be addressed similarly, the following expressions showing the associativity of *and* and the non-associativity of *not-and*:

```
      ∧/,((D∘.∧D)∘.∧D)=(D∘.∧(D∘.∧D))
1
      ∧/,((D∘.⍲D)∘.⍲D)=(D∘.⍲(D∘.⍲D))
0
```

A proof by a sequence of identities is presented by listing a sequence of expressions, annotating each expression with the supporting evidence for its equivalence with its predecessor. For example, a formal proof of the identity A.1 suggested by the first example treated would be presented as follows:

```
+/⍳N
+/⌽⍳N                         + is associative and commutative
((+/⍳N)+(+/⌽⍳N))÷2                                (X+X)÷2↔X
(+/((⍳N)+(⌽⍳N)))÷2            + is associative and commutative
(+/((N+1)⍴N))÷2                                       Lemma
((N+1)×N)÷2                                   Definition of ×
```

The fourth annotation above concerns an identity which, after observation of the pattern in the special case `(⍳5)+(⌽⍳5)`, might be considered obvious or might be considered worthy of formal proof in a separate lemma.

Inductive proofs proceed in two steps: 1) some identity (called the *induction hypothesis*) is assumed true for a fixed integer value of some parameter `N` and this assumption is used to prove that the identity also holds for the value `N+1`, and 2) the identity is shown to hold for some integer value `K`. The conclusion is that the identity holds for all integer values of `N` which equal or exceed `K`.

Recursive definitions often provide convenient bases for inductive proofs. As an example we will use the recursive definition of the binomial coefficient function `BC` given by A.3 in an inductive proof showing that the sum of the binomial coefficients of order `N` is `2*N`. As the induction hypothesis we assume the identity:

```
      +/BC N ↔ 2*N
```

and proceed as follows:

```
+/BC N+1
+/(X,0)+(0,X←BC N)                                      A.3
(+/X,0)+(+/0,X)             + is associative and commutative
(+/X)+(+/X)                                           0+Y↔Y
2×+/X                                               Y+Y↔2×Y
2×+/BC N                                    Definition of X
2×2*N                                   Induction hypothesis
2*N+1                                Property of Power (*)
```

It remains to show that the induction hypothesis is true for some integer value of `N`. From the recursive definition A.3, the value of `BC 0` is the value of the rightmost expression, namely `1`. Consequently, `+/BC 0` is `1`, and therefore equals `2*0`.

We will conclude with a proof that DeMorgan's law for scalar arguments, represented by:

```
      A∧B ↔ ~(~A)∨(~B)                                  A.4
```

and proved by exhaustion, can indeed be extended to vectors of arbitrary length as indicated earlier by the putative identity:

```
      ∧/V ↔ ~∨/~V                                       A.5
```

As the induction hypothesis we will assume that A.5 is true for vectors of length `(⍴V)-1`.

We will first give formal recursive definitions of the derived functions *and*-reduction and *or*-reduction (`∧/` and `∨/`), using two new primitives, *indexing*, and *drop*. Indexing is denoted by an expression of the form `X[I]`, where `I` is a single index or array of indices of the vector `X`. For example, if `X←2 3 5 7`, then `X[2]` is `3`, and `X[2 1]` is `3 2`. Drop is denoted by `K↓X` and is defined to drop `|K` (i.e., the magnitude of `K`) elements from `X`, from the head if `K>0` and from the tail if `K<0`. For example, `2↓X` is `5 7` and `¯2↓X` is `2 3`. The *take* function (to be used later) is denoted by `↑` and is defined analogously. For example, `3↑X` is `2 3 5` and `¯3↑X` is `3 5 7`.

The following functions provide formal definitions of *and*-reduction and *or*-reduction:

```
ANDRED:⍵[1]∧ANDRED 1↓⍵:0=⍴⍵:1                            A.6
ORRED :⍵[1]∨ ORRED 1↓⍵:0=⍴⍵:0                            A.7
```

The inductive proof of A.5 proceeds as follows:

```
∧/V
(V[1])∧(∧/1↓V)                    A.6
~(~V[1])∨(~∧/1↓V)                 A.4
~(~V[1])∨(~~∨/~1↓V)               A.5
~(~V[1])∨(∨/~1↓V)                 ~~X↔X
~∨/(~V[1]),(~1↓V)                 A.7
~∨/~(V[1],1↓V)                    ∨ distributes over ,
~∨/~V                             Definition of , (catenation)
```

2. Polynomials

If `C` is a vector of coefficients and `X` is a scalar, then the polynomial in `X` with coefficients `C` may be written simply as `+/C×X*¯1+⍳⍴C`, or `+/(X*¯1+⍳⍴C)×C`, or `(X*¯1+⍳⍴C)+.×C`. However, to apply to a non-scalar array of arguments `X`, the power function `*` should be replaced by the power table `∘.*` as shown in the following definition of the polynomial function:

```
P̲:(⍵∘.*¯1+⍳⍴⍺)+.×⍺                B.1
```

For example, `1 3 3 1 P̲ 0 1 2 3 4 ↔ 1 8 27 64 125`. If `⍴⍺` is replaced by `1↑⍴⍺`, then the function applies also to matrices and higher dimensional arrays of sets of coefficients representing (along the leading axis of `⍺`) collections of coefficients of different polynomials.

This definition shows clearly that the polynomial is a linear function of the coefficient vector. Moreover, if `⍺` and `⍵` are vectors of the same shape, then the pre-multiplier `⍵∘.*¯1+⍳⍴⍺` is the Vandermonde matrix of `⍵` and is therefore invertible if the elements of `⍵` are distinct. Hence if `C` and `X` are vectors of the same shape, and if `Y←C P̲ X`, then the inverse (curve-fitting) problem is clearly solved by applying the matrix inverse function `⌹` to the Vandermonde matrix and using the identity:

```
C ↔ (⌹X∘.*¯1+⍳⍴X)+.×Y
```

2.1 Products of Polynomials

The "product of two polynomials `B` and `C`" is commonly taken to mean the coefficient vector `D` such that:

```
D P̲ X ↔ (B P̲ X)×(C P̲ X)
```

It is well-known that `D` can be computed by taking products over all pairs of elements from `B` and `C` and summing over subsets of these products associated with the same exponent in the result. These products occur in the function table `B∘.×C`, and it is easy to show informally that the powers of `X` associated with the elements of `B∘.×C` are given by the addition table `E←(¯1+⍳⍴B)∘.+(¯1+⍳⍴C)`. For example:

```
      X←2
      B←3 1 2 3
      C←2 0 3
      E←(¯1+⍳⍴B)∘.+(¯1+⍳⍴C)
      B∘.×C            E            X*E
 6 0 9              0 1 2        1  2  4
 2 0 3              1 2 3        2  4  8
 4 0 6              2 3 4        4  8 16
 6 0 9              3 4 5        8 16 32
      +/,(B∘.×C)×X*E
518
      (B P̲ X)×(C P̲ X)
518
```

The foregoing suggests the following identity, which will be established formally in Section 4:

```
(B P̲ X)×(C P̲ X)↔+/,(B∘.×C)×X*(¯1+⍳⍴B)∘.+(¯1+⍳⍴C)        B.2
```

Moreover, the pattern of the exponent table `E` shows that elements of `B∘.×C` lying on diagonals are associated with the same power, and that the coefficient vector of the product polynomial is therefore given by sums over these diagonals. The table `B∘.×C` therefore provides an excellent organization for the manual computation of products of polynomials. In the present example these sums give the vector `D←6 2 13 9 6 9`, and `D P̲ X` may be seen to equal `(BP̲X)×(CP̲X)`.

Sums over the required diagonals of `B∘×C` can also be obtained by bordering it by zeros, skewing the result by rotating successive rows by successive integers, and then summing the columns. We thus obtain a definition for the polynomial product function as follows:

```
PP:+⌿(1-⍳⍴⍺)⌽⍺∘.×⍵,1↓0×⍺
```

We will now develop an alternative method based upon the simple observation that if `B PP C` produces the product of polynomials `B` and `C`, then `PP` is linear in both of its arguments. Consequently,

```
PP:⍺+.×A+.×⍵
```

where `A` is an array to be determined. `A` must be of rank `3`, and must depend on the exponents of the left argument `(¯1+⍳⍴⍺)`, of the result `(¯1+⍳⍴1↓⍺,⍵)`, and of the right argument. The "deficiencies" of the right exponent are given by the difference table `(⍳⍴1↓⍺,⍵)∘.-⍳⍴⍵`, and comparison of these values with the left exponents yields `A`. Thus

```
A←(¯1+⍳⍴⍺)∘.=((⍳⍴1↓⍺,⍵)∘.-⍳⍴⍵)
```

and

```
PP:⍺+.×((¯1+⍳⍴⍺)∘.=(⍳⍴1↓⍺,⍵)∘.-⍳⍴⍵)+.×⍵
```

Since `⍺+.×A` is a matrix, this formulation suggests that if `D←B PP C`, then `C` might be obtained from `D` by pre-multiplying it by the inverse matrix `(⌹B+.×A)`, thus providing division of polynomials.

Since `B+.×A` is not square (having more rows than columns), this will not work, but by replacing `M←B+.×A` by either its leading square part `(2ρ⌊/ρM)↑M`, or by its trailing square part `(-2ρ⌊/ρM)↑M`, one obtains two results, one corresponding to division with low-order remainder terms, and the other to division with high-order remainder terms.

2.2 Derivative of a Polynomial

Since the derivative of `X*N` is `N×X*N-1`, we may use the rules for the derivative of a sum of functions and of a product of a function with a constant, to show that the derivative of the polynomial `C P̲ X` is the polynomial `(1↓C×¯1+⍳ρC) P̲ X`. Using this result it is clear that the integral is the polynomial `(A,C÷⍳ρC) P̲ X`, where `A` is an arbitrary scalar constant. The expression `1⌽C×¯1+⍳ρC` also yields the coefficients of the derivative, but as a vector of the same shape as `C` and having a final zero element.

2.3 Derivative of a Polynomial with Respect to Its Roots

If `R` is a vector of three elements, then the derivatives of the polynomial `×/X-R` with respect to each of its three roots are `-(X-R[2])×(X-R[3])`, and `-(X-R[1])×(X-R[3])`, and `-(X-R[1])×(X-R[2])`. More generally, the derivative of `×/X-R` with respect to `R[J]` is simply `-(X-R)×.*J≠⍳ρR`, and the vector of derivatives with respect to each of the roots is `-(X-R)×.*I∘.≠I←⍳ρR`.

The expression `×/X-R` for a polynomial with roots `R` applies only to a scalar `X`, the more general expression being `×/X∘.-R`. Consequently, the general expression for the matrix of derivatives (of the polynomial evaluated at `X[I]` with respect to root `R[J]`) is given by:

```
      -(X∘.-R)×.*I∘.≠I←⍳ρR                    B.3
```

2.4 Expansion of a Polynomial

Binomial expansion concerns the development of an identity in the form of a polynomial in `X` for the expression `(X+Y)*N`. For the special case of `Y=1` we have the well-known expression in terms of the binomial coefficients of order `N`:

```
      (X+1)*N ←→ ((0,⍳N)!N)P̲ X
```

By extension we speak of the expansion of a polynomial as a matter of determining coefficients `D` such that:

```
      C P̲ X+Y ←→ D P̲ X
```

The coefficients `D` are, in general, functions of `Y`. If `Y=1` they again depend only on binomial coefficients, but in this case on the several binomial coefficients of various orders, specifically on the matrix `J∘.!J←¯1+⍳ρC`.

For example, if `C←3 1 2 4`, and `C P̲ X+1←→D P̲ X`, then `D` depends on the matrix:

```
      0 1 2 3 ∘.! 0 1 2 3
1 1 1 1
0 1 2 3
0 0 1 3
0 0 0 1
```

and `D` must clearly be a weighted sum of the columns, the weights being the elements of `C`. Thus:

```
      D←(J∘.!J←¯1+⍳ρC)+.×C
```

Jotting down the matrix of coefficients and performing the indicated matrix product provides a quick and reliable way to organize the otherwise messy manual calculation of expansions.

If `B` is the appropriate matrix of binomial coefficients, then `D←B+.×C`, and the expansion function is clearly linear in the coefficients `C`. Moreover, expansion for `Y=¯1` must be given by the inverse matrix `⌹B`, which will be seen to contain the alternating binomial coefficients. Finally, since:

```
C P̲ X+(K+1) ←→ C P̲ (X+K)+1 ←→ (B+.×C) P̲ (X+K)
```

it follows that the expansion for positive integer values of `Y` must be given by products of the form:

```
      B+.×B+.×B+.×B+.×C
```

where the `B` occurs `Y` times.

Because `+.×` is associative, the foregoing can be written as `M+.×C`, where `M` is the product of `Y` occurrences of `B`. It is interesting to examine the successive powers of `B`, computed either manually or by machine execution of the following inner product power function:

```
      IPP:⍺+.×⍺ IPP ⍵-1:⍵=0:J∘.=J←¯1+⍳1↑ρ⍺
```

Comparison of `B IPP K` with `B` for a few values of `K` shows an obvious pattern which may be expressed as:

```
      B IPP K ←→ B×K*0⌈-J∘.-J←¯1+⍳1↑ρB
```

The interesting thing is that the right side of this identity is meaningful for non-integer values of `K`, and, in fact, provides the desired expression for the general expansion `C P̲ X+Y`:

```
C P̲(X+Y) ←→ (((J∘.!J)×Y*0⌈-J∘.-J←¯1+⍳ρC)+.×C)P̲ X          B.4
```

The right side of B.4 is of the form `(M+.×C)P̲ X`, where `M` itself is of the form `B×Y*E` and can be displayed informally (for the case `4=ρC`) as follows:

```
1 1 1 1              0 1 2 3
0 1 2 3              0 0 1 2
0 0 1 3      ×Y*     0 0 0 1
0 0 0 1              0 0 0 0
```

Since `Y*K` multiplies the single-diagonal matrix `B×(K=E)`, the expression for `M` can also be written as the inner product `(Y*J)+.×T`, where `T` is a rank `3` array whose `K`th plane is the matrix `B×(K=E)`. Such a rank three array can be formed from an upper triangular matrix `M` by making a rank `3` array whose first plane is `M` (that is, `(1=⍳1↑⍴M)∘.×M`) and rotating it along the first axis by the matrix `J∘-J`, whose `K`th superdiagonal has the value `-K`. Thus:

```
      DS:(I∘.-I)⌽[1](1=I←⍳1↑⍴⍵)∘.×⍵                    B.5

      DS  K∘.!K←¯1+⍳3
1 0 0
0 1 0
0 0 1

0 1 0
0 0 2
0 0 0

0 0 1
0 0 0
0 0 0
```

Substituting these results in B.4 and using the associativity of `+.×`, we have the following identity for the expansion of a polynomial, valid for non-integer as well as integer values of `Y`:

```
C P̲ X+Y  ←→  ((Y*J)+.×(DS J∘.!J←¯1+⍳⍴C)+.×C)P̲ X          B.6
```

For example:

```
      Y←3
      C←3 1 4 2
      M←(Y*J)+.×DS J∘.!J←¯1+⍳⍴C
      M
 1  3  9 27
 0  1  6 27
 0  0  1  9
 0  0  0  1
      M+.×C
96 79 22 2
      (M+.×C) P̲ X←2
358
      C P̲ X+Y
358
```

3. Representations

The subjects of mathematical analysis and computation can be *represented* in a variety of ways, and each representation may possess particular advantages. For example, a positive integer `N` may be represented simply by `N` check-marks; less simply, but more compactly, in Roman numerals; even less simply, but more conveniently for the performance of addition and multiplication, in the decimal system; and less familiarly, but more conveniently for the computation of the least common multiple and the greatest common divisor, in the prime decomposition scheme to be discussed here.

Graphs, which concern connections among a collection of elements, are an example of a more complex entity which possesses several useful representations. For example, a simple directed graph of `N` elements (usually called *nodes*) may be represented by an `N` by `N` boolean matrix `B` (usually called an *adjacency* matrix) such that `B[I;J]=1` if there is a connection *from* node `I` *to* node `J`. Each connection represented by a `1` in `B` is called an *edge*, and the graph can also be represented by a `+/,B` by `N` matrix in which each row shows the nodes connected by a particular edge.

Functions also admit different useful representations. For example, a permutation function, which yields a reordering of the elements of its vector argument `X`, may be represented by a *permutation vector* `P` such that the permutation function is simply `X[P]`, by a *cycle* representation which presents the structure of the function more directly, by the boolean matrix `B←P∘=⍳⍴P` such that the permutation function is `B+.×X`, or by a *radix* representation `R` which employs one of the columns of the matrix `1+(⌽⍳N)⊤¯1+⍳!N←⍴X`, and has the property that `2|+/R-1` is the parity of the permutation represented.

In order to use different representations conveniently, it is important to be able to express the transformations between representations clearly and precisely. Conventional mathematical notation is often deficient in this respect, and the present section is devoted to developing expressions for the transformations between representations useful in a variety of topics: number systems, polynomials, permutations, graphs, and boolean algebra.

3.1 Number Systems

We will begin the discussion of representations with a familiar example, the use of different representations of positive integers and the transformations between them. Instead of the *positional* or *base-value* representations commonly treated, we will use *prime decomposition*, a representation whose interesting properties make it useful in introducing the idea of logarithms as well as that of number representation [6, Ch.16].

If `P` is a vector of the first `⍴P` primes and `E` is a vector of non-negative integers, then `E` can be used to represent the number `P×.*E`, and all of the integers `⍳⌈/P` can be so represented. For example, `2 3 5 7 ×.* 0 0 0 0` is `1` and `2 3 5 7 ×.* 1 1 0 0` is `6` ar.d:

```
      P
2 3 5 7
      ME
 0 1 0 2 0 1 0 3 0 1
 0 0 1 0 0 1 0 0 2 0
 0 0 0 0 1 0 0 0 0 1
 0 0 0 0 0 0 1 0 0 0
      P×.*ME
1 2 3 4 5 6 7 8 9 10
```

The similarity to logarithms can be seen in the identity:

```
×/P×.*ME ←→ P×.*+/ME
```

which may be used to effect multiplication by addition.

Moreover, if we define `GCD` and `LCM` to give the greatest common divisor and least common multiple of elements of vector arguments, then:

```
      GCD P×.*ME ←→ P×.*⌊/ME
      LCM P×.*ME ←→ P×.*⌈/ME

      ME                V←P×.*ME
 2 1 0                  V
 3 1 2          18900 7350 3087
 2 2 0                  GCD V                           LCM V
 1 2 3          21                         926100
                        P×.*⌊/ME                        P×.*⌈/ME
                21                         926100
```

In defining the function `GCD`, we will use the operator `/` with a boolean argument `B` (as in `B/`). It produces the *compression* function which selects elements from its right argument according to the *ones* in `B`. For example, `1 0 1 0 1/ι5` is `1 3 5`. Moreover, the function `B/` applied to a matrix argument compresses rows (thus selecting certain columns), and the function `B⌿` compresses columns to select rows. Thus:

```
GCD:GCD M,(M←⌊/R)|R:1≥ρR←(ω≠0)/ω:+/R
LCM:(×/X)÷GCD X←(1↑ω),LCM 1↓ω:0=ρω:1
```

The transformation to the value of a number from its prime decomposition representation (`VFR`) and the inverse transformation to the representation from the value (`RFV`) are given by:

```
VFR:α×.*ω
RFV:D+α RFV ω÷α×.*D:∧/~D←0=α|ω:D
```

For example:

```
      P VFR 2 1 3 1
10500
      P RFV 10500
2 1 3 1
```

3.2 Polynomials

Section 2 introduced two representations of a polynomial on a scalar argument `X`, the first in terms of a vector of coefficients `C` (that is, `+/C×X*¯1+ιρC`), and the second in terms of its roots `R` (that is, `×/X-R`). The coefficient representation is convenient for adding polynomials (`C+D`) and for obtaining derivatives (`1↓C×¯1+ιρC`). The root representation is convenient for other purposes, including multiplication which is given by `R1,R2`.

We will now develop a function `CFR` (Coefficients from Roots) which transforms a roots representation to an equivalent coefficient representation, and an inverse function `RFC`. The development will be informal; a formal derivation of `CFR` appears in Section 4.

The expression for `CFR` will be based on Newton's symmetric functions, which yield the coefficients as sums over certain of the products over all subsets of the arithmetic negation (that is, `-R`) of the roots `R`. For example, the coefficient of the constant term is given by `×/-R`, the product over the entire set, and the coefficient of the next term is a sum of the products over the elements of `-R` taken `(ρR)-1` at a time.

The function defined by A.2 can be used to give the products over all subsets as follows:

```
P←(-R)×.*M←T ρR
```

The elements of `P` summed to produce a given coefficient depend upon the number of elements of `R` excluded from the particular product, that is, upon `+⌿~M`, the sum of the columns of the complement of the boolean "subset" matrix `TρR`.

The summation over `P` may therefore be expressed as `((0,ιρR)∘.=+⌿~M)+.×P`, and the complete expression for the coefficients `C` becomes:

```
C←((0,ιρR)∘.=+⌿~M)+.×(-R)×.*M←T ρR
```

For example, if `R←2 3 5`, then

```
      M                                  +⌿~M
 0 0 0 0 1 1 1 1                 3 2 2 1 2 1 1 0
 0 0 1 1 0 0 1 1                       (0,ιρR)∘.=+⌿~M
 0 1 0 1 0 1 0 1                 0 0 0 0 0 0 0 1
      (-R)×.*M                   0 0 0 1 0 1 1 0
1 ¯5 ¯3 15 ¯2 10 6 ¯30           0 1 1 0 1 0 0 0
                                 1 0 0 0 0 0 0 0
      ((0,ιρR)∘.=+⌿~M)+.×(-R)×.*M←T ρR
¯30 31 ¯10 1
```

The function `CFR` which produces the coefficients from the roots may therefore be defined and used as follows:

```
      CFR:((0,ιρω)∘.=+⌿~M)+.×(-ω)×.*M←T ρω          C.1

      CFR 2 3 5
¯30 31 ¯10 1
      (CFR 2 3 5) P X←1 2 3 4 5 6 7 8
¯8 0 0 ¯2 0 12 40 90
      ×/X∘.-2 3 5
¯8 0 0 ¯2 0 12 40 90
```

The inverse transformation `RFC` is more difficult, but can be expressed as a successive approximation scheme as follows:

```
RFC:(¯1+ιρ1↓ω)G ω
G:(α-Z)G ω:TOL≥⌈/|Z←α STEP ω:α-Z
STEP:(⌹(α∘.-α)×.*I∘.≠I←ιρα)+.×(α∘.*¯1+ιρω)+.×ω

      ⎕←C←CFR 2 3 5 7
210 ¯247 101 ¯17 1
      TOL←1E¯8
      RFC C
7 5 2 3
```

The order of the roots in the result is, of course, immaterial. The final element of any argument of

`RFC` must be `1`, since any polynomial equivalent to `×/X-R` must necessarily have a coefficient of `1` for the high order term.

The foregoing definition of `RFC` applies only to coefficients of polynomials whose roots are all real. The left argument of `G` in `RFC` provides (usually satisfactory) initial approximations to the roots, but in the general case some at least must be complex. The following example, using the roots of unity as the initial approximation, was executed on an APL system which handles complex numbers:

```
      (*○0J2×(¯1+⍳N)÷N←⍴1↓ω)Gω                    C.2

       ⎕←C←CFR  1J1  1J¯1  1J2  1J¯2
10 ¯14 11 ¯4 1
      RFC C
1J¯1 1J2 1J1 1J¯2
```

The monadic function `○` used above multiplies its argument by pi.

In Newton's method for the root of a scalar function `F`, the next approximation is given by `A←A-(F A)÷DF A`, where `DF` is the derivative of `F`. The function `STEP` is the generalization of Newton's method to the case where `F` is a vector function of a vector. It is of the form `(⌹M)+.×B`, where `B` is the value of the polynomial with coefficients `ω`, the original argument of `RFC`, evaluated at `α`, the current approximation to the roots; analysis similar to that used to derive B.3 shows that `M` is the matrix of derivatives of a polynomial with roots `α`, the derivatives being evaluated at `α`.

Examination of the expression for `M` shows that its off-diagonal elements are all zero, and the expression `(⌹M)+.×B` may therefore be replaced by `B÷D`, where `D` is the vector of diagonal elements of `M`. Since `(I,J)↓N` drops `I` rows and `J` columns from a matrix `N`, the vector `D` may be expressed as `×/0 1↓(¯1+⍳⍴α)⌽α∘.-α`; the definition of the function `STEP` may therefore be replaced by the more efficient definition:

```
STEP:((α∘.*¯1+⍳⍴ω)+.×ω)÷×/0 1↓(¯1+⍳⍴α)⌽α∘.-α          C.3
```

This last is the elegant method of Kerner [7]. Using starting values given by the left argument of `G` in C.2, it converges in seven steps (with a tolerance `TOL←1E¯8`) for the sixth-order example given by Kerner.

3.3 Permutations

A vector `P` whose elements are some permutation of its indices (that is, `∧/1=+/P∘.=⍳⍴P`) will be called a *permutation* vector. If `D` is a permutation vector such that `(⍴X)=⍴D`, then `X[D]` is a permutation of `X`, and `D` will be said to be the *direct* representation of this permutation.

The permutation `X[D]` may also be expressed as `B+.×X`, where `B` is the boolean matrix `D∘.=⍳⍴D`. The matrix `B` will be called the *boolean* representation of the permutation. The transformations between direct and boolean representations are:

```
BFD:ω∘.=⍳⍴ω              DFB:ω+.×⍳1↑⍴ω
```

Because permutation is associative, the composition of permutations satisfies the following relations:

```
  (X[D1])[D2] ←→ X[(D1 [D2])]
B2+.×(B1+.×X) ←→ (B2+.×B1)+.×X
```

The inverse of a boolean representation `B` is `⍉B`, and the inverse of a direct representation is either `⍋D` or `D⍳⍳⍴D`. (The *grade* function `⍋` grades its argument, giving a vector of indices to its elements in ascending order, maintaining existing order among equal elements. Thus `⍋3 7 1 4` is `3 1 4 2` and `⍋3 7 3 4` is `1 3 4 2`. The *index-of* function `⍳` determines the smallest index in its left argument of each element of its right argument. For example, `'ABCDE'⍳'BABE'` is `2 1 2 5`, and `'BABE'⍳'ABCDE'` is `2 1 5 5 4`.)

The *cycle* representation also employs a permutation vector. Consider a permutation vector `C` and the segments of `C` marked off by the vector `C=⌊\C`. For example, if `C←7 3 6 5 2 1 4`, then `C=⌊\C` is `1 1 0 0 1 1 0`, and the blocks are:

```
7
3 6 5
2
1 4
```

Each block determines a "cycle" in the associated permutation in the sense that if `R` is the result of permuting `X`, then:

```
R[7] is X[7]
R[3] is X[6]        R[6] is X[5]        R[5] is X[3]
R[2] is X[2]
R[1] is X[4]        R[4] is X[1]
```

If the leading element of `C` is the smallest (that is, `1`), then `C` consists of a single cycle, and the permutation of a vector `X` which it represents is given by `X[C]←X[1⌽C]`. For example:

```
   X←'ABCDEFG'
   C←1 7 6 5 2 4 3
   X[C]←X[1⌽C]
   X
GDACBEF
```

Since `X[Q]←A` is equivalent to `X←A[⍋Q]`, it follows that `X[C]←X[1⌽C]` is equivalent to `X←X[(1⌽C)[⍋C]]`, and the direct representation vector `D` equivalent to `C` is therefore given (for the special case of a single cycle) by `D←(1⌽C)[⍋C]`.

In the more general case, the rotation of the complete vector (that is, `1⌽C`) must be replaced by rotations of the individual subcycles marked off by

`C=⌊\C`, as shown in the following definition of the transformation to direct from cycle representation:

```
      DFC:(ω[⍋X++\X←ω=⌊\ω])[⍋ω]
```

If one wishes to catenate a collection of disjoint cycles to form a single vector `C` such that `C=⌊\C` marks off the individual cycles, then each cycle `CI` must first be brought to *standard form* by the rotation `(¯1+CI⍳⌊/CI)⌽CI`, and the resulting vectors must be catenated in descending order on their leading elements.

The inverse transformation from direct to cycle representation is more complex, but can be approached by first producing the matrix of all powers of `D` up to the `⍴D`th, that is, the matrix whose successive columns are `D` and `D[D]` and `(D[D])[D]`, etc. This is obtained by applying the function `POW` to the one-column matrix `D∘.+,0` formed from `D`, where `POW` is defined and used as follows:

```
      POW:POW D,(D←ω[;1])[ω]:≤/⍴ω:ω

      ⎕←D←DFC C←7,3 6 5,2,1 4
4 2 6 1 3 5 7
      POW D∘.+,0
 4 1 4 1 4 1 4
 2 2 2 2 2 2 2
 6 5 3 6 5 3 6
 1 4 1 4 1 4 1
 3 6 5 3 6 5 3
 5 3 6 5 3 6 5
 7 7 7 7 7 7 7
```

If `M←POW D∘.+,0`, then the cycle representation of `D` may be obtained by selecting from `M` only "standard" rows which begin with their smallest elements (`SSR`), by arranging these remaining rows in descending order on their leading elements (`DOL`), and then catenating the cycles in these rows (`CIR`). Thus:

```
      CFD:CIR DOL SSR POW ω∘.+,0

        SSR:(∧/M=1⌽M←⌊\ω)⌿ω
        DOL:ω[⍒ω[;1];]
        CIR:(,1,∧\0 1↓ω≠⌊\ω)/,ω

      DFC C←7,3 6 5,2,1 4
4 2 6 1 3 5 7
      CFD DFC C
7 3 6 5 2 1 4
```

In the definition of `DOL`, indexing is applied to matrices. The indices for successive coordinates are separated by semicolons, and a blank entry for any axis indicates that all elements along it are selected. Thus `M[;1]` selects column `1` of `M`.

The cycle representation is convenient for determining the number of cycles in the permutation represented (`NC:+/ω=⌊\ω`), the cycle lengths (`CL:X-0,¯1↓X←(1⌽ω=⌊\ω)/⍳⍴ω`), and the *power* of the permutation (`PP:LCM CL ω`). On the other hand, it is awkward for composition and inversion.

The `!N` column vectors of the matrix `(⌽⍳N)⊤¯1+⍳!N` are all distinct, and therefore provide a potential *radix* representation [8] for the `!N` permutations of order `N`. We will use instead a related form obtained by increasing each element by `1`:

```
      RR:1+(⌽⍳ω)⊤¯1+⍳!ω

      RR 4
1 1 1 1 1 1 2 2 2 2 2 2 3 3 3 3 3 3 4 4 4 4 4 4
1 1 2 2 3 3 1 1 2 2 3 3 1 1 2 2 3 3 1 1 2 2 3 3
1 2 1 2 1 2 1 2 1 2 1 2 1 2 1 2 1 2 1 2 1 2 1 2
1 1 1 1 1 1 1 1 1 1 1 1 1 1 1 1 1 1 1 1 1 1 1 1
```

Transformations between this representation and the direct form are given by:

```
      DFR:ω[1],X+ω[1]≤X←DFR 1↓ω:0=⍴ω:ω
      RFD:ω[1],RFD X-ω[1]≤X←1↓ω:0=⍴ω:ω
```

Some of the characteristics of this alternate representation are perhaps best displayed by modifying `DFR` to apply to all columns of a matrix argument, and applying the modified function `MF` to the result of the function `RR`:

```
      MF:ω[,1;],[1]X+ω[(1 ⍴X)⍴1;]≤X←MF 1 0↓ω:0=1↑⍴ω:ω
      MF RR 4
1 1 1 1 1 1 2 2 2 2 2 2 3 3 3 3 3 3 4 4 4 4 4 4
2 2 3 3 4 4 1 1 3 3 4 4 1 1 2 2 4 4 1 1 2 2 3 3
3 4 2 4 2 3 3 4 1 4 1 3 2 4 1 4 1 2 2 3 1 3 1 2
4 3 4 2 3 2 4 3 4 1 3 1 4 2 4 1 2 1 3 2 3 1 2 1
```

The direct permutations in the columns of this result occur in *lexical* order (that is, in ascending order on the first element in which two vectors differ); this is true in general, and the alternate representation therefore provides a convenient way for producing direct representations in lexical order.

The alternate representation also has the useful property that the parity of the direct permutation `D` is given by `2|+/¯1+RFD D`, where `M|N` represents the residue of `N` modulo `M`. The parity of a direct representation can also be determined by the function:

```
      PAR:2|+/,(I∘.>I←⍳⍴ω)∧ω∘.>ω
```

3.4 Directed Graphs

A simple directed graph is defined by a set of `K` nodes and a set of directed connections from one to another of pairs of the nodes. The directed connections may be conveniently represented by a `K` by `K` boolean *connection* matrix `C` in which `C[I;J]=1` denotes a connection *from* the `I`th node *to* the `J`th.

For example, if the four nodes of a graph are represented by `N←'QRST'`, and if there are connections from node `S` to node `Q`, from `R` to `T`, and from `T` to `Q`, then the corresponding connection matrix is given by:

```
0 0 0 0
0 0 0 1
1 0 0 0
1 0 0 0
```

A connection from a node to itself (called a self-loop) is not permitted, and the diagonal of a connection matrix must therefore be zero.

If `P` is any permutation vector of order `⍴N`, then `N1←N[P]` is a reordering of the nodes, and the corresponding connection matrix is given by `C[P;P]`. We may (and will) without loss of generality use the numeric labels `⍳⍴N` for the nodes, because if `N` is any arbitrary vector of names for the nodes and `L` is any list of numeric labels, then the expression `Q←N[L]` gives the corresponding list of names and, conversely, `N⍳Q` gives the list `L` of numeric labels.

The connection matrix `C` is convenient for expressing many useful functions on a graph. For example, `+/C` gives the *out-degrees* of the nodes, `+⌿C` gives the *in-degrees*, `+/,C` gives the number of connections or *edges*, `⍉C` gives a related graph with the directions of edges reversed, and `C∨⍉C` gives a related "symmetric" or "undirected" graph. Moreover, if we use the boolean vector `B←∨/(⍳1↑⍴C)∘.=L` to represent the list of nodes `L`, then `B∨.∧C` gives the boolean vector which represents the set of nodes directly reachable from the set `B`. Consequently, `C∨.∧C` gives the connections for paths of length two in the graph `C`, and `C∨C∨.∧C` gives connections for paths of length one or two. This leads to the following function for the *transitive closure* of a graph, which gives all connections through paths of any length:

```
TC:TC Z:∧/,ω=Z←ω∨ω∨.∧ω:Z
```

Node `J` is said to be *reachable* from node `I` if `(TC C)[I;J]=1`. A graph is *strongly-connected* if every node is reachable from every node, that is `∧/,TC C`.

If `D←TC C` and `D[I;I]=1` for some `I`, then node `I` is reachable from itself through a path of some length; the path is called a *circuit*, and node `I` is said to be contained in a circuit.

A graph `T` is called a *tree* if it has no circuits and its in-degrees do not exceed `1`, that is, `∧/1≥+⌿T`. Any node of a tree with an in-degree of `0` is called a *root*, and if `K←+/0=+⌿T`, then `T` is called a `K`-rooted tree. Since a tree is circuit-free, `K` must be at least `1`. Unless otherwise stated, it is normally assumed that a tree is *singly-rooted* (that is, `K=1`); multiply-rooted trees are sometimes called *forests*.

A graph `C` *covers* a graph `D` if `∧/,C≥D`. If `G` is a strongly-connected graph and `T` is a (singly-rooted) tree, then `T` is said to be a *spanning tree* of `G` if `G` covers `T` and if all nodes are reachable from the root of `T`, that is,

```
(∧/,G≥T) ∧ ∧/R∨R∨.∧TC T
```

where `R` is the (boolean representation of the) root of `T`.

A *depth-first spanning tree* [9] of a graph `G` is a spanning tree produced by proceeding from the root through immediate descendants in `G`, always choosing as the next node a descendant of the latest in the list of nodes visited which still possesses a descendant not in the list. This is a relatively complex process which can be used to illustrate the utility of the connection matrix representation:

```
DFST:((,1)∘.=K) R ω∧K∘.∨~K←α=⍳1↑⍴ω                    C.4

R:(C,[1]α)Rω∧P∘.∨~C←<\U∧P∨.∧ω
 :~∨/P←(<\α∨.∧ω∨.∧U←~∨⌿α)∨.∧α
 :ω
```

Using as an example the graph `G` from [9]:

```
             G                                 1 DFST G
0 0 1 1 0 0 0 0 0 0 0 0          0 0 1 1 0 0 0 0 0 0 0 0
0 0 0 0 1 0 0 0 0 0 0 0          0 0 0 0 1 0 0 0 0 0 0 0
0 1 0 0 1 1 0 0 0 0 0 0          0 1 0 0 0 1 0 0 0 0 0 0
0 0 0 0 0 0 1 1 0 0 0 0          0 0 0 0 0 0 1 1 0 0 0 0
0 0 0 0 0 0 0 0 1 0 0 0          0 0 0 0 0 0 0 0 1 0 0 0
0 0 0 0 0 0 0 0 1 0 0 0          0 0 0 0 0 0 0 0 0 0 0 0
0 0 0 0 0 0 0 0 0 1 0 0          0 0 0 0 0 0 0 0 0 1 0 0
0 0 0 0 0 0 0 0 0 1 1 0          0 0 0 0 0 0 0 0 0 0 1 0
0 0 1 0 0 0 0 0 0 0 0 1          0 0 0 0 0 0 0 0 0 0 0 1
1 0 0 0 0 0 0 0 0 0 0 1          0 0 0 0 0 0 0 0 0 0 0 0
0 0 0 0 0 0 0 0 0 1 0 0          0 0 0 0 0 0 0 0 0 0 0 0
1 0 0 0 0 0 0 0 0 0 0 0          0 0 0 0 0 0 0 0 0 0 0 0
```

The function `DFST` establishes the left argument of the recursion `R` as the one-row matrix representing the root specified by the left argument of `DFST`, and the right argument as the original graph with the connections *into* the root `K` deleted. The first line of the recursion `R` shows that it continues by appending on the top of the list of nodes thus far assembled in the left argument the next child `C`, and by deleting from the right argument all connections into the chosen child `C` except the one from its parent `P`. The child `C` is chosen from among those reachable from the chosen parent (`P∨.∧ω`), but is limited to those as yet untouched (`U∧P∨.∧ω`), and is taken, arbitrarily, as the first of these (`<\U∧P∨.∧ω`).

The determinations of `P` and `U` are shown in the second line, `P` being chosen from among those nodes which have children among the untouched nodes (`ω∨.∧U`). These are permuted to the order of the nodes in the left argument (`α∨.∧ω∨.∧U`), bringing them into an order so that the last visited appears first, and `P` is finally chosen as the first of these.

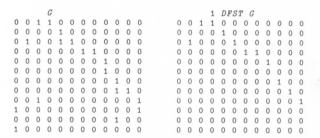

The last line of `R` shows the final result to be the resulting right argument `ω`, that is, the original graph with all connections into each node broken except for its parent in the spanning tree. Since the final value of α is a square matrix giving the nodes of the tree in reverse order as visited, substitution of ω,⌽[1]α (or, equivalently, ω,⊖α) for ω would yield a result of shape 1 2×ρG containing the spanning tree followed by its "preordering" information.

Another representation of directed graphs often used, at least implicitly, is the list of all node pairs V,W such that there is a connection from V to W. The transformation to this list form from the connection matrix may be defined and used as follows:

```
      LFC:(,ω)/1+D⊤¯1+⍳×/D←ρω
    C                          LFC C
 0 0 1 1                 1 1 2 3 3 4
 0 0 1 0                 3 4 3 2 4 1
 0 1 0 1
 1 0 0 0
```

However, this representation is deficient since it does not alone determine the number of nodes in the graph, although in the present example this is given by ⌈/,LFC C because the highest numbered node happens to have a connection. A related boolean representation is provided by the expression (LFC C)∘.=⍳1↑ρC, the first plane showing the out- and the second showing the in-connections.

An *incidence* matrix representation often used in the treatment of electric circuits [10] is given by the difference of these planes as follows:

```
      IFC:-⌿(LFC ω)∘.=⍳1↑ρω
```

For example:

```
      (LFC C)∘.=⍳1↑ρC                  IFC C
 1 0 0 0                        1  0 ¯1  0
 1 0 0 0                        1  0  0 ¯1
 0 1 0 0                        0  1 ¯1  0
 0 0 1 0                        0 ¯1  1  0
 0 0 1 0                        0  0  1 ¯1
 0 0 0 1                       ¯1  0  0  1

 0 0 1 0
 0 0 0 1
 0 0 1 0
 0 1 0 0
 0 0 0 1
 1 0 0 0
```

In dealing with non-directed graphs, one sometimes uses a representation derived as the *or* over these planes (∨⌿). This is equivalent to |IFC C.

The incidence matrix I has a number of useful properties. For example, +/I is zero, +⌿I gives the *difference* between the in- and out-degrees of each node, ρI gives the number of edges followed by the number of nodes, and ×/ρI gives their product. However, all of these are also easily expressed in terms of the connection matrix, and more significant properties of the incidence matrix are seen in its use in electric circuits. For example, if the edges represent components connected between the nodes, and if V is the vector of node voltages, then the branch voltages are given by I+.×V; if BI is the vector of branch currents, the vector of node currents is given by BI+.×I.

The inverse transformation from incidence matrix to connection matrix is given by:

```
      CFI:Dρ(¯1+⍳×/D)∊D⊥(1 ¯1∘.=ω)+.×¯1+⍳1↓D←⌊\⌽ρω
```

The *set membership* function ∊ yields a boolean array, of the same shape as its left argument, which shows which of its elements belong to the right argument.

3.5 Symbolic Logic

A boolean function of N arguments may be represented by a boolean vector of 2*N elements in a variety of ways, including what are sometimes called the *disjunctive, conjunctive, equivalence,* and *exclusive-disjunctive* forms. The transformation between any pair of these forms may be represented concisely as some 2*N by 2*N matrix formed by a related inner product, such as T∨.∧⍉T, where T←T̲ N is the "truth table" formed by the function T̲ defined by A.2. These matters are treated fully in [11, Ch.7].

4. Identities and Proofs

In this section we will introduce some widely used identities and provide formal proofs for some of them, including Newton's symmetric functions and the associativity of inner product, which are seldom proved formally.

4.1 Dualities in Inner Products

The dualities developed for reduction and scan extend to inner products in an obvious way. If DF is the dual of F and DG is the dual of G with respect to a monadic function M with inverse MI, and if A and B are matrices, then:

```
      A F.G B ←→ MI (M A) DF.DG (M B)
```

For example:

```
      A∨.∧B ←→ ~(~A)∧.∨(~B)
      A∧.=B ←→ ~(~A)∨.≠(~B)
      A⌊.+B ←→ -(-A)⌈.+(-B)
```

The dualities for inner product, reduction, and scan can be used to eliminate many uses of boolean negation from expressions, particularly when used in conjunction with identities of the following form:

```
      A∧(~B)  ↔ A>B
(~A)∧B        ↔ A<B
(~A)∧(~B)     ↔ A⍱B
```

4.2 Partitioning Identities

Partitioning of an array leads to a number of obvious and useful identities. For example:

```
×/3 1 4 2 6 ↔ (×/3 1) × (×/4 2 6)
```

More generally, for any associative function `F`:

```
F/V ↔ (F/K↑V) F (F/K↓V)
F/V,W ↔ (F/V) F (F/W)
```

If `F` is commutative as well as associative, the partitioning need not be limited to prefixes and suffixes, and the partitioning can be made by compression by a boolean vector `U`:

```
F/V ↔ (F/U/V) F (F/(~U)/V)
```

If `E` is an empty vector `(0=⍴E)`, the reduction `F/E` yields the identity element of the function `F`, and the identities therefore hold in the limiting cases `0=K` and `0=∨/U`.

Partitioning identities extend to matrices in an obvious way. For example, if `V`, `M`, and `A` are arrays of ranks `1`, `2`, and `3`, respectively, then:

```
V+.×M ↔ ((K↑V)+.×(K,1↓⍴M)↑M)+(K↓V)+.×(K,0)↓M     D.1
(I,J)↓A+.×V ↔ ((I,J,0)↓A)+.×V                    D.2
```

4.3 Summarization and Distribution

Consider the definition and and use of the following functions:

```
N̲:(∨⌿<\ω∘.=ω)/ω       D.3
S̲:(N̲ω)∘.=ω            D.4
```

```
      A←3 3 1 4 1
      C←10 20 30 40 50

      N̲ A           S̲ A             (S̲ A)+.×C
3 1 4           1 1 0 0 0      30 80 40
                0 0 1 0 1
                0 0 0 1 0
```

The function `N̲` selects from a vector argument its *nub*, that is, the set of distinct elements it contains. The expression `S̲ A` gives a boolean "summarization matrix" which relates the elements of `A` to the elements of its nub. If `A` is a vector of account numbers and `C` is an associated vector of costs, then the expression `(S̲ A)+.×C` evaluated above sums or "summarizes" the charges to the several account numbers occurring in `A`.

Used as postmultiplier, in expressions of the form `W+.×S̲ A`, the summarization matrix can be used to *distribute* results. For example, if `F` is a function which is costly to evaluate and its argument `V` has repeated elements, it may be more efficient to apply `F` only to the nub of `V` and distribute the results in the manner suggested by the following identity:

```
F V ↔ (F N̲ V)+.×S̲ V       D.5
```

The order of the elements of `N̲ V` is the same as their order in `V`, and it is sometimes more convenient to use an *ordered* nub and corresponding *ordered* summarization given by:

```
Q̲N̲:N̲ω[⍋ω]        D.6
Q̲S̲:(Q̲N̲ω)∘.=ω     D.7
```

The identity corresponding to D.5 is:

```
F V ↔ (F Q̲N̲ V)+.×Q̲S̲ V      D.8
```

The summarization function produces an interesting result when applied to the function `T̲` defined by A.2:

```
+/S̲+⌿T̲ N ↔ (0,⍳N)!N
```

In words, the sums of the rows of the summarization matrix of the column sums of the subset matrix of order `N` is the vector of binomial coefficients of order `N`.

4.4 Distributivity

The distributivity of one function over another is an important notion in mathematics, and we will now raise the question of representing this in a general way. Since multiplication distributes to the right over addition we have a×(b+q)↔ab+aq , and since it distributes to the left we have (a+p)×b↔ab+pb. These lead to the more general cases:

```
(a+p)×(b+q) ↔ ab+aq+pb+pq
(a+p)×(b+q)×(c+r) ↔ abc+abr+aqc+aqr+pbc+pbr+pqc+pqr
(a+p)×(b+q)×...×(c+r) ↔ ab...c+....+pq...r
```

Using the notion that `V←A,B` and `W←P,Q` or `V←A,B,C` and `W←P,Q,R`, etc., the left side can be written simply in terms of reduction as `×/V+W`. For this case of three elements, the right side can be written as the sum of the products over the columns of the following matrix:

```
V[0]  V[0]  V[0]  V[0]  W[0]  W[0]  W[0]  W[0]
V[1]  V[1]  W[1]  W[1]  V[1]  V[1]  W[1]  W[1]
V[2]  W[2]  V[2]  W[2]  V[2]  W[2]  V[2]  W[2]
```

The pattern of `V`'s and `W`'s above is precisely the pattern of *zeros* and *ones* in the matrix `T←T̲⍴V`, and so the products down the columns are given by `(V×.*~T)×(W×.*T)`. Consequently:

```
×/V+W ↔ +/(V×.*~T)×W×.*T←T̲ ⍴V      D.9
```

We will now present a formal inductive proof of D.9, assuming as the induction hypothesis that D.9 is true for all V and W of shape N (that is, `∧/N=(⍴V),⍴W`) and proving that it holds for shape N+1, that is, for X,V and Y,W, where X and Y are arbitrary scalars.

For use in the inductive proof we will first give a recursive definition of the function T̲, equivalent to A.2 and based on the following notion: if `M←T̲ 2` is the result of order 2, then:

```
      M
0 0 1 1
0 1 0 1
      0,[1]M            1,[1]M
0 0 0 0           1 1 1 1
0 0 1 1           0 0 1 1
0 1 0 1           0 1 0 1

      (0,[1]M),(1,(1)M)
0 0 0 0 1 1 1 1
0 0 1 1 0 0 1 1
0 1 0 1 0 1 0 1
```

Thus:

```
      T̲:(0,[1]T),(1,[1]T←T̲ω-1):0=ω:0 1⍴0                    D.10

+/((C←X,V)×.*~Q)×D×.*Q←T̲⍴(D←Y,W)
+/(C×.*~Z,U)×D×.*(Z←0,[1] T),U←1,[1] T←T̲⍴W                     D.10
+/((C×.*~Z),C×.*~U)×(D×.*Z),D×.*U                            Note 1
+/((C×.*~Z),C×.*~U)×((Y*0)×W×.*T),(Y*1)×W×.*T               Note 2
+/((C×.*~Z),C×.*~U)×(W×.*T),Y×W×.*T                     Y*0 1↔1,Y
+/((X×V×.*~T),V×.*~T)×(W×.*T),Y×W×.*T                       Note 2
+/(X×(V×.*~T)×W×.*T),(Y×(V×.*~T)×W×.*T)                     Note 3
+/(X××/V+W),(Y××/V+W)                          Induction hypothesis
+/(X,Y)××/V+W                                  (X×S),(Y×S)↔(X,Y)×S
×/(X+Y),(V+W)                                      Definition of ×/
×/(X,V)+(Y,W)                                    + distributes over ,
```

Note 1: `M+.×N,P ↔ (M+.×N),M+.×P` (partitioning identity on matrices)

Note 2: `V+.×M ↔ ((1↑V)+.×(1,1↓⍴M)↑M)+(1↓V)+.×1 0↓M` (partitioning identity on matrices and the definition of C, D, Z, and U)

Note 3: `(V,W)×P,Q ↔ (V×P),W×Q`

To complete the inductive proof we must show that the putative identity D.9 holds for some value of N. If N=0, the vectors A and B are empty, and therefore `X,A ↔ ,X` and `Y,B ↔ ,Y`. Hence the left side becomes `×/X+Y`, or simply `X+Y`. The right side becomes `+/(X×.*~Q)×Y×.*Q`, where `~Q` is the one-rowed matrix `1 0` and Q is `0 1`. The right side is therefore equivalent to `+/(X,1)×(1,Y)`, or `X+Y`. Similar examination of the case N=1 may be found instructive.

4.5 Newton's Symmetric Functions

If X is a scalar and R is any vector, then `×/X-R` is a polynomial in X having the roots R. It is therefore equivalent to some polynomial `C P̲ X`, and assumption of this equivalence implies that C is a function of R. We will now use D.8 and D.9 to derive this function, which is commonly based on Newton's symmetric functions:

```
×/X-R
×/X+(-R)
+/(X×.*~T)×(-R)×.*T←T̲ ⍴R                                     D.9
(X×.*~T)+.×P←(-R)×.*T                                Def of +.×
(X*S←+⌿~T)+.×P                                           Note 1
((X*Q̲N̲ S)+.×Q̲S̲ S)+.×P                                      D.8
(X*Q̲N̲ S)+.×((Q̲S̲ S)+.×P)                      +.× is associative
(X*0,⍳⍴R)+.×((Q̲S̲ S)+.×P)                                 Note 2
((Q̲S̲ S)+.×P)P̲ X                                B.1 (polynomial)
((Q̲S̲ +⌿~T)+.×((-R)×.*T←T̲ ⍴R))P̲ X                    Defs of S
                                                          and P
```

Note 1: If X is a *scalar* and B is a boolean vector, then `X×.*B ↔ X*+/B`.

Note 2: Since T is boolean and has ⍴R rows, the sums of its columns range from 0 to ⍴R, and their ordered nub is therefore `0,⍳⍴R`.

4.6 Dyadic Transpose

The dyadic transpose, denoted by ⍉, is a generalization of monadic transpose which permutes axes of the right argument, and (or) forms "sectors" of the right argument by coalescing certain axes, all as determined by the left argument. We introduce it here as a convenient tool for treating properties of the inner product.

The dyadic transpose will be defined formally in terms of the selection function

```
      SF:(,ω)[1+(⍴ω)⊥α-1]
```

which selects from its right argument the element whose indices are given by its vector left argument, the shape of which must clearly equal the rank of the right argument. The rank of the result of `K⍉A` is `⌈/K`, and if I is any suitable left argument of the selection `I SF K⍉A` then:

```
      I SF K⍉A ↔ (I[K]) SF A                                  D.11
```

For example, if M is a matrix, then `2 1 ⍉M ↔ ⍉M` and `1 1 ⍉M` is the diagonal of M; if T is a rank three array, then `1 2 2 ⍉T` is a matrix "diagonal section" of T produced by running together the last two axes, and the vector `1 1 1 ⍉T` is the principal body diagonal of T.

The following identity will be used in the sequel:

```
      J⍉K⍉A ↔ (J[K])⍉A                                       D.12
```

Proof:

```
I SF J⍉K⍉A
(I[J]) SF K⍉A                              Definition of ⍉ (D.11)
((I[J])[K]) SF A                                  Definition of ⍉
(I[(J[K])]) SF A                             Indexing is associative
I SF(J[K])⍉A                                      Definition of ⍉
```

4.7 Inner Products

The following proofs are stated only for matrix arguments and for the particular inner product `+.×`. They are easily extended to arrays of higher rank and to other inner products `F.G`, where `F` and `G` need possess only the properties assumed in the proofs for `+` and `×`.

The following identity (familiar in mathematics as a sum over the matrices formed by (outer) products of columns of the first argument with corresponding rows of the second argument) will be used in establishing the associativity and distributivity of the inner product:

```
        M+.×N ←→ +/1 3 3 2 ⍉ M∘.×N                 D.13
```

Proof: `(I,J)SF M+.×N` is defined as the sum over `V`, where `V[K] ←→ M[I;K]×N[K;J]`. Similarly,

```
        (I,J)SF +/1 3 3 2 ⍉ M∘.×N
```

is the sum over the vector `W` such that

```
W[K] ←→ (I,J,K)SF 1 3 3 2 ⍉ M∘.×N
```

Thus:

```
W[K]
(I,J,K)SF 1 3 3 2 ⍉M∘.×N
(I,J,K)[1 3 3 2]SF M∘.×N                           D.12
(I,K,K,J)SF M∘.×N                        Def of indexing
M[I;K]×N[K;J]                       Def of Outer product
V[K]
```

Matrix product distributes over addition as follows:

```
        M+.×(N+P) ←→ (M+.×N)+(M+.×P)               D.14
```

Proof:

```
M+.×(N+P)
+/(J← 1 3 3 2)⍉M∘.×N+P                             D.13
+/J⍉(M∘.×N)+(M∘.×P)                × distributes over +
+/(J⍉M∘.×N)+(J⍉M∘.×P)              ⍉ distributes over +
(+/J⍉M∘.×N)+(+/J⍉M∘.×P)             + is assoc and comm
(M+.×N)+(M+.×P)                                    D.13
```

Matrix product is associative as follows:

```
        M+.×(N+.×P) ←→ (M+.×N)+.×P                 D.15
```

Proof: We first reduce each of the sides to sums over sections of an outer product, and then compare the sums. Annotation of the second reduction is left to the reader:

```
M+.×(N+.×P)
M+.×+/1 3 3 2⍉N∘.×P                                D.12
+/1 3 3 2⍉M∘.×+/1 3 3 2⍉N∘.×P                      D.12
+/1 3 3 2⍉+/M∘.×1 3 3 2⍉N∘.×P      × distributes over +
+/1 3 3 2⍉+/1 2 3 5 5 4⍉M∘.×N∘.×P                Note 1
+/+/1 3 3 2 4 ⍉1 2 3 5 5 4⍉M∘.×N∘.×P             Note 2
+/+/1 3 3 4 4 2⍉M∘.×N∘.×P                          D.12
+/+/1 3 3 4 4 2⍉(M∘.×N)∘.×P            × is associative
+/+/1 4 4 3 3 2⍉(M∘.×N)∘.×P       + is associative and
                                           commutative

(M+.×N)+.×P
(+/1 3 3 2⍉M∘.×N)+.×P
+/1 3 3 2⍉(+/1 3 3 2⍉M∘.×N)∘.×P
+/1 3 3 2⍉+/1 5 5 2 3 4⍉(M∘.×N)∘.×P
+/+/1 3 3 2 4⍉1 5 5 2 3 4⍉(M∘.×N)∘.×P
+/+/1 4 4 3 3 2⍉(M∘.×N)∘.×P
```

Note 1: `+/M∘.×J⍉A ←→ +/((⍳⍴⍴M),J+⍴⍴M)⍉M∘.×A`

Note 2: `J⍉+/A ←→ +/(J,1+⌈/J)⍉A`

4.8 Product of Polynomials

The identity B.2 used for the multiplication of polynomials will now be developed formally:

```
(B P X)×(C P X)
(+/B×X*E←¯1+⍳⍴B)×(+/C×X*F←¯1+⍳⍴C)                  B.1
+/+/(B×X*E)∘.×(C×X*F)                           Note 1
+/+/(B∘.×C)×((X*E)∘.×(X*F))                     Note 2
+/+/(B∘.×C)×(X*(E∘.+F))                         Note 3
```

Note 1: `(+/V)×(+/W)←→+/+/V∘.×X` because `×` distributes over `+`and `+` is associative and commutative, or see [12,P21] for a proof.

Note 2: The equivalence of `(P×V)∘.×(Q×W)` and `(P∘.×Q)×(V∘×W)` can be established by examining a typical element of each expression.

Note 3: `(X*I)×(X*J)←→X*(I+J)`

The foregoing is the proof presented, in abbreviated form, by Orth [13, p.52], who also defines functions for the composition of polynomials.

4.9 Derivative of a Polynomial

Because of their ability to approximate a host of useful functions, and because they are closed under addition, multiplication, composition, differentiation, and integration, polynomial functions are very attractive for use in introducing the study of calculus. Their treatment in elementary calculus is, however, normally delayed because the derivative of a polynomial is approached indirectly, as indicated in Section 2, through a sequence of more general results.

The following presents a derivation of the derivative of a polynomial directly from the expression for the slope of the secant line through the points `X, F X` and `(X+Y),F(X+Y)`:

```
((C P X+Y)-(C P X))÷Y
((C P X+Y)-(C P X+0))÷Y
((C P X+Y)-((0*J)+.×(A←DS J∘.!J←¯1+⍳⍴C)+.×C) P X)÷Y   B.6
((((Y*J)+.×M) P X)-((0*J)+.×M←A+.×C) P X)÷Y           B.6
((((Y*J)+.×M)-(0*J)+.×M) P X)÷Y             P dist over -
((((Y*J)-0*J)+.×M) P X)÷Y                  +.× dist over -
(((0,Y*1↓J)+.×M) P X)÷Y                            Note 1
(((Y*1↓J)+.× 1 0 ↓M) P X)÷Y                           D.1
(((Y*1↓J)+.×(1 0 0 ↓A)+.×C) P X)÷Y                    D.2
((Y*1↓J-1)+.×(1 0 0 ↓A)+.×C) P X           (Y*A)÷Y←→Y*A-1
((Y*¯1+⍳¯1+⍴C)+.×(1 0 0 ↓A)+.×C) P X             Def of J
(((Y*¯1+⍳¯1+⍴C)+.× 1 0 0 ↓A)+.×C) P X                D.15
```

Note 1: `0*0←→1←→Y*0` and `∧/0=0*1↓J`

The derivative is the limiting value of the secant slope for `Y` at zero, and the last expression above can be evaluated for this case because if `E←¯1+⍳¯1+⍴C` is the vector of exponents of `Y`, then all elements of `E` are non-negative. Moreover, `0*E` reduces to a `1` followed by zeros, and the inner product with `1 0 0↓A` therefore reduces to the first plane of `1 0 0↓A` or, equivalently, the second plane of `A`.

If `B←J∘.!J←¯1+⍳⍴C` is the matrix of binomial coefficients, then `A` is `DS B` and, from the definition of `DS` in B.5, the second plane of `A` is `B×1=-J∘.-J`, that is, the matrix `B` with all but the first super-diagonal replaced by zeros. The final expression for the coefficients of the polynomial which is the derivative of the polynomial `C P ω` is therefore:

```
      ((J∘.!J)×1=-J∘.-J←¯1+⍳⍴C)+.×C
```

For example:

```
      C ← 5 7 11 13
      (J∘.!J)×1=-J∘.-J←¯1+⍳⍴C
 0 1 0 0
 0 0 2 0
 0 0 0 3
 0 0 0 0
      ((J∘.!J)×1=-J∘-J←¯1+⍳⍴C)+.×C
7 22 39 0
```

Since the superdiagonal of the binomial coefficient matrix `(⍳N)∘.!⍳N` is `(¯1+⍳N-1)!⍳N-1`, or simply `⍳N-1`, the final result is `1⌽C×¯1+⍳⍴C` in agreement with the earlier derivation.

In concluding the discussion of proofs, we will re-emphasize the fact that all of the statements in the foregoing proofs are executable, and that a computer can therefore be used to identify errors. For example, using the canonical function definition mode [4 , p.81], one could define a function `F` whose statements are the first four statements of the preceding proof as follows:

```
   ∇F
[1] ((C P X+Y)-(C P X))÷Y
[2] ((C P X+Y)-(C P X+0))÷Y
[3] ((C P X+Y)-((0*J)+.×(A←DS J∘.!J←¯1+⍳⍴C)+.×C) P X)÷Y
[4] ((((Y*J)+.×M) P X)-((0*J)+.×M←A+.×C) P X)÷Y
   ∇
```

The statements of the proof may then be executed by assigning values to the variables and executing `F` as follows:

```
      C←5 2 3 1
      Y←5
      X←3              X←⍳10
      F                F
132              66 96 132 174 222 276 336 402 474 552
132              66 96 132 174 222 276 336 402 474 552
132              66 96 132 174 222 276 336 402 474 552
132              66 96 132 174 222 276 336 402 474 552
```

The annotations may also be added as comments between the lines without affecting the execution.

5. Conclusion

The preceding sections have attempted to develop the thesis that the properties of executability and universality associated with programming languages can be combined, in a single language, with the well-known properties of mathematical notation which make it such an effective tool of thought. This is an important question which should receive further attention, regardless of the success or failure of this attempt to develop it in terms of APL.

In particular, I would hope that others would treat the same question using other programming languages and conventional mathematical notation. If these treatments addressed a common set of topics, such as those addressed here, some objective comparisons of languages could be made. Treatments of some of the topics covered here are already available for comparison. For example, Kerner [7] expresses the algorithm C.3 in both ALGOL and conventional mathematical notation.

This concluding section is more general, concerning comparisons with mathematical notation, the problems of introducing notation, extensions to APL which would further enhance its utility, and discussion of the mode of presentation of the earlier sections.

5.1 Comparison with Conventional Mathematical Notation

Any deficiency remarked in mathematical notation can probably be countered by an example of its rectification in some particular branch of mathematics or in some particular publication; comparisons made here are meant to refer to the more general and commonplace use of mathematical notation.

APL is similar to conventional mathematical notation in many important respects: in the use of functions with explicit arguments and explicit results, in the concomitant use of composite expressions which apply functions to the results of other functions, in the provision of graphic symbols for the more commonly used functions, in the use of vectors, matrices, and higher-rank arrays, and in the use of operators which, like the derivative and the convolution operators of mathematics, apply to functions to produce functions.

In the treatment of functions APL differs in providing a precise formal mechanism for the definition of new functions. The direct definition form used in this paper is perhaps most appropriate for purposes of exposition and analysis, but the canonical form referred to in the introduction, and defined in [4, p.81], is often more convenient for other purposes.

In the interpretation of composite expressions APL agrees in the use of parentheses, but differs in eschewing hierarchy so as to treat all functions (user-defined as well as primitive) alike, and in adopting a single rule for the application of both monadic and dyadic functions: the right argument of a function is the value of the entire expression to its right. An important consequence of this rule is that any portion of an expression which is free of parentheses may be read *analytically* from left to

Fig. 3.

$$\sum_{j=1}^{n} j \cdot 2^{-j}$$

$$1 \cdot 2 \cdot 3 \ + \ 2 \cdot 3 \cdot 4 \ + \ \ldots \ n \ terms \longleftrightarrow \frac{1}{4} n(n+1)(n+2)(n+3)$$

$$1 \cdot 2 \cdot 3 \cdot 4 \ + \ 2 \cdot 3 \cdot 4 \cdot 5 \ + \ \ldots \ n \ terms \longleftrightarrow \frac{1}{5} n(n+1)(n+2)(n+3)(n+4)$$

$$\frac{\left[\frac{x-a}{N}\right]^{-q}}{\Gamma(-q)} \sum_{j=0}^{N-1} \frac{\Gamma(j-q)}{\Gamma(j+1)} f\left(x - j\left[\frac{x-a}{N}\right]\right)$$

right (since the leading function at any stage is the "outer" or overall function to be applied to the result on its right), and *constructively* from right to left (since the rule is easily seen to be equivalent to the rule that *execution* is carried out from right to left).

Although Cajori does not even mention rules for the order of execution in his two-volume history of mathematical notations, it seems reasonable to assume that the motivation for the familiar hierarchy (power before × and × before + or -) arose from a desire to make polynomials expressible without parentheses. The convenient use of vectors in expressing polynomials, as in `+/C×X*E`, does much to remove this motivation. Moreover, the rule adopted in APL also makes Horner's efficient expression for a polynomial expressible without parentheses:

```
+/3 4 2 5×X*0 1 2 3 ↔ 3+X×4+X×2+X×5
```

In providing graphic symbols for commonly used functions APL goes much farther, and provides symbols for functions (such as the power function) which are implicitly denied symbols in mathematics. This becomes important when operators are introduced; in the preceding sections the inner product `×.*` (which must employ a symbol for power) played an equal role with the ordinary inner product `+.×`. Prohibition of elision of function symbols (such as ×) makes possible the unambiguous use of multi-character names for variables and functions.

In the use of arrays APL is similar to mathematical notation, but more systematic. For example, `V+W` has the same meaning in both, and in APL the definitions for other functions are extended in the same element-by-element manner. In mathematics, however, expressions such as `V×W` and `V*W` are defined differently or not at all.

For example, `V×W` commonly denotes the *vector product* [14, p.308]. It can be expressed in various ways in APL. The definition

```
VP:((1⌽α)×¯1⌽ω)-(¯1⌽α)×1⌽ω
```

provides a convenient basis for an obvious proof that `VP` is "anticommutative" (that is, `V VP W ↔ W VP V`), and (using the fact that `¯1⌽X ↔ 2⌽X` for 3-element vectors) for a simple proof that in 3-space `V` and `W` are both orthogonal to their vector product, that is, `∧/0=V+.×V VP W` and `∧/0=W+.×V VP W`.

APL is also more systematic in the use of operators to produce functions on arrays: reduction provides the equivalent of the sigma and pi notation (in `+/` and `×/`) and a host of similar useful cases; outer product extends the outer product of tensor anaysis to functions other than ×, and inner product extends ordinary matrix product (`+.×`) to many cases, such as `∨.∧` and `⌊.+`, for which ad hoc definitions are often made.

The similarities between APL and conventional notation become more apparent when one learns a few rather mechanical substitutions, and the translation of mathematical expressions is instructive. For example, in an expression such as the first shown in Figure 3, one simply substitutes `⍳N` for each occurrence of j and replaces the sigma by `+/`. Thus:

`+/(⍳N)×2*-⍳N` , or `+/J×2*-J←⍳N`

Collections such as Jolley's *Summation of Series* [15] provide interesting expressions for such an exercise, particularly if a computer is available for execution of the results. For example, on pages 8 and 9 we have the identities shown in the second and third examples of Figure 3. These would be written as:

```
+/×/(¯1+⍳N)∘.+⍳3 ←→ (×/N+0,⍳3)÷4
+/×/(¯1+⍳N)∘.+⍳4 ←→ (×/N+0,⍳4)÷5
```

Together these suggest the following identity:

```
+/×/(¯1+⍳N)∘.+⍳K ←→ (×/N+0,⍳K)÷K+1
```

The reader might attempt to restate this general identity (or even the special case where `K=0`) in Jolley's notation.

The last expression of Figure 3 is taken from a treatment of the fractional calculus [16, p.30], and represents an approximation to the qth order derivative of a function f. It would be written as:

```
(S*-Q)×+/(J!J-1+Q)×F X-(J←¯1+⍳N)×S←(X-A)÷N
```

The translation to APL is a simple use of `⍳N` as suggested above, combined with a straightforward identity which collapses the several occurrences of the gamma function into a single use of the binomial coefficient function `!`, whose domain is, of course, not restricted to integers.

In the foregoing, the parameter `Q` specifies the order of the derivative if positive, and the order of the integral (from `A` to `X`) if negative. Fractional values give fractional derivatives and integrals, and the following function can, by first defining a function `F` and assigning suitable values to `N` and `A`, be used to experiment numerically with the derivatives discussed in [16]:

```
OS:(S*-α)×+/(J!J-1+α)×Fω-(J←¯1+⍳N)×S←(ω-A)÷N
```

Although much use is made of "formal" manipulation in mathematical notation, truly formal manipulation by explicit algorithms is very difficult. APL is much more tractable in this respect. In Section 2 we saw, for example, that the derivative of the polynomial expression `(ω∘.*¯1+⍳⍴α)+.×α` is given by `(ω∘.*¯1+⍳⍴α)+.×1⌽α×¯1+⍳⍴α`, and a set of functions for the formal differentiation of APL expressions given by Orth in his treatment of the calculus [13] occupies less than a page. Other examples of functions for formal manipulation occur in [17, p.347] in the modeling operators for the vector calculus.

Further discussion of the relationship with mathematical notation may be found in [3] and in the paper "Algebra as a Language" [6, p.325].

A final comment on printing, which has always been a serious problem in conventional notation. Although APL does employ certain symbols not yet generally available to publishers, it employs only 88 basic characters, plus some composite characters formed by superposition of pairs of basic characters. Moreover, it makes no demands such as the inferior and superior lines and smaller type fonts used in subscripts and superscripts.

5.2 The Introduction of Notation

At the outset, the ease of introducing notation in context was suggested as a measure of suitability of the notation, and the reader was asked to observe the process of introducing APL. The utility of this measure may well be accepted as a truism, but it is one which requires some clarification.

For one thing, an ad hoc notation which provided exactly the functions needed for some particular topic would be easy to introduce in context. It is necessary to ask further questions concerning the total bulk of notation required, the degree of structure in the notation, and the degree to which notation introduced for a specific purpose proves more generally useful.

Secondly, it is important to distinguish the difficulty of describing and of learning a piece of notation from the difficulty of mastering its implications. For example, learning the rules for computing a matrix product is easy, but a mastery of its implications (such as its associativity, its distributivity over addition, and its ability to represent linear functions and geometric operations) is a different and much more difficult matter.

Indeed, the very suggestiveness of a notation may make it seem harder to learn because of the many properties it suggests for exploration. For example, the notation `+.×` for matrix product cannot make the rules for its computation more difficult to learn, since it at least serves as a reminder that the process is an addition of products, but any discussion of the properties of matrix product in terms of this notation cannot help but suggest a host of questions such as: Is `∨.∧` associative? Over what does it distribute? Is `B∨.∧C ←→ ⍉(⍉C)∨.∧⍉B` a valid identity?

5.3 Extensions to APL

In order to ensure that the notation used in this paper is well-defined and widely available on existing computer systems, it has been restricted to current APL as defined in [4] and in the more formal standard published by STAPL, the ACM SIGPLAN Technical Committee on APL [17, p.409]. We will now comment briefly on potential extensions which would increase its convenience for the topics treated here, and enhance its suitability for the treatment of other topics such as ordinary and vector calculus.

One type of extension has already been suggested by showing the execution of an example (roots of a polynomial) on an APL system based on complex numbers. This implies no change in function symbols, although the domain of certain functions will have to be extended. For example, `|X` will give the magnitude of complex as well as real arguments, `+X` will give the conjugate of complex arguments as well as the trivial result it now gives for real arguments, and the elementary functions will be appropriately extended, as suggested by the use of `*` in the cited example. It also implies the possibility of meaningful inclusion of primitive functions for zeros of polynomials and for eigenvalues and eigenvectors of matrices.

A second type also suggested by the earlier sections includes functions defined for particular purposes which show promise of general utility. Examples include the *nub* function `N̲`, defined by D.3, and the *summarization* function `S̲`, defined by D.4. These and other extensions are discussed in [18]. McDonnell [19, p.240] has proposed generalizations of *and* and *or* to non-booleans so that `A∨B` is the GCD of `A` and `B`, and `A∧B` is the LCM. The functions `GCD` and `LCM` defined in Section 3 could then be defined simply by `GCD:∨/ω` and `LCM:∧/ω`.

A more general line of development concerns operators, illustrated in the preceding sections by the reduction, inner-product, and outer-product. Discussions of operators now in APL may be found in [20] and in [17, p.129], proposed new operators for the vector calculus are discussed in [17, p.47], and others are discussed in [18] and in [17, p.129].

5.4 Mode of Presentation

The treatment in the preceding sections concerned a set of brief topics, with an emphasis on clarity rather than efficiency in the resulting algorithms. Both of these points merit further comment.

The treatment of some more complete topic, of an extent sufficient for, say, a one- or two-term course, provides a somewhat different, and perhaps more realistic, test of a notation. In particular, it provides a better measure of the amount of notation to be introduced in normal course work.

Such treatments of a number of topics in APL are available, including: high school algebra [6], elementary analysis [5], calculus, [13], design of digital systems [21], resistive circuits [10], and crystallography [22]. All of these provide indications of the ease of introducing the notation needed, and one provides comments on experience in its use. Professor Blaauw, in discussing the design of digital systems [21], says that "APL makes it possible to describe what really occurs in a complex system", that "APL is particularly suited to this purpose, since it allows expression at the high architectural level, at the lowest implementation level, and at all levels between", and that "....learning the language pays of (sic) in- and outside the field of computer design".

Users of computers and programming languages are often concerned primarily with the efficiency of execution of algorithms, and might, therefore, summarily dismiss many of the algorithms presented here. Such dismissal would be short-sighted, since a clear statement of an algorithm can usually be used as a basis from which one may easily derive more efficient algorithms. For example, in the function `STEP` of section 3.2, one may significantly increase efficiency by making substitutions of the form `B⌹M` for `(⌹M)+.×B`, and in expressions using `+/C×X*¯1+⍳⍴C` one may substitute `X⊥⌽C` or, adopting an opposite convention for the order of the coefficients, the expression `X⊥C`.

More complex transformations may also be made. For example, Kerner's method (C.3) results from a rather obvious, though not formally stated, identity. Similarly, the use of the matrix `α` to represent permutations in the recursive function `R` used in obtaining the depth first spanning tree (C.4) can be replaced by the possibly more compact use of a list of nodes, substituting indexing for inner products in a rather obvious, though not completely formal, way. Moreover, such a recursive definition can be transformed into more efficient non-recursive forms.

Finally, any algorithm expressed clearly in terms of arrays can be transformed by simple, though tedious, modifications into perhaps more efficient algorithms employing iteration on scalar elements. For example, the evaluation of `+/X` depends upon every element of `X` and does not admit of much improvement, but evaluation of `∨/B` could stop at the first element equal to `1`, and might therefore be improved by an iterative algorithm expressed in terms of indexing.

The practice of first developing a clear and precise definition of a process without regard to efficiency, and then using it as a guide and a test in exploring equivalent processes possessing other characteristics, such as greater efficiency, is very common in mathematics. It is a very fruitful practice which should not be blighted by premature emphasis on efficiency in computer execution.

Measures of efficiency are often unrealistic because they concern counts of "substantive" functions such as multiplication and addition, and ignore the housekeeping (indexing and other selection processes) which is often greatly increased by less straightforward algorithms. Moreover, realistic measures depend strongly on the current design of computers and of language embodiments. For example, because functions on booleans (such as `∧/B` and `∨/B`) are found to be heavily used in APL, implementers have provided efficient execution of them. Finally, overemphasis of efficiency leads to an unfortunate circularity in design: for reasons of efficiency early programming languages reflected the characteristics of the early computers, and each generation of computers reflects the needs of the programming languages of the preceding generation.

Acknowledgments. I am indebted to my colleague A.D. Falkoff for suggestions which greatly improved the organization of the paper, and to Professor Donald McIntyre for suggestions arising from his reading of a draft.

Appendix A. Summary of Notation

Fω	SCALAR FUNCTIONS			αFω
ω	Conjugate	+	Plus	
0-ω	Negative	-	Minus	
(ω>0)-ω<0	Signum	×	Times	
1÷ω	Reciprocal	÷	Divide	
ω⌈-ω	Magnitude	|	Residue	ω-α×ωω÷α+α=0
Integer part	Floor	P	Minimum	(ω×ω<α)+α×ω≥α
- -ω	Ceiling	⌈	Maximum	-(-α)--ω
2.71828...*ω	Exponential	*	Power	×/ωρα
Inverse of *	Natural log	⍟	Logarithm	(⍟ω)÷⍟α
×/1+⍳ω	Factorial	!	Binomial	(!ω)÷(!α)×!ω-α
3.14159...×ω	Pi times	○		

Boolean: ∨ ⍱ ~ (and, or, not-and, not-or, not)
Relations: < ≤ = ≥ > ≠ (αRω is 1 if relation R holds).

	Sec. Ref.	V↔2 3 5 M↔1 2 3 / 4 5 6
Integers	1	⍳5↔1 2 3 4 5
Shape	1	ρV↔3 ρM↔2 3 2 3ρ⍳6↔M 2ρ4↔4 4
Catenation	1	V,V↔2 3 5 2 3 5 M,M↔1 2 3 1 2 3 / 4 5 6 4 5 6
Ravel	1	,M↔1 2 3 4 5 6
Indexing	1	V[3 1]↔5 2 M[2;2]↔5 M[2;]↔4 5 6
Compress	3	1 0 1/V↔2 5 0 1⌿M↔4 5 6
Take,Drop	1	2↑V↔2 3 ¯2↑V↔1↓V↔3 5
Reversal	1	⌽V↔5 3 2
Rotate	1	2⌽V↔5 2 3 ¯2⌽V↔3 5 2
Transpose	1, 4	⍉ω reverses axes α⍉ω permutes axes
Grade	3	⍋3 2 6 2↔2 4 1 3 ⍒3 2 6 2↔3 1 2 4
Base value	1	10⊥V↔235 V⊥V↔50
&inverse	1	10 10 10⊤235↔2 3 5 V⊤50↔2 3 5
Membership	3	V∊3↔0 1 0 V∊5 2↔1 0 1
Inverse	2, 5	⌹ω is matrix inverse α⌹ω↔(⌹ω)+.×α
Reduction	1	+/V↔10 +/M↔6 15 +⌿M↔5 7 9
Scan	1	+\V↔2 5 10 +\M↔2 3ρ1 3 6 4 9 15
Inner prod	1	+.× is matrix product
Outer prod	1	0 3∘.+1 2 3↔M
Axis	1	F[I] applies F along axis I

Appendix B. Compiler from Direct to Canonical Form

This compiler has been adapted from [22, p.222]. It will not handle definitions which include `α` or `:` or `ω` in quotes. It consists of the functions `FIX` and `F9`, and the character matrices `C9` and `A9`:

```
FIX
0ρ⎕FX F9 ⍞

D←F9 E;F;I;K
F←(,(E='ω')∘.≠5↑1)/,E,(⌽4,ρE)ρ' Y9 '
F←(,(F='α')∘.≠5↑1)/,F,(⌽4,ρF)ρ' X9 '
F←1↓ρD←(0,+/¯6,I)↓(-(3×I)++\I←':'=F)⌽F,(⌽6,ρF)ρ' '
D←3⌽C9[1+(1+'α'∊E),I,0;],⍉D[;1,(I←2↓⍳F),2]
K←K+2×K<1⌽K←I∧K∊(>⌿1 0⌽'←⎕'∘.=E)/K←+\~I←E∊A9
F←(0,1+ρE)⌈ρD←D,(F,ρE)↑⍉0 ¯2↓K⌽' ',E,[1.5]';'
D←(F↑D),[1]F[2] '⍝',E
      C9                    A9
   Z9←                   012345678
  Y9Z9←                  9ABCDEFGH
  Y9Z9←X9                IJKLMNOPQ
 )/3→(0=1↑,              RSTUVWXYZ
    →0,0ρZ9←             A̲B̲C̲D̲E̲F̲G̲H̲I̲
                         J̲K̲L̲M̲N̲O̲P̲Q̲R̲
                         S̲T̲U̲V̲W̲X̲Y̲Z̲⎕
```

Example:

```
      FIX
FIB:Z,+/¯2↑Z←FIBω-1:ω=1:1

      FIB 15
1 1 2 3 5 8 13 21 34 55 89 144 233 377 610

      ⎕CR'FIB'
Z9←FIB Y9;Z
→(0=1↑,Y9=1)/3
→0,0ρZ9←1
Z9←Z,+/¯2↑Z←FIB Y9-1
⍝FIB:Z,+/¯2↑Z←FIBω-1:ω=1:1
```

References

1. Boole, G. *An Investigation of the Laws of Thought*, Dover Publications, N.Y., 1951. Originally published in 1954 by Walton and Maberly, London and by MacMillan and Co., Cambridge. Also available in Volume II of the *Collected Logical Works of George Boole*, Open Court Publishing Co., La Salle, Illinois, 1916.
2. Cajori, F. *A History of Mathematical Notations*, Volume II, Open Court Publishing Co., La Salle, Illinois, 1929.
3. Falkoff, A.D., and Iverson, K.E. The Evolution of APL, *Proceedings of a Conference on the History of Programming Languages*, ACM SIGPLAN, 1978.
4. *APL Language*, Form No. GC26-3847-4, IBM Corporation.
5. Iverson, K.E. *Elementary Analysis*, APL Press, Pleasantville, N.Y., 1976.
6. Iverson, K.E. *Algebra: an algorithmic treatment*, APL Press, Pleasantville, N.Y., 1972.
7. Kerner, I.O. Ein Gesamtschrittverfahren zur Berechnung der Nullstellen von Polynomen, *Numerische Mathematik*, Vol. 8, 1966, pp. 290-294.
8. Beckenbach, E.F., ed. *Applied Combinatorial Mathematics* , John Wiley and Sons, New York, N.Y., 1964.
9. Tarjan, R.E, Testing Flow Graph Reducibility, *Journal of Computer and Systems Sciences*, Vol. 9 No. 3, Dec. 1974.
10. Spence, R. *Resistive Circuit Theory*, APL Press, Pleasantville, N.Y., 1972.
11. Iverson, K.E. *A Programming Language*, John Wiley and Sons, New York, N.Y., 1962.
12. Iverson, K.E. *An Introduction to APL for Scientists and Engineers*, APL Press, Pleasantville, N.Y.
13. Orth, D.L. *Calculus in a new key*, APL Press, Pleasantville, N.Y., 1976.

14. Apostol, T.M. *Mathematical Analysis,* Addison Wesley Publishing Co., Reading, Mass., 1957.
15. Jolley, L.B.W. *Summation of Series,* Dover Publications, N.Y.
16. Oldham, K.B., and Spanier, J. *The Fractional Calculus,* Academic Press, N.Y., 1974.
17. *APL Quote Quad,* Vol. 9, No. 4, June 1979, ACM STAPL.
18. Iverson, K.E., *Operators and Functions,* IBM Research Report RC 7091, 1978.
19. McDonnell, E.E., A Notation for the GCD and LCM Functions, *APL 75, Proceedings of an APL Conference,* ACM, 1975.
20. Iverson, K.E., Operators, *ACM Transactions on Programming Languages And Systems,* October 1979.
21. Blaauw, G.A., *Digital System Implementation,* Prentice-Hall, Englewood Cliffs, N.J., 1976.
22. McIntyre, D.B., The Architectural Elegance of Crystals Made Clear by APL, *An APL Users Meeting,* I.P. Sharp Associates, Toronto, Canada, 1978.

1979 ACM Turing Award Lecture

Delivered at ACM '79, Detroit, Oct. 29, 1979

The 1979 ACM Turing Award was presented to Kenneth E. Iverson by Walter Carlson, Chairman of the Awards Committee, at the ACM Annual Conference in Detroit, Michigan, October 29, 1979.

In making its selection, the General Technical Achievement Award Committee cited Iverson for his pioneering effort in programming languages and mathematical notation resulting in what the computing field now knows as APL. Iverson's contributions to the implementation of interactive systems, to the educational uses of APL, and to programming language theory and practice were also noted.

Born and raised in Canada, Iverson received his doctorate in 1954 from Harvard University. There he served as Assistant Professor of Applied Mathematics from 1955–1960. He then joined International Business Machines, Corp. and in 1970 was named an IBM Fellow in honor of his contribution to the development of APL.

Dr. Iverson is presently with I.P. Sharp Associates in Toronto. He has published numerous articles on programming languages and has written four books about programming and mathematics: *A Programming Language* (1962), *Elementary Functions* (1966), *Algebra: An Algorithmic Treatment* (1972), and *Elementary Analysis* (1976).

8 *The Inductive Method of Introducing APL*

THE INDUCTIVE METHOD OF INTRODUCING APL

Kenneth E. Iverson
I.P. Sharp Associates
Toronto, Ontario

Because APL is a language, there are, in the teaching of it, many analogies with the teaching of natural languages. Because APL is a **formal** language, there are also many differences, yet the analogies prove useful in suggesting appropriate objectives and techniques in teaching APL.

For example, adults learning a language already know a native language, and the initial objective is to learn to translate a narrow range of thoughts (concerning immediate needs such as the ordering of food) from the native language in which they are conceived, into the **target** language being learned. Attention is therefore directed to imparting effective use of a small number of words and constructs, and not to the memorization of a large vocabulary. Similarly, a student of APL normally knows the terminology and procedures of some area of potential application of computers, and the inital objective should be to learn enough to translate these procedures into APL. Obvious as this may seem, introductory courses in APL (and in other programming languages as well) often lack such a focus, and concentrate instead on exposing the student to as much of the vocabulary (i.e., the primitive functions) of APL as possible.

This paper treats some of the lessons to be drawn from analogies with the teaching of natural languages (with emphasis on the inductive method of teaching), examines details of their application in the development of a three-day introductory course in APL, and reports some results of use of the course. Implications for more advanced courses are also discussed briefly.

1. The Inductive Method

Grammars present general rules, such as for the conjugation of verbs, which the student learns to apply (by **deduction**) to particular cases as the need arises. This form of presentation contrasts sharply with the way the mother tongue is learned from repeated use of particular instances, and from the more or less conscious formulation (by **induction**) of rules which summarize the particular cases.

The inductive method is now widely used in the teaching of natural languages. One of the better-known methods is that pioneered by Berlitz [1] and now known as the "direct" method. A concise and readable presentation and analysis of the direct method may be found in Diller [2].

A class in the purely inductive mode is conducted entirely in the target language, with no use of the student's mother tongue. Expressions are first learned by imitation, and concepts are imparted by such devices as pointing, pictures, and pantomime; students answer questions, learn to ask questions, and experiment with their own statements, all with constant and immediate reaction from the teacher in the form of correction, drill, and praise, expressed, of course, in the target language.

In the analogous conduct of an APL course, each student (or, preferably, each student pair) is provided with an APL terminal, and with a series of printed sessions which give explicit expressions to be "imitated" by entering them on the terminal, which suggest ideas for experimentation, and which pose problems for which the student must formulate and enter appropriate expressions. Part of such a session is shown as an example in Figure 1.

SESSION 1: NAMES AND EXPRESSIONS

The left side of each page provides examples to be entered on the keyboard, and the right side provides comments on them. Each expression entered must be followed by striking the RETURN key to signal the APL system to execute the expression.

```
      AREA←8×2                          The name AREA is assigned to the result
      HEIGHT←3                          of the multiplication, that is 16
      VOLUME←HEIGHT×AREA
      HEIGHT×AREA                       If no name is assigned to the result, it
48                                      is printed
      VOLUME
48
      3×8×2
48
      LENGTH←8 7 6 5                    Names may be assigned to lists
      WIDTH←2 3 4 5
      LENGTH×WIDTH
16 21 24 25
      PERIMETER←2×(LENGTH+WIDTH)    Parentheses specify the order in which
      PERIMETER                         parts of an expression are to be
20 20 20 20                             executed
      1.12×1.12×1.12                    Decimal numbers may be used
1.404928
      1.12*3                            Yield of 12 percent for 3 years
1.404928
```

SAMPLE PORTION OF SESSION

Figure 1

Because APL is a formal "imperative" language, the APL system can execute any expression entered on the terminal, and therefore provides most of the reaction required from a teacher. The role of the instructor is therefore reduced to that of tutor, providing explicit help in the event of severe difficulties (such as failure of the terminal), and general discussion as required. As compared to the case of a natural language, the student is expected, and is better able, to assess his own performance.

Applied to natural languages, the inductive method offers a number of important advantages:

1. Many dull but essential details (such as pronunciation) required at the outset are acquired in the course of doing more interesting things, and without explicit drill in them.

2. The fun of constantly looking for the patterns or rules into which examples can be fitted provides a stimulation lacking in the explicit memorization of rules, and the repeated examples provide, as always, the best mnemonic basis for remembering general rules.

3. The experience of committing error after error, seeing that they produce no lasting harm, and seeing them corrected through conversation, gives the student a confidence and a willingness to try that is difficult to impart by more formal methods.

4. The teacher need not be expert in two languages, but only in the target language.

Analogous advantages are found in the teaching of APL:

1. Details of the terminal keyboard are absorbed gradually while doing interesting things from the very outset.

2. Most of the syntactic rules, and the extension of functions to arrays, can be quickly gleaned from examples such as those presented in Figure 1.

3. The student soon sees that most errors are harmless, that the nature of most are obvious from the simple error messages, and that any adverse effects (such as an open quote) are easily rectified by consulting a manual or a tutor.

4. The tutor need only know APL, and does not need to be expert in areas such as financial management or engineering to which students wish to apply APL, and need not be experienced in lecturing.

2. The Use Of Reference Material

In the pure use of the inductive method, the use of reference material such as grammars and dictionaries would be forbidden. Indeed, their use is sometimes discouraged because the conscious application of grammatical rules and the conscious pronunciation of words from visualization of their spellings promotes uneven delivery. However, if a student is to become independent and capable of further study on his own, he must be introduced to appropriate reference material.

Effective use of reference material requires some practice, and the student should therefore be introduced to it early. Moreover, he should not be confined to a single reference; at the outset, a comprehensive dictionary is too awkward and confusing, but a concise dictionary will soon be found to be too limited.

In the analogous case of APL, the role of both grammar and dictionary is played by the reference manual. A concise manual limited to the core language [3] should be supplemented by a more conprehensive manual (such as Berry [4]) which covers all aspects of the particular system in use. Moreover, the student should be led immediately to locate the two or three main summary tables in the manual, and should be prodded into constant use of the manual by explicit questions (such as "what is the name of the function denoted by the comma"), and by glimpses of interesting functions.

3. Order Of Presentation

Because the student is constantly striving to impose a structure upon the examples presented to him, the order of presentation of concepts is crucial, and must be carefully planned. For example, use of the present tense should be well established before other tenses and moods are introduced. The care taken with the order of presentation should, however, be unobtrusive, and the student may become aware of it only after gaining experience beyond the course, if at all.

We will address two particular difficulties with the order of presentation, and exemplify their solutions in the context of APL. The first is that certain expressions are too complex to be treated properly in detail at the point where they are first useful. These can be handled as "useful expressions" and will be discussed in a separate section.

The second difficulty is that certain important notions are rendered complex by the many guises in which they appear. The general approach to such problems is to present the essential notion early, and return to it again and again at intervals to reinforce it and to add the treatment of further aspects.

For example, because students often find difficulty with the notion of literals (i.e., character arrays), its treatment in APL is often deferred, even though this deferral also makes it necessary to defer important practical notions such as the production of reports. In the present approach, the essential notion is introduced early, in the manner shown in Figure 2. Literals are then returned to in several contexts: in the representation of function definitions; in discussion of literal digits and the functions (⍕ and ⍎) which are used to transform between them and numbers in the production of reports; and in their use with indexing to produce barcharts.

Function definition is another important idea whose treatment is often deferred because of its seeming complexity. However, this complexity inheres not in the notion itself, but in the mechanics of the general del form of definition usually employed. This complexity includes a new mode of keyboard entry with its own set of error messages, a set of rules for function headers, confusion due to side-effects resulting from failure to localize names used or to definitions which print results but have no explicit results, and the matter of suspended functions.

All of this is avoided by representing each function definition by a character vector in the direct form of definition [5 6]. For example, a student first uses the function *ROUND* provided in a workspace, then shows its definition, and then defines an equivalent function called *R* as follows:

```
      ROUND 24.78 31.15 28.59
25 31 29

      SHOW 'ROUND'
ROUND:⌊.5+⍵
```

SESSION 4: LITERALS

```
      JANET←5                       Janet received 5 letters today
      MARY←8

      MARY⌈JANET                    The maximum received by one of them
8
      MARY⌊JANET                    The minimum
5
      MARY>JANET                    Mary received more than Janet
1
      MARY=JANET                    They did not receive an equal number
0
```

What sense can you make of the following sentences:

JANET has 5 letters and *MARY* has 8

JANET has 5 letters and *MARY* has 4

'*JANET*' has 5 letters and '*MARY*' has 4

The last sentence above uses quotation marks in the usual way to make a **literal reference** to the (letters in the) name itself as opposed to what it denotes. The second points up the potential ambiguity which is resolved by quote marks.

```
      LIST←24.6 3 17
      ⍴LIST
3
      WORD←'LIST'
      ⍴WORD
4
      SENTENCE←'LIST THE NET GAINS'
```

INTRODUCTION OF LITERALS

Figure 2

```
      DEFINE 'R:⌊.5+W'

      R 24.78 31.15
25 31
```

The function *DEFINE* compiles the definition provided by its argument into an appropriate del form, localizes any names which appear to the left of assignment arrows in the definition, provides a "trap" or "lock" appropriate to the particular APL system so that the function defined behaves like a primitive and cannot be suspended, and appends the original argument in a comment line for use by the function *SHOW*.

This approach makes it possible to introduce simple function definition very early and to use it in a variety of interesting contexts before introducing conditional and recursive definitions (also in the direct form), and the more difficult del form.

4. Teaching Reading

It is usually much easier to **read** and comprehend a sentence than it is to **write** a sentence expressing the same thought. Inductive teaching makes much use of such reading, and the student is encouraged to scan an entire passage, using pictures, context, and other clues, to grasp the overall theme before invoking the use of a dictionary to clarify details.

Because the entry of an APL expression on a terminal immediately yields the overall result for examination by the student, this approach is particularly effective in teaching APL. For example, if the student's workspace has a table of names of countries, and a table of oil imports by year by country by month, then the sequence:

```
      N←25
      B←+/[1]+/[3] OIL

      COUNTRIES,'.⎕'[1+B∘.≥(⌈/B)×(⍳N)÷N]
```

produces the following result, which has the obvious interpretation as a barchart of oil imports:

```
ARABIA   ⎕⎕⎕⎕⎕⎕⎕⎕⎕⎕⎕⎕⎕⎕⎕⎕⎕⎕⎕⎕.....
NIGERIA  ⎕⎕⎕⎕⎕⎕⎕⎕⎕⎕⎕⎕⎕⎕⎕⎕⎕⎕.......
CANADA   ⎕⎕⎕⎕⎕⎕⎕⎕⎕⎕⎕⎕⎕⎕⎕..........
INDONESIA⎕⎕⎕⎕⎕⎕⎕⎕⎕................
IRAN     ⎕⎕⎕⎕⎕⎕⎕⎕.................
LIBYA    ⎕⎕⎕⎕⎕⎕⎕⎕.................
ALGERIA  ⎕⎕⎕⎕⎕⎕⎕⎕.................
OTHER    ⎕⎕⎕⎕⎕⎕⎕⎕⎕⎕⎕⎕⎕⎕⎕⎕⎕⎕⎕⎕⎕⎕⎕⎕⎕
```

Moreover, because the simple syntax makes it easy to determine the exact sequence in which the parts of the sentence are executed, a detailed understanding of the expression can be gained by executing it piece-by-piece, as illustrated in Figure 3. Finally, such critical reading of an expression can lead the student to formulate his own definition of a useful related function as follows:

```
      DEFINE ⍞
BARCHART:'.⎕'[1+⍵∘.≥((⍳⍺)÷⍺)×⌈/⍵]
```

5. Useful Expressions

As remarked in Section 3, some expressions are too useful and important to be deferred to the point that would be dictated by the complexity of their structure. In APL such expressions can be handled by introducing them as defined functions whose use may be grasped immediately, but whose internal definition may be left for later study.

For example, files can be introduced in terms of the functions *GET*, *TO*, *RANGE*, and *REMOVE*, illustrated in Figure 4. These can be grasped and used effectively by the

```
      N                                   The width of the barchart
25
      Q←(⍳N)÷N                            Numbers from 0 to 1 in 25 equal steps
                                                  (display if desired)
      ⌈/B                                 The largest value to be charted
      C←(⌈/B)×Q                           Numbers from 0 to the largest value to be
                                          charted

      S←B∘.≥C                             Comparison of each value of B with
      S                                   each value in the range to be charted
1 1 1 1 1 1 1 1 1 1 1 1 1 1 1 1 1 1 1 1 0 0 0 0 0
1 1 1 1 1 1 1 1 1 1 1 1 1 1 1 1 1 1 0 0 0 0 0 0 0
1 1 1 1 1 1 1 1 1 1 1 1 1 1 1 0 0 0 0 0 0 0 0 0 0
1 1 1 1 1 1 1 1 1 0 0 0 0 0 0 0 0 0 0 0 0 0 0 0 0
1 1 1 1 1 1 1 1 0 0 0 0 0 0 0 0 0 0 0 0 0 0 0 0 0
1 1 1 1 1 1 1 1 0 0 0 0 0 0 0 0 0 0 0 0 0 0 0 0 0
1 1 1 1 1 1 1 1 0 0 0 0 0 0 0 0 0 0 0 0 0 0 0 0 0
1 1 1 1 1 1 1 1 1 1 1 1 1 1 1 1 1 1 1 1 1 1 1 1 1

      3 21↑1+S                            Examine a piece of 1+S
2 2 2 2 2 2 2 2 2 2 2 2 2 2 2 2 2 2 2 2 1
2 2 2 2 2 2 2 2 2 2 2 2 2 2 2 2 2 2 1 1 1
2 2 2 2 2 2 2 2 2 2 2 2 2 2 2 1 1 1 1 1 1
```

DETAILED EXECUTION OF AN EXPRESSION

Figure 3

student at an earlier stage and with much greater ease than can the underlying language elements from which they must be constructed in most APL systems.

A further example is provided by the function needed to compile, display, and edit the character vectors used in direct definition of functions. For example, an editing function which deletes each position indicated by a slash, and inserts ahead of the position of the first comma any text which follows it (in the manner provided for del editing in many APL systems) is illustrated in Figure 5.

Deferral of the internal details of the definition of these essential functions can, in fact, be turned to advantage, because they provide interesting exercises in reading (using the techniques of Section 4) the definitions of functions whose purposes are already clear from repeated use. For example, critical reading of the following definition of the function *EDIT* is very helpful in grasping the important idea of recursive definition:

```
EDIT:EDIT(A DELETE K↑ω),(1↓K↓A),(K←+/∧\A≠',')↓ω:0=ρA←⍞,0ρ⎕←ω:ω
```

```
DELETE:(~(ρω)↑'/'=α)/ω
```

Analysis of the complete set of functions provided for the compilation from direct definition form also provides an interesting exercise in reading, but one which would not be completed, or perhaps even attempted, until after completion of an introductory course. Extensive leads to other interesting reading, of both workspaces and published material, should be given the student to encourage further growth after the conclusion of formal course work.

If the first dimension of an array (list, table, or list of tables) has the value *N*, (for example, `1↑ρOIL` is 7), then it may be distributed to *N* items of a file by a single operation. For example:

```
      OIL TO 'IMPORTS 72 73 74 75 76 77 78'
```

*Use the function *GET* to retrieve individual items from the *IMPORTS* file to verify the effect of the preceding expression.

```
      COUNTRIES TO 'IMPORTS 1'   Non-numeric data may be entered
```

The functions *RANGE* and *REMOVE* are useful in managing files:

```
      RANGE 'IMPORTS'                  Gives range of indices
1 72 73 74 75 76 77 78'

      REMOVE 'IMPORTS 73 75 77'   Removes odd years

      RANGE 'IMPORTS'
1 72 74 76 78
```

FUNCTIONS FOR USING FILES

Figure 4

```
      TEXT←'DDELLLETN AND INSRTION'
      Z←EDIT TEXT                Apply EDIT to erroneous text
DDELLLETN AND INSRTION                 Line printed by the function
/   //   ,IO                     Line entered on keyboard
DELETION AND INSRTION                  Line printed by the function
                 ,E              Line entered on keyboard
DELETION AND INSERTION                 Line printed by the function
                                 Empty line entered on keyboard (carriage
                                 return alone) ends execution of EDIT

      DEFINE 'REVISE:DEFINE EDIT SHOW ω'   Define a function for revision

      REVISE 'SUM'
SUM:+/[α]ω
///,MAX
MAX:+/[α]ω
    /,⌈
MAX:⌈/[α]ω
```

FUNCTIONS FOR EDITING AND REVISION

Figure 5

Advanced Courses

Advanced language courses can also employ the inductive method, but the greater the student's mastery of a language, the greater the potential benefits of the deductive approach and of explicit analysis of the structure of the language. A point sometimes made in the advanced treatment of natural languages is that grammar and related matters can now be discussed **in the target language**, avoiding distractions and distortions which might be introduced by use of the mother tongue.

Similar remarks apply to advanced APL courses. In particular, the use of APL in its own discussion and in the introduction of the more complex functions is quite productive. For example, reduction is very useful in discussing the inner product, and inner product and grade are helpful in analyzing dyadic transpose.

Conduct Of The Course

The introductory course on which these remarks are based evolved through four versions offered over a period of several months. The resulting course covers three contiguous days, and has been offered a number of times in the final form.

Most students appear to work better in pairs than when assigned individually to terminals. Because there are no lectures, each pair can work at their own pace. Observations and student comments show that they find it more stimulating than a lecture course, and tend to come early and work late. Moreover, they learn to consult manuals much more than in a lecture course, and exhibit a good deal of independence by the end of the three days.

Acknowledgements

I am indebted to a number of my colleagues at I.P. Sharp Associates, to Mr. Roland Pesch for his development of the file functions used, to Mr. Pesch and Mr. Michael Berry for assistance and advice in the early versions of the course, and to Ms. Nancy Neilson and Dr. Paul Berry for comments arising from their use of the course. I am also indebted to several members of the staff of the Berlitz School of Languages in Toronto, to Ms. Grace Palumbo and Ms. G. Dunn for discussions of the direct method, and to Ms. N. Eracleous for patient demonstrations of it.

References

[1] Berlitz, M.D., **Methode Berlitz**, Berlitz and Co., New York, 1887.

[2] Diller, Karl Conrad, **The Language Teaching Controversy**, Newbury House Publishers, Inc., Rowley, Massachusetts, 1978.

[3] **APL Language**, IBM Form #GC26-3847, IBM Corporation.

[4] Berry, P.C., **SHARP APL Reference Manual**, I.P. Sharp Associates.

[5] Iverson, K.E., **Elementary Analysis**, APL Press, 1976.

[6] Iverson, K.E., Programming Style in APL, **An APL Users Meeting**, I.P. Sharp Associates, 1978.

layout/design	**Arlene E. Azzarello**
cover	**Ron Rios,** ArtComp Graphics, Sunnyvale, CA
production	**Pete McDonnell, MollieO Patrick**
printing & binding	Consolidated Publications, Inc., Sunnyvale, CA